11/16/2022

To paul

Thank you
for buying
the book
KAN-6

ENDORSEMENTS

January 9, 2011, was a memorable day as Sudan's Lost Boys made their way to Chicago to cast their votes for South Sudan's independence. I was privileged to provide buses for the boys from Michigan to be there. Among those voting that day was Dominic Malual, a young man whose story of courage and faith is recounted in *Barefoot in the Boot*. The ravages of war at the hands of terrorists later drove Dominic to join the US Army in the fight against terrorism in Iraq. This compelling story by my own countryman fills me with immense pride.

Luol Ajou Deng
Born in Wau, Sudan (now South Sudan)
Pro basketball player, NBA Los Angeles Lakers

Dominic and Luol Deng in Nebraska (2016).

Dominic Malual's story is inspiring. Imagine the courage required to set out on foot, fleeing war that had taken family and friends, for an unknown land. Then imagine that you are only seven years old. We get glimpses into life in the village, the hardships along the route, the anxieties of resettlement, and the hardships of adjusting to life in a foreign land. *Barefoot in the Boot* is a challenge to those of us with settled lives, national political stability, and relative affluence. I stand in awe of the strength of the "Lost Boys" and the personal story of Dominic.

George K. Heartwell
Former Mayor, City of Grand Rapids, Michigan

**Mayor Heartwell and Dominic at the Grand Rapids visit of
South Sudan's Vice President James Wanni Igga in 2013.**

A uniquely enlightening autobiography revealing the comprehensive story of one of the Lost Boys of Sudan. God's protective hand is seen in each episode of Malual's arduous journey to freedom.

Dr. John Koetsier
Grand Rapids, Michigan

My brother Manute Bol was not just one of the tallest NBA basketball players, but was a true humanitarian worker who devoted his time to supporting his people during the South Sudan civil war. Ultimately, his vision was to construct forty-one schools throughout the former states of South Sudan. Manute did build schools, supplied buses, and encouraged his people. He specifically was devoted to the Lost Boys and Girls of southern Sudan, and he visited them often to encourage them in their new lives in America. Manute was considered an icon and a hero worldwide. Before his health deteriorated, all he wanted was to witness the historic referendum taking place in southern Sudan, making his South Sudan an independent country. Unfortunately, he could not make it, as Manute passed away thirteen months before South Sudan gained its independence. I am so pleased that my cousin Dominic Malual is getting his own story told, and that he and the other Lost Boys and Girls of southern Sudan are continuing the work that my brother started.

Nybol Bol
Sister to Manute Bol

BAREFOOT IN THE BOOT

A Lost Boy's Journey to Freedom

DOMINIC MALUAL; DOROTHY FANBERG BAKKER

WESTBOW
P R E S S®
A DIVISION OF THOMAS NELSON
& ZONDERVAN

WestBow Press books may be ordered through booksellers or by contacting:

WestBow Press
A Division of Thomas Nelson & Zondervan
1663 Liberty Drive
Bloomington, IN 47403
www.westbowpress.com
1 (866) 928-1240

Because of the dynamic nature of the Internet, any web addresses or
links contained in this book may have changed since publication and
may no longer be valid. The views expressed in this work are solely those
of the author and do not necessarily reflect the views of the publisher,
and the publisher hereby disclaims any responsibility for them.

Any people depicted in stock imagery provided by Getty Images are
models, and such images are being used for illustrative purposes only.
Certain stock imagery © Getty Images.

ISBN: 978-1-9736-2072-3 (sc)
ISBN: 978-1-9736-2074-7 (hc)
ISBN: 978-1-9736-2073-0 (e)

Library of Congress Control Number: 2018902581

Print information available on the last page.

WestBow Press rev. date: 05/22/2018

TABLE OF CONTENTS

APPRECIATION TO MY FRIENDS AND FAMILIES

First of all, I thank Almighty God from the bottom of heart for my entire life, because he is the giver of everything. Did I know that one day I would be living in America? No. Only God has the key for my life.

As a child of war, I must thank people who made differences in my life from the refugee camp to America. Thanks to my uncle, Manute Bol, who saved southern Sudanese refugees from hunger during the civil war in Sudan. Thanks to the United Nations and the United States of America for bringing the Lost Boys and Girls of southern Sudan to America. I thank the Ethiopian people, who welcomed us to their country during our struggle. And I thank the Kenyan people for their generosity in welcoming us to their country and allowing us to attend their schools. Thank you to the people of Uganda for welcoming my people to their country, and thanks to all other countries in the world who opened their arms to welcome my people.

My South Sudanese Friends and Families

Thanks to my cousin Nyanguek Anyiel with her kids; her husband, Maluak Ayuel; Aunt Alony Mayol with her husband, Agoth Alor; and their kids; Aunt Nyankol Ajing with her husband, Monychol Bol; with their children, who were all taking care of me before I was hospitalized in the refugee camp.

Thanks to Majok Nyuol Koul, who was with me in the camp hospital for more than a month because of tapeworm in my stomach. I thank Kuol Awut, who put his hands on my mouth so that I could throw up in them at the hospital. Thanks to my cousin

Deng Majok Kang, who would help us in the camp when we had nothing to eat. These people shaped my life in the camp. I thank my cousin Malual Ajak, who held our hands at night when we were traveling from southern Sudan to Ethiopia. I thank Ring Chol Ring, who was our leader when we were traveling in big groups going to Ethiopia. Malual and Ring were our parents on our travels; they never slept without having us at least eat something to save our lives in the jungles and beyond. They contributed something good to my life. They would tell me that one day I would be somebody in life if I continued doing well in school and behaved well in any situation.

My American Friends and Families

I can't find words to describe my happiness to my American families. They opened their arms and welcomed us to their homes as their biological children. I would like to thank Mama Rita, Dad Gary, their children, and Aunt Dorothy with her kids. Mama Rita and Dad Gary were foster parents to my cousin James Mum Ajuong and his brother Mayom Ajuong in 2000. When I arrived in Virginia in 2001, my cousins told their foster parents I had arrived in Virginia. Mama Rita called her college friends Penny and Vincent Combs and told them about our being new in Virginia. Penny immediately came to our apartment to visit us; from there Penny became our American mother in Virginia. She was involved in our transition to American life. Thanks to Mama Penny and her husband and their children for helping us in our new country.

Our American families always give us the best advice on our journey. Thanks to Mama Sally Bolte and her husband, who gave us our first special car in America—a Honda Accord. Mama Rita and Dad Gary took care of my cousins, and later they became my foster parents when I moved from Virginia to Michigan in 2003. They never fail us when we need help from them. The VanderVens gave us a van, and later in 2006, Mama Rita told me to marry my girlfriend before I was deployed to Iraq, which I did. In 2016, when we wanted to buy our first home, we called Mama Rita, and she helped us find a home and did most of the VA paperwork. Thank you, Mama Rita, for taking your time to help us get our first home.

In 2010, Mama Rita introduced me to her aunt Dorothy to edit my journal for my book. Aunt Dorothy is a very strong and generous lady. Although she was taking care of her disabled husband at the time, she didn't say no to me. She spent years editing my journal and even paid for it to be published. Aunt Dorothy also gave me five hundred dollars to buy a cow for my mother, which I did before my mother died. Thank you so much, Aunt Dorothy! I want to thank Aunt Dorothy's niece Judy who introduced me to her husband, Ken Hopper. Ken is a wonderful artist, who created the beautiful cover for my book! Thank you to Mama Rita for helping edit the early drafts of the book and selecting the pictures for the book.

My American families are blessed with caring hearts; they are always there for me and my family to help us. They guided us through tough times and easy times, and they are important in my life. I also would like to thank Mr. Duffy, a gentleman who paid our rent and school costs for almost two years with his daughter, Colleen Duffy, and her uncle Pat, in Holland, Michigan.

Thanks to Aunt Ayak Malek Majok, who took my wife in when I was deployed to Iraq. Thank you, too, Ann Dennis, my wife's foster mother, who always takes our kids to her house for holidays and took care of them for two months when we traveled to Africa. May God bless all my American families and give them more ages.

Thanks to friends who took their time to write something in my book: former Grand Rapids Mayor George Heartwell, Luol Deng of the NBA, Dr. John Koetsier, and my cousin Nybol Bol.

My greatest thanks goes to my wife, Mahalet, who stood strong when I was deployed to Iraq. She is a great woman, an amazing wife, and a wonderful mother to our children, Achuei, Hawathiya, Malual, and Lina. My life's journey would not be possible without all of you!

My family: Hawathiya, Malual,
Dominic, Mahalet, Lina and Achuei

Dominic (second from left) visits his
family for the first time in
20 years (southern Sudan 2009).

Mahalet and children with
foster mom, Ann Dennis.

(Top to bottom/ left to right) Grant
Keeven, Penny and Vince Combs,
Tara, Carter and Scott Keeven,
Vincent and Taylor Combs.

Mama Rita VanderVen and
Aunt Dorothy Bakker

A TRIBUTE TO MANUTE BOL

I would like to pay a special tribute to Manute Bol, the man I refer to as my uncle. We share a common grandfather in our lineage, but it is our Sudanese custom to show respect by referring to an older kinsman as "Uncle" rather than cousin. Manute's father, a leader in our Dinka tribe, gave him the name "Manute," which means "special blessing" in Dinka. A special blessing is exactly what Manute was to all of us!

Most remember Manute as a basketball player, for his ten years with the NBA. If they remember him in that role, they likely recall that he was a man of extreme height—seven foot seven. But I remember him as man of great generosity and compassion, a true humanitarian.

When Manute came to our refugee camp in Kakuma, Kenya, I was thrilled to see a family member come to visit. At that time, I knew nothing of his fame as an American athlete. In fact, I thought *he* too may have become a victim of the horrific raids that had driven us from our villages. Thank God, Manute's physical stature assured him of a place in the world of basketball. Manute selflessly used the earnings from his career to help the people of southern Sudan who had become impoverished by the relentless raids and genocide. Working with the organization Sudan Sunrise, he helped finance the building of schools and a hospital—a work that is still ongoing in South Sudan.

After I arrived as a Lost Boy in Richmond, Virginia, I reconnected with my cousins in Grand Rapids, Michigan, and later moved there. Manute would come to Grand Rapids to attend family functions and would hang out with us at our apartment. He was there for our high school graduations and told us to take our education seriously. He gave us hope and urged us to *never* forget our culture and our families back in Sudan.

Manute called my cousins' foster mom "Mama Rita," just as we did. Once, Rita booked him a room at the Marriott, where my cousins and I could all go to visit. She brought food for us and ironed Manute's shirts for him. My cousin Mayom was taking pictures and asked my wife, Mahalet, if she would like to take a picture with Manute, but she refused. Being a shy person and very petite, I think she was overwhelmed by both his height and his fame.

Sadly, Manute passed away at the age of forty-seven, leaving a tremendous hole in our lives and in the world. One very important thing he told us was to thank our American families for opening their arms and taking us in and giving us an opportunity for a good life. May God bless our memory of this great man!

Dominic Malual

Manute Bol (center) on one of his many visits to Grand Rapids, Michigan.(Left to right) Malual Mayol Awak, Dad Gary, Cousin Mayom Ajuong, Mama Rita, Angelo Deng, and Dominic Malual.

Manute joins a VanderVen family celebration. (Center, top to bottom) Manute, Dad V, Dominic M, (right of center, top to bottom) Tyler V, Malual Awak, Mayom Majok, James Mum, (far right, top to bottom) Steve Schwanda, Kerstin V, Quinn V.

Malual Malual Mayom was my father and mentor, whose patience and persistence prepared me to survive the ravages of civil war. Without his guidance, I might never have withstood the arduous trek through the forests, rivers, and deserts of Africa. And my mother, Hawathiya Monchikon Wol, loved me and never gave up her dream that I would one day return.

My mother, Hawathiya Monchikon Wol.

PROLOGUE

In times of war, where there is a gun there is a brave gunner. I speak as a gunner of the 2-12 Cavalry of the US Army, a personal security detail of the battalion commander, and an infantryman for Operation Iraqi Freedom (OIF) in 2006 and 2008. I also was a Lost Boy from southern Sudan, and I am the father of four beautiful children, the husband of a beautiful woman from the horn of Africa, I will let you know a little about my background, and then you can read the rest for yourself. As a child who witnessed the horror of civil war in Sudan and as a man who served as an American soldier in the Iraq war, I have gone through two wars that I will *never* forget. It has been a journey of more than two decades, and my heart is torn between my people in South Sudan and those in the United States of America, which I have come to love.

I was born in southern Sudan in 1982. However, I didn't know the year of my birth until I was reunited with my mother in 2009. I was the sixth of seven children born to my daddy, Malual Malual Mayom, and his first wife, Hawathiya Monchikon Wol. My parents named me Deng Malual. My mother was from Abyei County—just north of the county of Twic, where my daddy and I both were born.

Sudan has always known war, but after gaining independence from the British in 1956, our people hoped things would be better—but they weren't. The Arab Sudanese government made improvements in the cities and villages in the north, while southern Sudan was totally ignored. Because of this injustice, the faculty and students of the Southern Political University started a rebellion against the government. Fighting continued until 1972, when leaders from northern Sudan signed a peace agreement with southern Sudanese leaders like Lagu, Abel Alier, and Deng Nhial. Soon afterward, soldiers from the northern army, who called themselves "Arabs of the Northern Sudan," captured Deng Nhial and beheaded him.

John Garang de Mabior replaced the assassinated leader and led an attack on the South Sudan city of Mading Bor, where soldiers from the north were living, under the late commander Kerubino Kuanyin Bol. The southern soldiers were known as the Sudan People's Liberation Army, or the SPLA, and were trained in Ethiopia to fight the northern soldiers. This was the situation in my country when I was born.

CHAPTER 1

A Child of the Cattle Camps

They called me "Deng Achel Anguam," the first of many nicknames I would acquire along the way. There was a special reason behind the name. When I was born, my mother had already given birth to two daughters and three sons, and she had nursed each one for more than a year. But when my time came, she was unable to nurse me, because her breasts became swollen and she could not produce milk. Fortunately, however, she had a cow that she got milk from to feed me. That cow was called "Achel Anguam," which in the language of my tribe, the Dinkas of southern Sudan, means "black cow with the horns facing downward." Since that cow provided my nourishment, my mother nicknamed me after her. It's fairly common for Dinka people to name a child after the color of a cow, but in my case, people who didn't know thought I was given the name because my own mother had passed away.

My mother had one more baby after me—my sister Abuk, who was born when I was five. My mother had no problem nursing her, but first, let me tell you about Abuk. She was my mother's seventh child, so for my mom, pregnancy was a familiar experience. The people in our village, and especially our own family, anxiously awaited the birth of my mother's baby, but Abuk didn't come at the expected time. My mother had felt my sister moving and kicking in her belly for several months, but she just wasn't ready to come out into the world.

Three months passed beyond Mother's due date, but there was still no baby.

1

"I think your baby is *dead*," one of the village women told her. "No," Mother said. "My baby is okay. I can feel it *moving*."

More months went by. My mother looked very pregnant, but she wasn't gaining additional weight and she seemed to be in reasonably good health. But by this time, everyone was becoming quite concerned for her. Month after month the family watched her, and they struggled to find a way to make her deliver the baby. As her pregnancy approached twenty-four months, they called her a "human elephant," because that's about how long it takes an elephant to give birth.

With nowhere else to turn, my daddy finally made the decision to take my mother to a hospital. This was a big decision on his part, because our people rely on traditional or tribal practitioners for medical issues, but no one as yet had been able to help my mother. The closest hospital was many miles away in Wau City, and we had no means of transportation of our own. So my daddy had to hire a truck—the equivalent of taking a bus—in a nearby community to get my mother to the hospital. This was an important event for us, and a whole family entourage accompanied my parents on foot to see them off. I was there too, trudging along the dusty road while keeping close to my mother's side.

This was definitely a new experience for me, and when we reached our destination, I was a little frightened by the strange animal that stood quietly waiting for us. It seemed harmless enough, but I was curious about the odd-looking round legs and huge eyes of the beast. Then my daddy's friend Rind Deng stepped inside and sat down. "What kind of animal is *this*?" I asked my big brother, Mayom. "And why do you sit inside it instead of riding on top?"

"It's not an animal," he said, amused at my question. "It's a *thurumbil*," he explained, speaking the Dinka word for "motor vehicle." I had never seen any type of machinery before, and I was in awe of this thing that was going to take my mother to Wau City to get our new baby.

We said our good-byes, and my daddy helped my mother into

the cab of the truck, where she sat alongside the driver. Then Daddy and his friend Rind Deng and my brother Mayom climbed into the truck bed along with more than a dozen other passengers who were also going to Wau. Then I returned home with the other family members who had seen my parents off.

The roads of South Sudan are extremely treacherous in places, and on the way the driver lost control of the truck, causing it to roll down an embankment. It was a terrible accident that left ten passengers dead. My father suffered a deep cut on his thigh, and his friend Rind bit his tongue and nearly severed it. My brother Mayom was saved by landing safely in the top branches of a tree, and my mother was saved by God.

The survivors were all taken to the hospital in Wau City for treatment. The men had their wounds cleaned and stitched, and the doctors tended to my mother. After a thorough examination, they agreed that her baby was definitely well past due, but they told my daddy that, unfortunately, there was nothing they could do for her there. "The reason the baby won't come," one doctor explained, "is because it can't. It is *attached* to her back, right by her spine. This is unheard of. I've delivered many babies but have never seen anything like this before. Surgery is not an option; it would be too dangerous to even risk." They told Daddy to take my mother home and consult traditional tribal doctors (witch doctors) or powerful spiritual leaders to cure my mother of her long pregnancy. So once the men had been released from the hospital and could travel, they returned home with my mother.

When they arrived back in our village days later, with my poor mother still pregnant, the people felt sad for her, especially after they heard of the accident and all that the family had been through. After they were told what the doctor had said about the baby being attached inside my mother, they said someone with "powerful eyes" must have done this to her and caused the baby to stick inside her.

Then someone told my daddy about a man named Apuk, who was from a sub-Dinka tribe. They said Apuk had powerful eyes and should be able to help by neutralizing the work of the first man's powerful eyes. This, they said, would allow my mother to finally deliver her baby. So my daddy sent someone from our family to find this man. He was located in a village many miles away, but he agreed to come. He traveled on foot for seven days to reach our home.

Apuk was all business when he arrived, and he seemed to know exactly what to do. He asked for someone in my family to heat some cow's butter until it had melted and separated, and to bring him just the clear oil from it. Then, with my mother kneeling on her hands and knees like a goat, he took his thumb and pressed hard on her spine so that it left a slight indentation in her flesh. Then he slowly poured about a cup of the warm oil into the spot, and using his *powerful eyes*, he caused the oil to go directly into her body as if there had been a hole in that spot. He said that was all he needed to do, and the baby would come soon.

A place was made in our home for the medicine man to sleep while he stayed and waited for the baby to arrive. About five days passed, and then one night my mother safely delivered a baby girl. There were no complications, and she was a healthy baby of normal size. This surprised many people, because they fully expected the infant to either be very large or to be born with some kind of birth defect.

I remember how I was awakened rather abruptly one morning by an annoying, squalling sound. I got up from my sleeping mat and called to my mother, "Who's making that noise?"

"It's a baby," she told me.

"Did the baby come out last night?" I asked.

"Yes, it did," she said. "You have a baby sister."

I hurried over to where my mother sat cradling a small bundle in her lap. I pulled the cover back to peek and was frightened. "No!" I said, pulling my hand back from the bundle. "That's not a baby; that's a baby *lion!*"

A group of family members was gathered there to see my mom and her baby girl, who had been so long in coming. They were laughing at me for thinking my sister was a baby lion. But I was the only young child in the family at that time, and I had never seen a newborn before. All of the babies I remembered seeing were plump, bright-eyed infants several months old—not scrunched-up creatures like the one my mother was holding. I guess I was also a little disappointed that the baby I had been waiting for didn't seem to care about meeting me. My parents named my sister Abuk, which is the Dinka translation of "Eve." But they nicknamed her "Nyankuekyiech," which means "the girl who was stuck in her mother's womb."

The medicine man's work was finished, and he was pleased to have brought relief to my poor mother. All he asked for in exchange for his services was a goat, which my father gave him before he began the weeklong trek back to his own village. "When your daughter grows up and has children of her own, tell her to give me a cow," the man told my father. My sister is now married and has five children of her own, but she learned that the medicine man that helped bring about her birth has since died.

But back to Abuk. I continued to insist that my baby sister was a lion. And as little and helpless as she was, to *me* she was something to be feared, and I kept a safe distance from her - especially at night when I slept. At bedtime, I would retreat to the barn, where I would curl up and fall asleep on the straw near the warmth of the fire that was kept for the animals. Then late at night my oldest sister, Achuei, would come out and pick me up and carry me inside the house and tuck me in bed. I made it clear that I wanted nothing to do with my *lion* sister, and this continued until Abuk was big enough to start crawling. It was then that I assumed the role of big brother and began playing with her.

I don't expect that many people will believe the story that has been passed down about my sister, but the people of my village confirm that it's true. There are powerful unexplainable forces at work in Africa that outsiders don't understand. Throughout the years, men with powerful eyes have been believed to put curses on people, doing terrible things to them. For instance, Dinka people believe that when someone pays you a compliment and something bad ensues, then what the person said was meant for evil rather than good, and they may actually have been putting a curse on you.

When I was quite young—maybe three years old—someone told my family that I had beautiful hair. Then the following day, a blister mysteriously appeared on the top of my head, making it look as if I'd been burned by fire. The blister spread quickly until it covered three-quarters of my scalp. I lost my hair and was in very bad shape with a burn that was slow to heal. My mother did everything she could to nurse the problem out of me until I recovered. But God didn't want me to die, and my head slowly healed and my hair grew back—except for the small spot on the top of my head where the blister had first started.

I was fortunate, because some wounds *refuse* to heal. I remember that when I was little, my uncle's wife had a wound on her leg that never healed. She had had the wound since she was ten years old, and it just stayed and stayed and caused her a lot of pain. When I went back to Sudan in 2009, I saw my aunt again and was astonished to see that she still had the ugly wound on her leg. She told me it had been there for *thirty* years.

What kind of wound, I've wondered, *never heals?* Even the woman in the Bible who bled for twelve years was healed by Jesus when she touched his clothes. My aunt's family worries about her because she is suffering so much and can't find a cure. I pray that someone with a kind heart will come forward and help this poor mother who suffers from this wound that refuses to heal.

There is much sickness in African villages, and the infant mortality rate is high. I had just turned four when I became very sick with a fever that lasted for more than two months. I lost weight and became so frail and thin that my family felt certain I was going to die. My mother did everything she knew to care for me, but I wasn't getting any better. She was pregnant with my sister Abuk at this time, and my family worried about her because she was not eating. She would just sit every day and hold me in her arms and weep because I was so close to death.

One day a neighbor lady named Ayur Briar, who was married to my daddy's cousin, came and took me from my mother's lap. She said to my mother, "You let *me* have the boy so he can die in *my* hands if God wants him." Just a few days later while I was in her care, the fever, which had lasted for weeks, finally broke. My appetite returned, and I slowly regained my strength. The recovery was miraculous, but the fever did a strange thing—it left me with amnesia. I had forgotten my mother completely and was convinced that Ayur was my mom. I stayed on in Ayur's home and called her Mommy because I truly believed I was her son.

My family was most grateful to Ayur. Had it not been for her, I might not have lived. But my mother was hurt by my rejection. She and my brothers and sisters all told me I belonged to *them*, but I didn't believe them. So Ayur continued to care for me until I was completely well and strong again. And it was she who finally convinced me that she was *not* my mother. She told me how she had taken me from my *real* mother, who had given up all hope that I would live and had wanted to die with me. Ayur told me I had been a *very* sick little boy and had come close to dying in my mother's arms.

I went back home and began to accept my mother and daddy as my *real* parents again. Of course, my mother was overjoyed because she had sacrificed so much for me. She used to say to me when I was young, "Son, when you grow up, you are going to be an ambassador in our family." I wasn't exactly sure what she meant by that—but I knew she had struggled very hard to care for me and had great hopes and plans for my future.

The next year I went through another painful ordeal. Someone gave me a vaccination on my right buttock, and it became infected and began to swell. I don't know if the vaccination was not given properly or if something just went wrong. But for four months I was miserable because I could neither lie nor sit on my right side. Then just as I had healed completely from the infection, something even *worse* was waiting to happen to me.

One day my mother sat making rope like they use in building the roofs of Sudanese houses, and I was napping on a straw mat at her feet. About ten feet away, my cousin Achuei Bol was cooking a pot of sorghum mixed with grain and beans. When the mixture was done, she picked up the heavy pot to show it to my mother. My mother told her not to bring it so close, because I was asleep on the floor. "It's okay," Achuei told her. But just as she reached us, the pot slipped, spilling the steaming contents onto my bare body. The hot sticky mixture immediately fused to my skin.

I remember the incident clearly. My mother was crying as she poured water on my back to stop the burning. I was in agony. I had never felt pain that intense in my life. When they removed the food from my back, sides, and buttocks, the skin came with it. I could feel the searing heat going all through my body, and it felt like my heart was on fire. It took three months for the burn to heal, which meant I had to spend my time either standingor sitting or lying on my stomach. Again, it was my mother who tended to me, nursing my wounds while trying to keep me comfortable.

My memories from my younger years are quite naturally about my mother, because most of my time was spent with her until I was old enough to go to the cattle camps. I have great memories of my daddy too. I remember him as a very kind man—a spiritual leader in our small village of Wunriang, a man everyone in the community looked up to with the greatest admiration and respect.

My daddy had six wives, my mother being the first, and more than twenty-five children in all. By our standards, my daddy was considered a *wealthy* man because of his large herds of cattle, and in southern Sudan a man's wealth is determined by the sizes of his herds. He also had goats and sheep as well as flocks of chickens—but his cattle were his pride. He was my hero. He was the one who taught me things a child needs to know, and I was indeed a curious child.

Once I was old enough to be out and away from my mother, I became my daddy's constant companion. His brothers used to ask him why he took me everywhere while I was still so young. He told them, "If you want to train a warrior, you don't train him when he is old. You let him test the fire when he is *young*, and he will know how to handle it when he grows up." There was much wisdom in those words, and I owe my later survival to his constant training.

My extended family occupied a large compound where each of my daddy's wives lived in a hut, or tukul, with her children. These homes were usually thirty to forty feet across and had walls made from mud and roofs made from straw or savannah grass. As a child, I was very interested in watching the construction of a new home because it was always a community event.

After a suitable spot had been chosen, the men would work smoothing the ground to make it perfectly level. Next, they would attach a long rope to a stake and drive it into the center of the plot; then they would tie a smaller stake to the other end of the rope to mark a large circle defining the perimeter of the house. Then they would drive poles into the ground at intervals around the circle to provide a framework for the structure. They would place small branches between the poles to make a base to hold the mud in place. It was now time for the women to take over.

The women would work together gathering mud into containers and would carry it to the building site and, using their hands, would apply it in layers between the poles. They would make a few small porthole-type openings high along the walls to let in a little light, while still keeping out the heat. And once the layers of mud had dried, the walls were sturdy and weatherproof. The last step in finishing the walls was to coat them inside and out with a smooth layer of fresh cow dung. This dried like varnish and made the mud water resistant.

Finally, the men would bend and tie fresh saplings to make rings of three or four sizes to form the framework of the cone-shaped roof of the house. Then they would assemble the roof frame and attach tight bundles of straw in rows to complete the building. I can remember my mother and my aunts cutting the tall savannah grass and tying it into small tightly wrapped bundles to be used in building and repairing the roofs. Depending on the size of the house, construction could take two weeks or more. But the work was *always* rewarded with an abundance of food, often including an ox roast. The finished houses were very durable and could last ten to twenty years.

I got myself in trouble when our new house was being built. It was the rainy season, and a pond had formed where the women were gathering clay for finishing the walls of the structure. The pond was some distance from the house and was about the size of a child's large swimming pool, with a depth of two to three feet. I had been forbidden to play in it because it was deep enough for me to drown and I had not yet learned to swim. But the temptation was too great, and I wandered off one day and was happily playing in the muddy water when my father saw me and came running. Before I had a chance to get out, he grabbed me and tossed me into the middle of the pond, making a great splash as I hit the water. I was terrified and screaming as I thrashed around while trying unsuccessfully to touch the ground with my feet. Then Daddy pulled me from the water. "Son," he said, "I did that so you will know not to jump around in the water when you don't know how to *swim*. If I hadn't seen you, you might have *drowned!* I wanted you to know what that would feel like so you'll never do it again." My daddy had a way of teaching me lessons I would never in my life forget.

The compounds were large—up to fifteen miles across—and there were distances of several miles between some of the homes. There were also large huts—some of them with open sides—which served as barns for a few cows and goats that provided milk for our families. These animals grazed close by, and it was the job of the women to milk them each morning and evening. We kept a garden too, and all the women pitched in to help with the planting and harvesting of okra, peanuts, and African beans. We also planted small fields of sorghum and sesame—ingredients needed for making breads and other Sudanese dishes. If the year was good, we could enjoy these crops at harvest time, but sometimes the heavy rains destroyed everything we planted.

As is the Sudanese custom, Daddy's six marriages had cost him sizable dowries to the families of his wives, and now his *own* daughters were becoming young women.

My oldest sister, Achuei, had reached the age when young men were becoming interested in her with marriage in mind. Three men were competing for her at the same time, and this is how it went: In the evening, after Achuei had finished all of her chores—helping my mother with the cooking, tending to the younger children, and cleaning the compound—she would go out to meet with one of her suitors. There was a big tree with large spreading branches about forty meters from our house, and the two would sit beneath it and talk at length during the evening. The young man would talk to my sister about his family background, and he would relate his ideas about raising children and talk about his beliefs. He would also tell her how the wives in his family were treated. That would be of great interest to her in choosing a husband. The following evening, the scene would be the same but with a *different* suitor. This routine would continue until my sister and my family arrived at a decision as to which man she should marry.

The reason three men were competing for Achuei was that she was considered a good catch. She was a hardworking, responsible girl. Not only that, our family was prominent because my father was the leader of the cattle keepers in the community.

I observed this drama with great curiosity and questioned my mother every evening about my sister's courtship. "Why are those men talking to Achuei?" I would ask. "What do they *want* from her? There are a lot of other girls in the village—why don't they go and talk to them?" When my mother told me they were hoping to marry her, I had more questions.

"Is she going to marry all *three* of them?"

My mother laughed at my questions. "Son," she said, "when you grow up, you will learn and will understand why those men are talking to your sister. But now you are just a child. Your time will come in the future."

A husband was finally chosen for Achuei—a young man named Deng—and things quickly became very busy at home. My mother and the other wives and neighbors were grinding grain to make flour for baking Sudanese flat breads, and they were preparing other traditional foods for the wedding feast. The event would take days of preparation.

Many people came to celebrate my sister's wedding, and it was indeed a festive occasion. There were dancing men decked out in leopard skins, jumping and leaping. Some were beating drums as they sang traditional wedding songs. And there were women in dresses made from animal hides festooned with intricate beading, clapping their hands as they joined in the revelry. Young children, too, gathered around and watched with amusement. Once the actual marriage ceremony took place, Achuei would be wearing a traditional African dress, natural white in color.

But meanwhile inside a hut in the compound, women from the groom's family were counseling my sister on how to take care of her husband. They explained to her the rules of family relationships and procedures. They told her if anyone in her husband's family ever insulted her, she was to keep her mouth shut and not return the insult. But if she ever insulted one of *his* family members, her family would be required to give his family an apology cow to pay for her misdeed. There were old women, young women, girls, and friends—all bombarding her with information that a new bride would need. And all the while, poor Achuei was crying because she had to leave her family and go away with her husband.

It was a great celebration indeed. Five oxen were slaughtered for the wedding feast and the seven days of festivities that followed. Much of the meat was prepared by roasting, and some of the blood was also cooked in the Dinka tradition. Three days into the wedding rituals, the elders from both the bride's and the groom's families met together, and I came to the meeting too and sat down beside my uncle. I listened intently, trying to understand what all the talk was about. Then I stood up among the elders and spoke. "Could I say something, please?" The men looked at me, wondering what this five-year-old boy could possibly have to say. Then an elderly gentleman from the groom's side nodded. "Go ahead, my child. Speak up."

I looked around the room and asked, "Who is the *father* of the bridegroom?"

A man named Chan spoke up. "Here I am, son."

I looked at the man and explained to him what was on my mind. "Now, *your* son is going to take *my* sister to be his wife," I said. "So I think *I* deserve to get a gift from you because my sister is very special to me and my family, just like I am."

The man was clearly amused by my comment; however, I could not have been more serious. "And just what kind of gift do you want, my son?"

"I need *three* gifts from you," I explained.

"And what might those gifts be?"

"I would like a pregnant cow and a male calf, and I want the calf *inside* the cow to be a female." Everyone burst out laughing at my most unusual request.

"You surprise me, my son," he said. "I have never talked to a young child like you before who had such things to say as you do." The man paused a moment and then continued. "I will give you the gifts you have requested, but I must tell you," he said, smiling, "the calf *inside* the pregnant cow will be either a female or a male. Only God can make that decision—not me. I think your request is a reasonable one," he added. "I will give you this gift when you have your *own* family or as a wedding gift. Just grow up, my son, and then I will give you your gift." After the man spoke, everyone applauded and cheered for me. It had been my first experience at negotiating a deal, and I felt pleased with the outcome. My business was finished, so I got up and left the elders to continue with their meeting.

Our people believe in looking out for their family members, and because of all the work involved in establishing a home and a cattle herd, it was customary for a wife's brother to go and live with the couple for a time. So when my second sister, Agom, got married, my brother Garang stayed with her and her husband for a year to help where he was needed—especially with the cattle. *All* our customs focused on caring for our family members.

My own mother had seven children—three girls and four boys—and I was second to the last born. As a little boy, I would go with my dad to see his other wives and my half brothers and half sisters, and I was always full of questions. I didn't quite understand the family structure, and I thought my dad's other wives were his sisters. I liked them all, and they were always nice to me. Then one day I *asked* him if those women were his sisters. He didn't speak right away but seemed to be searching for an answer. I asked him *three* times, "Daddy, are those women your *sisters?*"

"Call them your *mothers*," he said, "because they are my wives."

"Call them *Mother?*" I questioned. That was ridiculous! "I have *one* mother. Why should I call *them* my mothers, when I was born to *my* mother?"

"There are things you will understand when you grow up," he told me. "But now you are still young, my son."

After being enlightened about my extended family, I decided I would like to go and spend a week or two with my dad's third wife, Adior. After all, she was one of my *mothers*. So Daddy took me to her house, which was about ten miles away—a walk of several hours for my short legs.

Adior had recently given birth to a baby girl, and she had more breast milk than the baby could drink. She also had a little puppy. She would allow the baby to nurse until she was full, and then she would milk out what remained and set it down for the puppy to drink. I watched in disbelief each time Adior did this, but I said nothing. This was just too strange for me. I felt sure that if I asked for milk, she wouldn't give me cow's milk like I drank at home. No, she would give me a cup of *breast* milk to drink like she did the puppy. I said to myself, *You know what? I'm going back to my own mother—I can't do this anymore.*

At first, the visit had sounded like a good idea, but now I had second thoughts. For one thing, Adior didn't have children for me to play with. I hadn't gotten to know anyone else in her area, so I was lonely and bored. She was being very kind to me, but I was missing my friends—and she was giving *breast* milk to the puppy! I had never seen any of the other mothers do that before. I didn't want Adior to know how I felt, so out of courtesy I stayed with her for three days. Then I got up very early one morning and slipped out of the house without being noticed and began to walk home.

I was definitely scared as I started out. I had never walked such a distance alone, and I lost track of the path and came close to getting lost in the forest. I hoped I wouldn't meet any hungry lions or leopards, because I didn't have my daddy along to protect me. I began to get thirsty, and my stomach hurt because I was hungry—so I looked and found some wild tamarinds to eat. That helped a little, but I was still hungry. I missed the meals with bread that my mother always fixed for me. The walk seemed much *farther* than it had been when I walked it with my daddy. Finally, when I saw familiar surroundings, I was greatly relieved. I was thankful that I had reached home before dark, but because I had been wandering about while trying to find my way, the trip had taken me nine hours.

It had been a big adventure for me but very scary, and I told myself I would never do that again. My mother was greatly surprised when she saw me at the door. She didn't believe that I had walked home by myself, but I explained to her how I had left early that morning alone without telling Adior that I was leaving. When my daddy came home and found out what I had done, he was not at all happy and whipped me as a punishment. "Son," he said, "don't you know that wild animals could have *eaten* you—or you could have wandered and gotten lost in the forest, where we might never have *found* you?" I realized that without meaning to, I had almost caused a big problem in our family.

"What happened?" he wanted to know. "Why did you leave Adior and come home?"

"She was giving breast milk to the dog," I told him tearfully, "and I thought she was going to give me breast milk to drink like she did the puppy." At that, my daddy burst out laughing. He wasn't meaning to make fun of me, but the whole idea struck him as hilarious. When he later told the other family members what I had done, they had a good laugh too as they tried to picture me sneaking out of Adior's home that morning.

"You know I love you, son," he reassured me. "I whipped you because I don't want to ever lose you like that."

I got to know all my dad's wives before I became separated from the family, and they became my best mothers. Then when I went home to visit after twenty years, they all welcomed me. And when Adior mentioned the breast milk incident, we all laughed about it. What had troubled me so much back then was now quite amusing.

There was good reason for my father to be concerned about me walking through the forest without protection—lions were a constant threat. They are very intelligent animals and hard to outsmart. I remember an incident from my early childhood that involved a lion in the cattle camp.

A man whose camp was next to my father's camp witnessed a lion attacking and killing one of his cows. The lion then saw the man and ran off, leaving the carcass of the cow beneath a tree. The man knew the lion would eventually return to retrieve his prey, so he set a watch for the animal. He left the dead cow under the tree, and then he armed himself with a gun and watched from a distance for the lion's return. It was about ten o'clock that night when the lion came back. As he settled down next to the cow and began feeding on her, the man aimed his gun and shot the lion. The bullet struck the animal in the back, injuring but not killing him. Then he bolted and began to jump around in pain before disappearing into the dark.

The next morning the man recruited his brother and the other men who worked in his camp to help him hunt down the injured animal. Very soon a group of more than thirty warriors, armed with spears, set out looking for the lion. They found him about a half mile away, lying hidden in the tall grass. As they began to close in on him, he sprung toward them and grabbed the cattle owner by the leg and bit into it. It was as though he had recognized his assailant from the previous night. At that, the man's brother and the other men raced toward the lion with their spears and thrust them into the animal as they fell on top of him. After a few seconds, they were frightened by a low growling noise and thought they had failed to kill the lion. But it turned out to be a noise coming from the dead animal's throat as air escaped its lungs when the men fell upon him. The lion had taken a bite out of the cattle keeper's leg, but the man survived. He was just glad the dangerous predator had been killed before it could do any more harm to his herd. The cow, however, was not a total loss. The man was able to salvage a good part of the animal, and he shared it with the people in his camp.

It was a typical rainy morning in the cattle camp. The cows had been milked and untethered from their stakes and turned loose to graze—and I was swinging from the low vines under a large tree, waiting for my friends to come and join me at play. Then a stranger approached. There was nothing unusual about that, because many people traveled through the camps every day. But this man was alone and was moving in slow motion. It was as if every step was torture to his body. Our eyes met, and then he dropped to the ground a short distance from the tree where I was swinging. "Come," was all he said.

I jumped down from the swing and ran to the man to see what he wanted—but when I reached him, he was unable to speak. Then I raced to tell my daddy about the fallen stranger, and he ran quickly to the man's aid. "Hurry!" he told me. "Bring me some milk!" When

I returned, Daddy raised the man into a sitting position and got him to open his mouth and take a sip of milk. Sweat poured from the man's face, and he was breathing heavily as he took another large swallow. Then he looked up at my daddy and asked, "Who are you?"

"I'm Malual," Daddy answered. "I'm the owner of this cattle camp."

"You have a good little boy," the man said. "When he left to get you, I didn't think he would come back." He continued to drink milk as he told Daddy his story. He said he had been walking for four days without eating. The people in his family had no food, and some of them were dying, so he had set off for the city to get rations. It had been an arduous trek, and he had begun to lose all hope. Then he had miraculously spotted me and called to me with his last bit of strength. He stayed in the camp and rested for about three hours, and Daddy stayed with him, making sure he was comfortable. Then as the man got up to leave, he said, "Thank the little boy for me."

"Have a safe journey," Daddy told him. "And when you come back, stop and see me."

Several weeks had passed when the man came though the cattle camp again. He was leading a donkey laden with sorghum and other food supplies. He had with him several African man dresses and gave one to my daddy. He had also brought one for me in my size. "You not only saved my life," he told us. "You have saved the lives of my whole family."

"Let me tell you a story," Daddy told him, "a true story."

"A man went hunting one day and saw a lion in his path. As he came a little closer to the animal, he noticed that it had a piece of bone sticking out of its mouth. The bone had become stuck between the lion's teeth, causing it much pain. The man had to think quickly. Should he help the lion or kill it? Then he approached the suffering animal and pulled the bone from its mouth. He then turned and went back home.

When the man went outside the next morning, he saw a dead gazelle lying just yards from his door. Neighbors also saw the gazelle and were puzzled. They knew the man had not killed it, because there was no spear in it—so it had to have been placed there by the animal that had killed it. The next day the man went hunting again, and two hungry lions came racing, ready to pounce on him and kill him. But suddenly the lion he had befriended charged forward, letting out a loud cry as it dropped in front of the man, scaring the hungry pair away.

"You see," Daddy said, "whenever you do good by helping someone, that good deed will come back to you—but it may be through another person."

In those days, my daddy had more than a thousand head of cattle. The camps where the animals grazed were located about seven or eight miles from our village. When one area became bare, the men tending the camp would move on to another location where there was plenty of new grass and water for the animals. A crew of family members and other workers stayed at the camp tending the herds, milking the cows, and making sure they were safe. We might stay in a location for just a few weeks—or if the water and grass held out, it could be for several months.

The camp was a busy place, and with hundreds of milk cows to oversee, birthing was always taking place. Some cows gave birth without incident, but often a cow needed assistance. Daddy made sure I was trained to handle those emergencies.

"Come, Deng," Daddy called to me. "I need your help with a calf." I came running and positioned myself behind the laboring cow and *w*aited for the calf's feet to emerge. Once they appeared, I grabbed hold of the legs, trying to pull them steadily the way I had seen my father do.

"Daddy, I can't hold on!" I said. "My hands keep slipping!"

"Rub your hands in the sand," he said, "and they won't slip."

By now my hands were wet enough for the sand to cling to them, and I grabbed the calf's legs again. My hands held firm as I continued to tug. Then the cow gave a heave, and her calf dropped to the ground. There was no movement at first, and I wondered if the calf was dead. But the mother nudged the calf with her nose, and it struggled to its feet, its legs wobbling unsteadily. Then the cow licked the newborn calf's face with her long tongue, and it soon found its way and began nursing contentedly.

"It's a female!" I said excitedly. "Now we'll have another milk cow!" I couldn't help but think back to my request at Achuei's wedding. I had wanted a pregnant cow that would give birth to a female calf.

If a new calf was a male, I would be equally excited. "Wow!" I'd say. "It's a male!" Then I would make plans for training its horns once they began to surface. I would talk this way because it was customary to train a bull's horns to curve or to grow in a certain direction. The milk cows were our main source of income, but the bulls and oxen were a herdsman's pride, and he would go to great lengths to train the horns into spirals or other shapes. And if someone in the camp killed a lion, he would keep the tail as a trophy and use it to decorate the horn of an ox.

"I want to be the best cattle keeper in the whole village," I would say to my daddy. "I want to be just like you."

"And that's why I'm teaching you everything," he would tell me.

Yes, I was growing up—I no longer ran when a cow was calving. But I'd had a good reason to run before. My cousins and my half brothers used to grab me and pull me close to a cow that had just given birth. Then they would force me to open my mouth and would squirt warm milk from the cow, making me swallow it. I would struggle and try to free myself, but they were bigger and stronger than I was—plus they threatened me. "You swallow it, because if you don't, we're going to whip your buttocks!" How I hated the strong taste of it. They called it "green milk," and it was often given to children who were not well breastfed, as it was believed to be rich in vitamins.

My family also had a few goats, which were kept in the village, and I went out one day to see a mother goat that had just given birth to a pair of kids. But what I saw was very strange and disturbing.

Instead of allowing her kids to nurse, the mother had pushed them aside and was nursing on *herself.* I couldn't believe what I was seeing! Then I reasoned that *all* mothers must have to do that for the milk to flow. I raced back to the house and told my mother what I had just seen. "Did *you* do that?" I asked.

"No," she told me. Then she explained how it is natural for animals to nurse their young, and told me that what this goat was doing was not normal.

When my father was told about the goat, he made a leather cuff from cowhide and fastened it around the goat's neck to prevent her from nursing on herself and robbing her kids of their milk. After that, each time she gave birth, he would fasten the cuff to her to keep her from the disturbing habit.

In America people have hot dog–eating contests—but in the cattle camps, we had milk-drinking contests. It wasn't so much who could consume the most milk, but rather who could become the fattest. Usually one man from each family in the camp would enter the competition, and the men would sit under a tree and drink milk for several months. At the end of the designated time, judges would compare the men to see who was now the fattest. There was no financial award, but being deemed the fattest warrior was compensation enough.

I always wanted to do what I saw the grown-ups doing, so I joined the men during one of the milk-drinking contests. "What is this young boy doing here?" one of the men asked.

"It's *okay.* Let him do it," someone answered. And my father didn't care one way or the other, as long as I was where he could keep an eye on me. It had sounded like a wonderful challenge to me—and I had the best of intentions, but one month and a few pounds later I called it quits and dropped out of the contest. It wasn't the milk-drinking that got to me—it was the inactivity. I loved milk and actually lived on nothing but milk for about a year in the camp, but I needed to be free to explore and to play with my friends.

Our lives and activities revolved, to a great extent, around the weather—the rainy and the dry seasons. We didn't need a meteorologist to tell us when it was going to rain or from what direction a rainstorm would be coming. All we had to do was watch the cattle. They would stand and face the direction of the approaching rain. Then the smell of fresh rain would fill the air, well before the first drop could be felt.

When things began to turn dry and the water in a stream became too low for the cattle to drink from, my brothers and I would go looking for mudfish. They are interesting fish that can survive for weeks without water by burying themselves under mud or leaves until the rains come again. But during that time, we could easily find them by looking for the little mounds of mud that covered them. My brothers and I would hunt until we had gathered enough fish for a meal. Then we would take them home, and our family would prepare a fish stew from them that was quite tasty. Of course, my brothers and I were proud to have made such a contribution!

During the rainy season, I would sneak out and play under the trees. I say sneak because more dangers were present during this season and I was not supposed to venture out alone. Snakes were one of the dangers. One day I found a python coiled around the trunk of a tree. Of course, I didn't know it was a deadly python—I only knew it was the biggest and most beautiful snake I had ever seen! It must have measured twelve inches across, and it was the color of rich cream. Large brown spots decorated its enormous body. The snake never moved, so I thought it was dead. I wasn't used to observing snakes at such close range, and I was fascinated by it—so I stayed and watched it for a couple of hours. It's funny ... I was fascinated by the snake yet afraid at the same time. I would wander away for a while and then return again to look at the motionless snake. The longer it remained motionless, the more certain I was that it *was* dead.

Meanwhile, my family was out looking for me. My brother and sister—Garang and Agom—had been searching house to house and finally found me watching the snake. I could see that Agom was upset with me. "You are so lucky!" she said. "That snake is huge—it could have swallowed you up!" She and Garang took me home to Mother and told her where they had found me. She was relieved that I was safe after hearing their account, but she was at her wits' end with trying to keep me out of harm's way. She ordered me to stay in the house and not wander off again. "I don't want to *lose* you, my son," she said. I had gotten off easy. If my daddy had not been off in the cattle camp, he would have whipped me to teach me a lesson that could possibly save my life.

Then the very next day I went back to get one more look at the snake—but it was *gone.* That was when I realized that Agom was telling me the truth and the snake really *was* alive. They went looking for me again and knew where I most likely could be found. Now I was in *real* trouble. This time my mother was not so easy on me. She scolded me and whipped me for disobeying her again. But she knew that as determined as I was, she would have to take stronger measures to protect me. Then she and Garang came up with an idea. They fastened bells to my ankles so they could hear them and rein me in if I started to wander off.

I was still intent on exploring, but I first had to deal with the troublesome bells. Mud is wonderful. It can be used to build strong walls for houses—but when mud is stuffed inside of bells, they become *silent.* I stuffed the bells with mud and headed undetected to the riverbanks. I was skipping along barefoot at the water's edge, throwing rocks at the fish, when a neighbor saw me and took me home to my mother. With my brother Garang's help, she took a long rope—one about a hundred feet long—and tied it snugly around my ankle. Then Garang took the other end of the rope, attached a large bell to it, and fastened it to the high peak in the roof of the open cow barn. The bell would not ring unless I was pulling hard in an attempt to get away. And just to be *safe,* they hid all the knives from me in case I had any thoughts of cutting the rope! That strategy finally worked for the duration of the season.

I don't know why I was so obsessed with snakes. It really was a problem, because while many snakes were harmless, others were *deadly*—and I didn't know one from the other. My brother Ajuong and I were very close, and being *older*, he loved to tease me. There were large black-and-white snakes in the village that people claimed were harmless. Once when Ajuong and I found one of these snakes, I took a stick and touched its head and it *moved*. Then I touched its tail with the stick to see what it would do. "No, Deng," Ajuong said. "Not *that* way. Don't use a stick. You need to touch it with your *hands*." I compromised. I tossed the long stick aside and took a short stick and continued to poke at the reptile. While I was messing with the snake, Ajuong saw Daddy heading toward us and took off running, leaving me to face our dad alone.

Daddy grabbed me and held me up close to the snake, and I began to scream. Then he put me down. He had got his point across. I had no knowledge of snakes to tell which ones were dangerous— and if turned out to be harmless, there was no reason for me to be tormenting it.

On lazy afternoons, in a world far removed from smart phones, video games, and Air Jordan shoes, my cousins and I happily amused ourselves creating wonderful things from the natural resources in our village in Sudan—straw and clay. The only life we knew involved cattle, so during the rainy season when moist clay was plentiful, we constructed our own miniature villages complete with cows, bulls, and little round straw huts.

We started out by gathering a mound of workable clay, and from it we fashioned milk cows that stood about six or eight inches high. We knew the necessity of bulls in the cattle camps, so we created those too—animals with menacing horns ready to fight their opponents. The work was slow, but once we had completed our output for the day, we carefully placed them in the fire to harden. After the figures cured, we would color them using charcoal and ashes. Once our little herds were complete, we would place them to graze in a spot shaded by a large tree. Then following the routine of the cattle camps, we would bring them back later to be milked. We would engage the bulls in fights, the way we had seen bulls fight in the camps. We would eventually have several miniature villages constructed, which we would name after the nearby villages, including our own village of Wunriang. It was fun to make believe, but in reality we were learning to be herdsmen.

During the dry season when clay was difficult to dig, we played a different game. The boys in our village would compete with boys from a neighboring village to see who could gather the most rounds of dried cow dung. The competition would become very serious, with the team finding the fewest piles being the losers. This activity served a very useful purpose too, because cow dung was our main source of fuel for cooking and for the outdoor fires. We also burned wood, but the dried cow dung was plentiful and was favored because it kept disease-carrying mosquitoes away.

Our days were full of playing and of learning songs and dances. Humor, drama, and music came naturally to us, and we were constantly putting on shows in the evenings for ourselves and the other folks in the village. We would perform little skits based on things we had observed happening among the adults. One of us might pretend to be a man angrily accusing a neighbor of stealing an animal or some other item from his home. The two would argue it out, allowing the grown-ups watching to see how foolish the incident was in the first place. Or one of the boys might play the role of a revered spiritual leader counseling a villager about a problem. The most interesting skits were the playacting of young men negotiating with a man for the hand of his daughter in marriage—like how many cows is the young lady worth?

Our people love the traditional tribal dances. Late at night, after everyone was finished with their chores, they would bring out their drums and walk to what was called the "drum place," which was a large clearing just a few miles from our homes. The drums were our main source of music, so they were found in every home. There were small drums and large ones made from hollowed-out sections of logs and covered with tightly stretched cowhide. These drums were very loud and could be heard for miles.

Dancing was an activity the whole family could enjoy. While the grown-ups danced and sang under a moonlit sky, my friends and I would mimic the drummers—going through their exact motions with great animation. The dancing would last until about two o'clock in the morning, and we enjoyed every minute of it.

The workers from the cattle camps came to the dances too. They worked in shifts, so they could take turns enjoying a night out. While I was staying in the cattle camp, I went with a group of friends one night to the dance at the drum place. It was about ten o'clock when we arrived, and my friends and I played until we became exhausted and had to rest. I found a place to sit at the base of a large tree that had thick roots running above the ground. After positioning myself snugly between two large roots and leaning back, I became drowsy. I was unaware of my friends getting up and joining in the dancing without me, and as I reclined against the tree while half-awake, the rhythmic sound of the drums and the singing soon lulled me into a deep sleep.

About three o'clock in the morning I was awakened abruptly—but *not* by the sound of drums. It was a hideous, chuckling, cackling noise that sounded too close for comfort. *Hyenas!* They often roamed about the cattle camps while people slept—but I never feared them in the camp, because my daddy was there to protect me. But *this* night the noise of the hyenas had me nearly paralyzed with fear. Fortunately, I knew the direction of the cattle camp, and the moon's glow lit my path as I raced the two or three mile distance with speed fueled by fear. I was terrified of hyenas, and I wondered if I had not woken up and run when I did, they would have found me under the tree and *eaten* me. Needless to say, I never slept under the tree again at the dance.

I had learned to respect lions, snakes, and hyenas—but there were other less obvious dangers I had not yet dealt with. I loved the sweet taste of honey, and when I found a beehive in the cattle camp, I was excited. I was playing with my friends when I spotted the giant hive attached to the trunk of a tree. "See that hive?" I said. "We need to get that honey, but we need to get the bees away first." Smoke, I knew, would drive the bees away, but we weren't supposed to mess with the fire. "We can't use fire," I said, "but I don't think the bees like water either, so let's get water and chase them out."

We took some small gourd containers down to the river and filled them and carried them back to the "bee tree." Then we threw the water on the hive. I was right—the bees did *not* like water. They swarmed out of the hive like a cloud and flew directly at us, stinging us on our bodies, faces, and eyelids. I was in anguish. We ran and plunged into the river to get the bees off and to find relief from the stings. We were in really sad shape as our faces began to swell, and it took a full week for us to recover. But I was not finished. I was *angry* at the bees.

"Those bees almost killed me," I told my dad, "so I'm going to kill *them* instead!"

"You're going to kill the *bees?*" he said. "Don't mess with the bees, or those bees are going to kill *you*. Just leave the bees alone." A week and a half had passed since the bee attack, and I had recovered from the stings, but I was still angry about the incident and wanted to retaliate. I gathered a bundle of dried grass and carried fire from the camp to the beehive. I placed the dried grass under the hive and set fire to it. I had only intended to burn the hive and kill the bees—but the fire began to rage, filling the air with the smell of burned honey. The surrounding area was dry, and the flames spread quickly. Now I was *really* in trouble! I ran to my daddy. "See the fire?" I said, pointing off in the distance. There was no use denying it. "I *did* it!" I said.

A fire in the camp could be disastrous, and extinguishing it required expert teamwork, so my daddy quickly summoned his workers and shouted instructions. As an army of men tore large leafy branches from trees and began beating the flames; dozens more raced to the river and filled large gourds with water to douse the spreading inferno. All the people in the camp did their part, and after five grueling hours, the fire was finally out.

This time Daddy didn't whip me. He did something *worse*. He knew how much I enjoyed my freedom, so he made me sit for several days on the ground under a tree and under his watchful eye while all my friends *played*. All day long I could hear them laughing, singing, and playing games without me, and that was the worst of all punishments.

I had seen my older brothers and their friends doing something I thought was remarkable and decided to copy them. My friends and I were playing in the cattle camp near the pit where the cow dung was dumped. The pit was three feet or more across, and I decided to dare my friends to jump over it. "If anyone misses and falls in," I told them, "he will not get to drink his breakfast milk today." The boys all agreed to my terms, and I made the first jump, landing safely on the other side. Four more boys followed, and a couple of them barely cleared the rim of the pit.

One more boy tried but didn't succeed and fell directly into the stinking pit. He cried loudly until his father came and rescued him. The boy was a terrible mess, but things got even worse when his father whipped his buttocks for failing to do what the other boys had been able to do. The boy didn't get to drink his milk that day, and his father told him he had better learn to jump over the pit, or he would not be getting breakfast milk again until he *did*. The boy coached himself every day, practicing jumps until he triumphantly made it across the pit.

Day by day in the camp we amused ourselves with such antics. We would climb trees and then jump from them, seeing who could jump from the highest limb. Or we would race and see who could climb them the highest and quickest. We suffered a lot of tumbles from trees with weakened branches. One time I got stuck between the branches of a tree and was there for an hour before I succeeded in pulling myself lose. Meanwhile, the other boys watched and had a good laugh at my expense. I didn't know at the time that these kinds of games would prepare me for survival as a Lost Boy, in much the same way that boot camp prepares a soldier for war.

I'm not sure when I first saw it—but a monstrous form had emerged from the thick mud of the receding Anaam River as my friends and I played on its banks early one morning. Suddenly, people were shouting, *"Hippo! Hippo!"* That was the only signal needed to send men rushing to the beast, spears in hand, quickly toppling it into a motionless heap. The hippo had somehow wandered from its herd and away from the deeper water necessary for its survival. While the animals are not usually aggressive, we had learned to fear them because they kill more people than lions do in Africa.

Removing the carcass from the river was too great a task for even a band of Dinka warriors, so my daddy called for the men to bring knives and spears to butcher the hippo on-site. It was a big job—much more difficult than butchering an ox. My friends and I watched as great chunks of meat were cut from the animal, with the men being careful to save large pieces of hide to be dried and made into sturdy shields. Then they carried the meat up to the camp and prepared it for cooking. Hippo meat is quite tasty, but it is also tough and requires hours of slow cooking.

Our people have a strange tradition or belief about eating the meat of this animal. They believe it is okay to eat the meat of a hippo, but people must not eat it *alone*, lest they be cursed. According to their superstition, the consequence of eating hippo meat alone could result in a child being born resembling a hippo or an elephant. So after the meat had been prepared, everyone gathered around and waited for the countdown, "One, two, three—*go!*" At that signal, everyone tore a chunk of the meat and began to eat.

One of the most significant rituals of the Dinkas is the *rite of passage* for a young man to become a *warrior*. This was always a very solemn ceremony with maybe a hundred or more boys in their late teens lining up like military inductees to participate. Armed with spears and warriors' clubs and carrying trumpets made from animal horns, they would march single file and go from village to village, singing loudly along the way. Villagers would hear the songs as the young men approached and would gather to watch the future warriors. People understood the seriousness of the occasion and knew that they dared not interrupt the line of marchers by crossing through it.

The entire ceremony would last for several weeks, with the final day being the day when the candidates would get their *marks*, branding them as true warriors. This would take place in a large open field—one large enough to accommodate all of the family members who came to watch—or it might be held at the "Drum Place."

Elders of the villages, who had been trained to do the cutting, presided over the ritual. It was a delicate procedure and a genuine art. The marks—five lines evenly spaced, beginning in the center of the forehead, then arching slightly above the eyebrow—were cut to completely encircle the head. The lines had to be cut deep enough to leave raised scars, but precision was needed so as not to cut into large veins and cause serious bleeding. And of course, the marks had to have symmetry.

I was both excited and nervous as I watched a young man step forward and push his spear into the sand before sitting cross-legged on the ground. His face was stern as he squared his shoulders, and then he crossed his arms and stared straight ahead as if focusing on something unseen in the distance. I couldn't help but clench my teeth as the elder took a razor-sharp knife and proceeded to cut five marks, starting on the boy's forehead. I saw blood trickle from the marks and knew it must be painful; I wondered if the boy might even cry. But he didn't. Instead, without brushing the blood away, he stood up and grabbed his spear. He took a few steps, and then he poised himself and launched the spear far into the distance.

I watched the course of the missile and quickly ran with a group of young boys hoping to retrieve it. An older boy outran the rest of us and shouted with excitement as he grabbed the weapon. That was okay, because I was a fast runner and before the day was over I had collected *three* spears, which I could keep. A spear could go the distance of a football field or even farther. And if it was not found right away, it was considered an honor because it proved the ability of the thrower. It was like hitting a baseball out of the ballpark.

After receiving their warrior marks, the young men were taken to a center where they remained for about a month, or until their cuttings had healed and scars had formed. Food would be brought to the center, and often a father of one of the boys would butcher an ox on-site to serve in honor of his son who had completed the ritual with no sign of cowardice. It was the goal of most boys to someday become warriors. In fact, it was *expected* of them, unless they left the village to pursue an education. And when a young man went looking for a wife, a girl's family could judge his character by whether he had been marked.

No cattle camp was complete without a faithful cattle dog for protection and companionship. Our dog was Chibileu, a large brown African hunting dog. Chibileu was our family hero; he faithfully guarded the herds at night from perils such as hyenas, leopards, wolves, and wild dogs. He had a long muscular body and was very swift on his feet, running like a deer. He loved to hunt and would take off by himself and come back with rabbits, wild pigs, and large birds. It was not unusual for Chibileu to land a prize catch of deer, antelope, or gazelle. He had a way of letting us know, and we would then go out and collect the meat for our family's use. He was completely fearless in the face of animals that are usually dangerous to dogs—and he was always there to protect.

One day a band of baboons got into our cornfield and was destroying the crop. Ever alert, Chibileu ran out and began to fight them. Even though he was far outnumbered, he seemed to be getting the upper hand. Then my uncle, who had been watching, went to assist the dog. He was an excellent marksman, and he raced with his spear aimed and threw it hard at a baboon. But the animal saw my uncle coming and dodged, sending the spear instead, straight through Chibileu's heart. The dog fell to the ground and died instantly. When we saw what had happened, we could not believe it. My uncle was very remorseful because it was his spear that had killed our Chibileu.

We cried and cried over the death of Chibileu—we loved him so much. We took him and placed him in a grave as if he were a family member. To this day, we still remember our brave canine friend, who was with our family for many years.

It was bad enough that we had to protect the herds from things such as cheetahs and lions—but there were always the bad guys from the north, the government militia, who thought it was okay to take away our possessions. And the raids were becoming more and more violent. One day the government militia descended from the north and raided our village while we were at work in the cattle camp. After raiding the village, they came on to the camp and raided it too, and we fled for our lives. My mother, my uncle's wife, and I ran in one direction, and the rest of the families ran with the cows. The raiders ended up taking half of my daddy's cattle, and they killed my uncle in the process.

My mother, my aunt, and I escaped with our lives, but we got lost in the jungle for a whole month and came close to starving. One day I was feeling very weak from hunger and sat down beneath a tree on top of a large anthill. There was a big hole in the center of the mound, and I peered down into the hole to see what might be inside. All I could see was blackness, but I still felt that something *unseen* was in there. I took a long stick and stuck it down the hole and poked around, but nothing came out. Then I lay down on the anthill and said to my mother, "Why can't a rabbit come out of the hole so we can kill it and have *food* today?"

My mother said, "Don't worry about the hunger, son, because your stomach is *God's* plate. God can fill up your stomach at any time."

Immediately, a long snout poked out from the hole where I lay. Then a giant lizard slowly emerged. I wasn't sure at first what it was, but it was about six feet long and I thought it looked like a crocodile. We quickly ran after the animal to kill it. My aunt raced and got directly in front of it, and it stopped and closed its eyes. As we moved in closer, it started to run. My aunt ran and got in front of the lizard *again*, and it stopped and closed its eyes again. When it ran the third time, my aunt raced once more and stood in front of it. The lizard stopped and closed its eyes for the last time, and we took our tools and killed it for food.

The Dinkas believe that when a monitor lizard sees a woman whose firstborn child is a girl, it will *sleep* for her. My aunt's first three children were daughters, so she believed the animal slept when it saw her. For this reason, we were happy to have had my aunt with us. The lizard provided us food for at least a week. We had no way to cook the meat, but we ate some of it raw right away and allowed the rest to dry in strips to eat during the days ahead. I thank God for the miracle of the lizard that appeared to us that day, because without it we might have died from starvation.

Our family had been searching for us since the day of the cattle raid, and they feared we had been kidnapped by the Arab militia and taken to the north as slaves. But after a month of searching, they found us in the jungle. My aunt was so happy to be rescued, but her joy turned to grief when she was told that her husband had been killed during the raid.

After I was back in the village, I learned that James Mum, one of my cousins I played with, was missing. He lived only a few miles from me, and we often walked between our two homes and engaged in games of hide-and-seek with our village friends. I wondered whom he had fled with during the raid. If my mother, my aunt, and I had been found, maybe Mum would soon be found too. I hoped he was finding food. Maybe he had even found a lizard in a hole like I had.

Cattle at my village, Wunriang, southern Sudan (2009).

My mom's brother's wife milking cows in our village (2009).

Women returning with
grass for the huts.

Village women bundling
grass for the roof.

The women, friends and relatives, help attach the straw roof.

CHAPTER 2

Barefoot

It was early evening, and we had pulled off our sandals and stripped off our clothing—except for little shirts—and we were laughing and playing under the trees. Then suddenly the village erupted into total chaos. People were fleeing their homes screaming, while cows and goats ran through the village frightened and disoriented. Chickens squawked and fluttered helplessly, trying to avoid being trampled underfoot as bullets flew from all directions. In an instant, our peaceful village had become a *war zone*! Without stopping to put on our clothes or sandals, we ran into the forest to escape, without knowing *where* we were running to. That evening turned the pages of my life from playing carefree under the trees to journeying across several countries and eventually across the ocean.

During the previous raid, my mother and I had fled from the cattle camp, and it had been a frightening ordeal. But I had felt a little safer back in the village, because it was usually the cattle—our source of wealth—that the enemy wanted. I am thankful to my father. He understood that danger lurked everywhere, and he had taught me some valuable survival skills. "Deng," he had told me, "if you are ever in danger, either at home or in the cattle camp, just *hide*. A small boy like you can easily hide among the bushes or in the tall savannah grass." But he warned me to be very cautious about coming out into the open again. "Use your ears and eyes very wisely, and look around the area before coming out from your hiding place." Memories of the month I had spent lost in the forest with my mother and my aunt were still fresh in my mind. I hoped my escape *this* time would be much shorter.

As we ran, we expected to soon catch up with other family members. My mother had been making bread for our supper when the gunfire erupted—but the meal was never eaten. Now I wondered where she was. The sky was turning dark, and I was very hungry—but we had no supplies with us. After walking a good while, we approached a small village and people offered us a little food, but there were too many mouths to feed. A few miles farther we came to another village. I wondered if my mother might be there—or maybe my daddy or some of my siblings—but all of the people I could see were strangers. Again, the people shared a little bread with us, but again it was too little to ease our hunger. There was no milk to drink that night, and I had *always* had my milk.

We met up with other groups of people who were running, and I moved through the crowds again looking for my mother. I couldn't find her, and I began to cry. Other children were also desperately searching for family members—and *they* cried too. There were also adults in the group, and one of the men—a fellow named Ring Choi—became our leader. He did a good job of getting us organized, and he told us we should stop and get some sleep. I bedded down in the leaves, and suddenly my mother was there *feeding* me. She gave me some ground peanuts and pumpkin, and some African bread with molasses. It tasted so good! But I soon awakened because my empty stomach was hurting so badly. The wonderful meal from my mother had been only a *dream*.

About a month into our journey I found two of my cousins—Madit and Ajuong Arop. Madit was a few years older than I and was more like a big brother to me. It was comforting to have my cousins with me, but I still needed to find my parents. Meanwhile, the adults in our group kept telling us we were heading south toward what they called the "final place." It began to rain. Many of us had no clothing other than the thin little shirts we had left with, and the rains were *cold*. In order to sleep, we would make beds in the leaves and cover ourselves with them to help protect us from the rain. But the rains could be dangerous too. At times, some of the children were at risk of being swept away by torrential downpours as they slept.

After much walking, we reached the small city of Yoril. This place left me with many memories. It was the first place where we set up camp with prospects of staying any length of time. The local children in Yoril were having classes under the trees, and they welcomed us to join them, making it also my first experience with *school*. This was wonderful because next to survival itself, education was the most important thing in our lives. We learned the English alphabet and were being taught to read and write. We were told that in the absence of our mothers and fathers, *education* was now our parent. It would be our very key to survival.

It was my cousin Madit who helped me write my name in the sand using a stick as a pencil. Madit's father, Deng Malual Mayom, was my father's brother, and they lived close enough to our family in the village that we saw each other often. And now as Lost Boys, we had been traveling together for several months. Madit had quickly become my mentor, teaching me lessons I would need in my father's absence. "Deng," he told me, "*always* do what is right. If you keep doing good, it will keep you from going the wrong direction." Madit was not only a kind person; he was also very wise for his years. He believed in helping others, but he believed in using discretion. "If you are going to do something good and help a brother or other family member, be sure that what you are helping with is going to be *successful*." He didn't believe in putting a lot of effort into helping people who weren't serious about what they were attempting to do.

Even though we had settled into the camp in Yoril, food was still very scarce and people were dying every day. By this time, I had found two more of my cousins—Malual and Bol Mayombek. The three of us would scout around the area outside the camp in hopes of finding something for a meal. In our travels, we met an older lady who had a small farm not far from the camp. After we had talked and become acquainted with her, she told us she would like to adopt all three of us and have us live on the farm and be her children. We felt sorry for the lady because she was all alone. She told us she'd had three children, but two of them had died very young and the remaining son was away working in the cattle camps.

The lady had planted a large garden, and she needed help keeping the birds and monkeys from destroying her crops. My cousins and I made slingshots and kept watch over the garden, shooting birds that dared to enter the area and throwing rocks to scare the monkeys away. We were young, but we were good little hunters. We had a fire in the garden, and we would pluck the birds that we killed and roast them on sticks over the hot coals. We enjoyed working for the lady because she always gave us food for helping her and the activity there was somewhat like life had been in our own village. We spent most of our daytime hours in the lady's garden, but we always returned to the camp to spend the night.

We stayed about six months in Yoril, and because of the lady's help, we fared better than a lot of others in our group. In fact, after talking it over, we had finally decided to accept the woman's offer to adopt us. Then things turned bad in the camp. The enemy had found us and had begun raiding us daily by air, hoping to eradicate us. Our leader told us we would soon be heading to Ethiopia, where we should be safe from attacks. The news brought hope to us, because we thought it meant we were heading to the final place we'd been told about.

The air raids had been brutal in Yoril, and one day I had witnessed a harrowing sight. A local fisherman's head was cut off by an airplane bomb, and the man continued running for some distance in an open field before dropping. I didn't sleep at all that night, because every time I closed my eyes, my mind would replay the gruesome scene.

As our group quickly prepared to leave Yoril, my cousins and I told the lady with the garden that we had decided *not* to stay with her after all. We told her there was a good chance our parents had made it to Ethiopia and we needed to go there to search for them. She was saddened by the news of our plans for leaving and tried her best to dissuade us. Then she told us a story that made our curly hair stand on end. "Don't you *know*," she said, "the Malual Agueng Ber People are on the way, and they will *eat* you the moment you leave Yoril to go to Ethiopia?" Here is what she told us:

The Malual Agueng Ber are also known as "the lions' families." They have special genes that turn them into lions after death. Because of this, when one of their people dies, the family members dig a very deep grave to bury that person in. Then the family guards the grave for seven days, because at that time the dead person will try to come out of the grave—still in the form of a human, but with the mind and behavior of a lion. The family members then pile huge logs on the site to stop the dead from escaping the grave. If the dead person wins the battle, he begins at once to eat all his family members—beginning with the ones who had guarded the grave. He then kills and eats anyone who passes through his territory.

If the family members are strong and win the battle and kill the "human lion," he becomes completely dead and can no longer harm them. But they must burn the body to make sure it doesn't revive and eat them. They must be very careful to burn the body entirely, because just one drop of blood that escapes is enough to bring the body back to life, where it can continue to kill people.

The woman's face was stern and her eyes dark and piercing. "Yes," she said, "there are human lions on the way to Ethiopia, and they are fully aware of the journey of refugees who are leaving the camp. Now they have an open window too—they blend in with groups going to Ethiopia and eat people as they travel. Some of them have been caught eating dead bodies along the way." My cousins and I looked at each other in disbelief, but the woman could not have been more serious.

"It's easy to eat kids at night when they are traveling in a large group," she said, "because they can just grab them and run. Starving children don't weigh much, and they don't have the energy to fight back. And the grown-ups in the group no longer have energy to fight them either, so the human lions have this all figured out!" After the woman finished her grim tale, she looked at us again. "Now, it's your choice," she said. "You can go with your group, or you can stay here with me and I will take care of you and you will be my children forever."

The woman assured us that she wasn't trying to frighten us but felt we should be aware of the dangers that lay ahead if we undertook the journey to Ethiopia. After her bizarre story sunk in, I suddenly had the mind of a sleuth. Hadn't she told us that there were Malual Agueng Ber living close to Yoril? And wasn't her own farm close by? Of course—that was it! She was one of them! If we were to stay and become her children, once she died, she would doubtless rise from the dead—most likely as we slept—and proceed to eat us. Would she just grab us and eat us, I wondered, or would she prepare us like she would a goat? Regardless of how she planned to do it, it was a very unpleasant thought.

I discussed my theory with Malual and Bol, in the way nine-year-old boys discuss things. We all agreed that it added up. Where was the woman's husband? And why did her son never come home from the cattle camp? Why did no one ever come to visit? We definitely had to get away from the woman, but I told my cousins not to say anything to her about our plans. "If she finds out we're leaving," I said, "she'll eat us right away, and we'll never get to Ethiopia and find our families."

My cousins and I left secretly with the rest of the camp, and we were still near Yoril when we stopped to sleep for the night. In the morning when we woke up to begin walking again, one of the boys wouldn't get up. We called to him and shook him, but he didn't budge. We thought he was faking sleep, and we began to laugh at him, because his face showed no expression. We then noticed water coming from his mouth and thought it was strange, so we went and got a couple of the older boys to help wake him. After shaking the boy a little, one of them checked him more closely. "He's *dead*," he announced. "He must have died in his sleep."

Nobody knew *why* the boy had died, but it scared us to know that he had died in his sleep. If it happened to *him*, how safe was it for *us* to sleep? The young men then took the little boy's body and buried it in a garden near Yoril, and that was the end of one child's life. We all grieved for our little friend who had bravely walked so far with us. While we had been hearing reports daily of people dying, the little boy's death was the first I had personally witnessed, and it was very troubling to me.

Malual, Bol, and I continued to walk together as much as possible, along with my older cousin, Madit. Madit knew how tough it was for us to be away from our parents, and he was always encouraging us to stay strong and not give up. Then one day Madit became sick with a headache—but I knew he would be okay. He *had* to be, because he was the strong one among us. But in a matter of hours, Madit too was dead.

It was an extremely sad time for me because he was not only my *cousin*, but one of my best friends. However, the deaths of the little boy and Madit were only the beginning. One morning just days after we lost Madit, my cousin Ajuong Arop also complained of a mild headache. He didn't appear to be seriously ill, but still the men in our group monitored him very closely because there was no hospital nearby to take him to. But by afternoon Ajuong Arop had passed away too, and we were all heartbroken. When would the nightmare end?

Ajuong had a little brother, Malual Arop, traveling with us—and Ajuong's death was devastating to him. We worried about Malual because he cried so and could not be consoled. He mourned for more than two months for his big brother, but we never gave up on him. We constantly talked to him and encouraged him. We reminded him that *we* were his brothers too and that we would look after him and stick by him just as Ajuong had done. Some people told us that Ajuong had died from heat stroke, but we had no way of knowing the cause for sure.

We will never forget our cousins Madit and Ajuong because they left our village with the same hopes and dreams as those of us who survived—yet they died right in front of us. As young children, we were devastated by having to go through such struggles without the support and comfort of our parents. Still we had each other and were closely bonded through our grief.

With heavy hearts, we continued our journey to Ethiopia. On the way, we ran out of all the supplies that we had carried from Yoril for our survival. We walked barefoot, and our feet bled as we trekked across burning sands, rocky terrain, and the sharp stubble of broken roots on the forest floor. We walked at night as much as possible because the hot sun made us thirsty and water was often hard to find. The darkness also made us less visible to our enemies as we walked.

Then during the day, we would look for a shed or shelter of some kind to hide in. And we'd look for water—even *dirty* water for drinking—and we would try to rest. When nighttime came, the journey would start again. We walked in lines—hundreds of us—holding onto one another's shirts so we would not get lost in the darkness; but some children who were sleepwalking *still* got lost. That was when I found out you could walk while asleep.

Sometimes the lines were cut off by lions and other wild animals that had caught our scent while looking for food. One night as we went through the desert, I was sleepwalking and got cut off from the line for about one hundred meters. I suddenly awoke and realized that I was no longer in line with the others. I became terrified. I thought for certain it was the end of my life. Then I heard people talking in the distance, and I ran in the dark toward the voices and caught up with my group.

The continual walking was torturous to our feet. My cousin Malual Mayom's feet became terribly swollen and caused him so much pain that he told me one day he could *not* go on any longer. "Don't give up." I told him, remembering the words of Madit. "You've got to get to the final place. Don't give up *now!*" And for all the pain he was in, he kept plodding along, resting his feet only when we stopped to sleep.

There had been times when *I* had wanted to give up and turn back too. And there were also times when I knew I lacked the strength to turn back and I wanted to simply lie down and die. But the older boys would not let me turn back. "You will *die* if you go back to the village!" they warned me. And I would remember the terrible things I had seen the evening we left, and I would keep going. Earlier—before we had even reached Yoril—a cousin named Dut *did* turn back. Luckily, he made it back to our village alive, but only after a painful ordeal that he later told about.

One evening as we were traveling through the desert toward Ethiopia, one of the boys from our group was sleeping beneath an acacia tree. He overslept, and the rest of the group left without him, and he didn't realize they were gone. In the desert, there were always black crows flying and circling overhead because they are scavengers and knew people were constantly dying there. While the boy slept, the crows landed above him in the acacia tree, and one crow swooped down and plucked out one of the boy's eyes.

The boy jumped up crying and, holding a hand over his blood-smeared face, he ran until he caught up with the rest of the group. It was sad for the boy to lose an eye, but he did escape with his life. And we *all* learned a lesson. We never slept alone under acacia trees without someone monitoring us. I still hate the black crows of the desert; they seek out the dead as hyenas do, and they attack unwary people as they sleep. The African people associate the black desert crows with *devils.*

While we traveled through the land of other Dinka tribes, we faced some language barriers. At least five different dialects are spoken among the Dinkas, and the differences were confusing to us. For example, some Dinka groups call the lion *kor*, while others call the lion *chuer*, which translated into English means "thieves." When we reached the Dinka tribe that calls the lion *chuer*, they warned us to be careful because there were a lot of *chuer* in the area. We thought they were warning us to watch out for *thieves* who would take our belongings. We said, "What can they steal from *us?* We have *nothing*." They laughed at us because we didn't understand that they were warning us to watch out for the lions.

Although it was an unbearably sad and a difficult time for us, looking back, I think we should be amused by some of the experiences we endured. I often wish we could have had a video camera to capture some of those incidents. Our angels were there to protect us, and they prayed for God to block the deadly weapons of the devils from harming us.

As children, some as young as four or five, we didn't understand *distance*, so the older people in the group would keep setting new goals for the end of our journey. "Look at those mountains ahead," they would say. "They have fire on them—*that's* the place where we are going." And when we would finally reach those mountains, they would say, "Oh, the people just moved to the *next* mountain; the final place is just a little bit farther." If they had not told us these things, some of us would have just given up and died there in the desert.

Our black hair turned brown on our heads from the baking sun and from poor nutrition. Things inside our bodies were no longer in their right positions. You could count our ribs and bones through our skin. But when we finally reached Ethiopia, we thought we had at last reached a place on earth that was *safe*. There in Ethiopia we went to school and learned both the English and Arabic alphabets. The schools also taught us *survival* skills, such as how to hide from the enemy—and how to operate small assault weapons for our future protection.

We spent many months in Ethiopia, but it was far from the Utopia we had dreamed of. I was very disappointed that after so many months, I still had not located my parents and my siblings. And *death* stalked us relentlessly. People died from homesickness, cholera, malaria, traumas, and everything else that causes death.

I don't know what our grand people did in the past to cause the curse that is still plaguing us to this day. Our people are descended from Cush, the grandson of Noah in the Bible, and we went through many things that the Bible says would happen to Sudan. Chapter 17 of the book of Isaiah refers to the people of Cush, which is now Sudan and Ethiopia. The New Century Version of the Bible speaks of people who are tall and smooth-skinned. People from my tribe, Dinka, are noted for their exceptional height. My late uncle, Manute Bol, who played professional basketball, was seven foot seven inches tall.

While we were in Ethiopia, the leadership of the Ethiopian president, Mengistu, came to an end when his power was weak—and with that came the end of our dream. We were no longer safe, so we were forced to flee from that country—only to be left in the middle of *nowhere*. We had no choice at the time but to turn back to Sudan, and that proved to be another nightmare. It was a very dark time when we left Ethiopia. It was as though the sun had turned black and the days were like nights—that's how utterly hopeless we felt. We abandoned everything that could support human life and headed back to Sudan in total defeat.

Leaving Ethiopia was the worst nightmare of all for the Lost Boys of Sudan, and it was the worst nightmare of my childhood. We lost vast numbers of people, from children to old people, as we crossed the Ethiopian border back into Sudan. Thousands of our people were gunned down by the enemy, and great numbers more were swept away by rising rivers that overflowed their banks. The strong currents were hard to swim against, and people who didn't know how to swim were left in the rivers for good. But thanks to my daddy, I was not threatened by the rivers.

It was my daddy who had insisted I learn to swim. "Son," he warned me, "someday you will be by the river, and if you don't know how to swim, the river will own you *for good*." I was thankful for his warning and for his wisdom in teaching me, because his prediction came true with me crossing many rivers from Sudan to Ethiopia and back.

Back in our village, my brother Garang had learned to swim in his own way. He and his friends would fish together, and then his friends would take the fish and swim to the other side of the river, build a fire, and then roast and eat the fish. My brother couldn't swim, so he didn't get to eat with them, and this was indeed challenging to him. So finally, without his friends' knowledge, he learned to swim. Then one day the boys did as they had done before—they took the fish to the other side of the river and roasted it, leaving my poor brother alone on the river's opposite bank.

Garang then jumped into the river and was under water for almost four minutes. His friends saw him jump and thought he had drowned, so they jumped into the river to search for him. Meanwhile, he swam underwater and climbed out on the other side of the river. There, he stuffed himself with as much of the roast fish as he could eat, and then he tossed the rest into the river. His friends were really angry, but he told them, "You boys used to take advantage of me, but now *I* know how to swim. Now what is the *next* challenge?"

I would see my brother doing these things, but I didn't really want to be like him. Instead, I got close to my daddy and let *him* teach me. He showed me how to swim just a short distance at first, but not across the river. We went through this routine several times; then one day he took me to the middle of the river and left me there. I swam back to the shore because I was scared. The waters were home to crocodiles and hippos, and I didn't want to be eaten by those mean animals or be drowned in the river. My brother had learned to swim the *hard* way, but my daddy's lesson wasn't exactly easy either.

The crocodiles were rejoicing and the other beasts of the rivers were celebrating because we were back again for them to try to snatch and eat us. Thousands of people died in the rivers when we crossed them. Then the land animals, hunger, and diseases attacked us again. We lost a lot of people because there was no food or medicine. After crossing the rivers, we settled in the small cities of Pakok and Korchum, which were just inside the border of Sudan. The cities were not far from Pachala, where large numbers of refugees were already living. Hunger still followed wherever we went.

By the time we reached the camp in Pakok, our hands and our backs had little strength left; still we managed to cut down trees to clear an area for a small airport. The airport took us several months to complete, but finally the United Nations had a place where they could drop food for us. We were extremely thankful, because by that time we had suffered beyond belief. Yet with so many thousands to feed, the supplies from the UN could go only so far and we continued to scavenge for food.

In Pakok, we were surviving by hunting rats and insects and by collecting wild fruit, which grew close to a cornfield belonging to a man from Uganda. One day my cousin Deng Malual was hunting rats in the field and came across a small bag and picked it up. He looked inside and saw that it was filled with grains of corn—a prize find for a starving boy. He shouted for us to come and see the bag of corn he'd found, and we ran quickly to get a glimpse of his treasure.

The bag, however, had been placed in the field by the owner as a trap to catch the person who had stolen corn from him earlier that week. Deng's shout had alerted the man, and he was there in an instant, armed with a *hammer*. He saw Deng with the bag of corn and grabbed him and commenced to beat him with the hammer. We were terrified by the man and raced back to the camp crying for help. We saw our older cousin, Malual Ajak, and told him to come quickly and rescue our poor cousin Deng.

We arrived back at the scene and found Deng passed out lying on the ground. Malual Ajak picked the boy up to carry him back to camp, and Deng started to come to. He began pleading with him, "Please, Uncle Hammer, don't beat me again! I'm not a thief— I'm not the one who stole your corn. I just found the bag by the roadside." As frightening as the incident was, we couldn't help but laugh at Deng, because he was calling our cousin "Uncle Hammer," thinking he had been picked up by the owner of the field.

Even though the man had used his hammer to beat Deng, he had not used it with deadly force. It was because of *hunger*, not the beating, that Deng had passed out. We were all far too weak to sustain such a whipping. But our cousin Malual Ajak was very angry at the owner of the field for attacking a little boy the way he had.

The two men were ready to fight it out when other people who were there separated them and told them that fighting was not the way to settle the problem. As for Deng, within a few days he had pretty much recovered from the hammer attack.

Then the following week after Deng's incident with the farmer, I got lost in the bush while running after some rabbits. It was around 5 p.m., and the sun was going down, putting a brisk chill into the air. But as fast a runner as I was, I was no match for the rabbits and by the time I gave up the chase, the sky was completely dark. Because I had chased the rabbits in different directions, I was unable to find my way back to the camp, so I spent the night in the trees hiding from the ground animals. I could hear animal voices throughout the night and was too scared to even *try* to sleep. I was lucky that the monkeys and the leopards did not eat me in the trees, because monkeys—and especially baboons—can be deadly when they attack.

In the morning I saw some men passing by, and I jumped from the tree, shivering from the cold. The men told me they had been on a seven-day hunting trip and were carrying meat from the hunt with them. They were astonished when I told them I had spent the entire night alone in the trees. They gave me some of their meat and told me to *never* hunt by myself again. After I thanked the men for sharing their bounty, I found my way back to the camp. I was shaken by the scary adventure because it could very well have cost me *my* life instead of the rabbits'. But I was excited to have food to share with my starving friends.

Sometimes we wondered if *any* of us would survive the hunger and the terrible war of Sudan. The Sudanese government was getting weapons through the help of their Arab allies, intending to wipe us out of the land completely. But we, on the other hand, were defenseless—*nobody* was coming to *our* aid. Every time the United Nations tried to bring food to us in Pakok and Pachala, the northern government would lie to them telling them they were dropping food to the rebels of South Sudan, the SPLA. Then the United Nations would cut back and deliver only small amounts of rations to our camp, and the food couldn't begin to feed us.

In the Pakok camp, we were divided into small groups. I was in a group with my cousins Deng Malual, Malual Makuac, Ring Chol Ring, and a few other boys. Our group was called the Nayanganyiu, which simply means "small group of young boys." Our neighbors in the camp were the Marekrek group, made up of older boys.

One day as Deng Malual and Ring were cooking their food, boys from the Marekrek group came and took their food by force, leaving the young boys to go hungry.

"You know," Deng said, "those guys are going to *pay* for what they've done to us." They waited about a week until the incident had been all but forgotten and came up with a plan for revenge. They watched until they saw the older boys cooking their own food. They knew that if they tried to go and steal it, they would get beaten up, so they needed a different strategy. Deng told Ring, "Let's go over there while they're waiting for their food to cool, and I'll accuse them of stealing my blanket. Then while they're arguing with me, *you* come and grab their food and *run* with it."

Deng went over to the boys as planned. "This is *my* blanket," he said, looking at a blanket lying on a sleeping mat. "Why do you guys like to take other people's things? Is it just because you're *older*, or what?" While the two were arguing, Ring came and grabbed the pot of food and ran with it. Deng turned and raced after him. When the bullies saw that Deng and Ring had taken their food, they tried to chase them down.

Deng and Ring put on quite a show. They ran through the camp crying, "Come and *help* us, *please*! They are going to take away our food again!" Some of the older boys in the camp heard Deng and Ring and stopped the Marekrek boys. They gave them a stern warning that if they ever touched Deng and Ring, they would face consequences for it. All the time this was going on, the rest of us younger boys stood back laughing at them. They had been really convincing with their act and had taught the older boys a lesson.

My cousins and I were always looking for ways to get food—and we came up with a very clever idea. There was a river close by, and it was home to many crocodiles. The animals could provide food for us if we could just figure out a way to *catch* them. Then one day we checked the area where the packaging materials had been dumped after food and supplies had been dropped by the UN, and we found hundreds of feet of sturdy rope that had been discarded. We took the pieces of rope and laid them out on the ground in long strips. Then we took other pieces and crossed the ropes, tying them where they intersected, and made ourselves a huge net. We carried the net over to the river and attached it to the trees that stood in the water and made a giant trap.

The following morning, we checked and found a crocodile in our net. We killed the animal, dressed it, and shared the meat with our friends. During the weeks that followed, we were able to catch several more crocodiles that way, but we came close to having our net stolen by someone who had been watching us. After that, we made sure one of us stayed by the river at night to guard the net. The crocodile meat fed us for a good while—and because the creatures had fed on so many of *us* in the past, we were more than happy to return the favor!

As we continued the journey back from Ethiopia, hunger was *always* our number one enemy. Those were very dark days for us, because we were losing people left and right due to starvation. There in Pakok we tried everything we could think of to survive. That was when I found out that our stomachs can take *anything* when one is hungry. We ate leaves from trees, we ate roots, and we ate insects. And if there was nothing else to eat, we ate mud—yes, *mud*! When a person is starving, the pain becomes so unbearable that the presence of *anything* in the stomach brings a measure of relief.

Each day we had but *one* goal. That was simply to stay alive until the next day. There were also times while we traveled through the arid desert that no water could be found. The heat was intense, and the ground was so dry that boys drank their own urine to survive.

Looking back on those dreadful days, I am truly amazed that *any* of us lived to tell about it.

We were always checking out the places where trash was put, just in case any tiny grains of sorghum, beans, or corn had spilled onto the ground. Occasionally, we were in luck and found a few scattered seeds or grains. When we did, we would search the ground and pick up every piece, and then we would carry the handful back and cook it for a meal. We always said, if there had been a *chicken* in the camp, it would have died of starvation because with the way we scavenged, it wouldn't have stood a chance of finding anything on the ground to eat!

I was looking for food one day when I came across a dog gnawing on an old dried cow skin. I don't know where he had unearthed the skin, but it looked like it might have been a couple years old. The dog was lucky indeed to have found the skin at all. I knew the dog was hungry, but he couldn't *possibly* have been as hungry as *I* was. I went around behind him and crept up very slowly so that he wouldn't see me and take off running with the precious skin.

I had a stick in my hand, and while the dog concentrated on the cowhide he was chewing, I jumped up and gave him a sharp whack. The startled dog took off running with the skin clutched tightly in his jaws, but I grabbed hold of it and pulled on it with all my might. The dog was as determined to *keep* the skin as I was to *steal* it from him, and a tug-of-war ensued. When it looked as if the dog was winning, I gripped the skin even tighter with one hand and then grabbed my stick with the other and struck the dog on the head. The dog let go of the skin, and I grabbed it and raced toward home. The dog was hot on my trail, so I threw some stones at him and continued to run. "I'm a dog *too!*" I shouted. "Come again, and you will face the *real* war, my friend!"

When I got the skin home, I cut a piece off and hid the rest of it under my sleeping mat. Then I took a small container and got water from the nearby river. I cut the small piece in two and put half of it to soak in water to soften, and I put the other half in a pot of water to boil over the fire. I watched as the water bubbled around the dingy gray hide and couldn't wait to enjoy my meal! Just then my cousin Deng Malual, the boy who had called my cousin "Uncle Hammer," came to my place and saw me cooking the cow skin. He said, "Cousin, I'm *done* with this camp. There is nothing but *death* here. Let's go to Boma City."

"That's a *bad* idea," I told him. "We're too weak for that. We could be attacked on the way by lions."

"And just how long do you think you're going to survive on the dry *cow skin* you're cooking?" he asked.

"Deng," I told him, "when *my* time comes to die, I'd rather die *here* where there are people who will bury me than be buried in the stomachs of lions on the way to Boma City. *Please* stay and let me share this with you." Deng turned and walked away as I stirred the pot with the simmering cow skin. I looked for my cousin Deng the next morning and was told that he had left for Boma with a group of Lost Boys.

Two months later in the Pachala and Pakok camps, things got very ugly for us. The Sudanese government began bombing us and wanted to capture us there in our camp. We had the choice of being captured by the enemy or moving on to Boma. I had worried about my cousin Deng after he left and was greatly relieved when I located him later in the new camp.

"Why did you tell me we might end up in the stomachs of *lions* before we left?" he asked me. "That's *exactly* what happened to some of the boys who went with me."

"It was obvious," I said. "People were disappearing all the time on the way to Boma. The lions were used to hunting for people, because every day there were bodies lying outside of the camp."

Deng then told me how he himself had narrowly escaped being eaten by a hungry lion. The lions had attacked the boys on the way and killed ten of them. Deng had barely escaped one of the lions by scrambling up a tree—and the lion grabbed the boy next to him instead. Deng said he looked and saw the lion begin to tear the boy's body, and he quickly closed his eyes to shut out the grisly scene.

"I'm sorry for what happened to your friends," I said, "but I tried to tell you I was better off staying in the camp eating the dry cow skin." I credit that cow skin with keeping me alive until the UN finally dropped some meager rations for us.

"Deng," I said, "do you remember the time we tried to kill that *cow* while we were in the Pachala camp?" We had found a stray cow wandering near the camp one day and tried to kill it for meat, but we were too weak. We attempted to wrestle it down so we could cut its throat the way we normally would kill a cow, but the animal kept attacking us with its horns as it tried to get away from us. Then we grabbed it by one leg and cut it off, and the cow escaped and went running on three legs.

That was a terrible thing to do—we had been taught to kill animals in a humane manner—but when you're starving, you don't think about those things. We assumed that the animal would quickly bleed to death and be out of its misery—but we were wrong. The next day we found the cow looking very weak as it hobbled on three legs, and we were able to catch and kill it. We could then enjoy having meat for many days knowing that the poor animal was no longer suffering.

As days, weeks, months, and more than a year went by, some children among us died while they were sleeping, and some died when they were *sneezing*. It was scary when somebody sneezed; you expected that he or she would die like the others who had died sneezing. In those days, many of the Lost Boys became very skinny like skeletons. And now that we have plenty to eat, it is still hard for some of us to gain weight. For the past decade, Lost Boys of Sudan have eaten high-calorie fast foods here in the United States, hoping to gain weight, but they have failed. Their bodies seem to be locked into a pattern that cannot absorb fat.

We continued to move from place to place, setting up camp near the towns of Kapoeta and Nairus. By this time, we had been walking for several years, and I still had not located my parents or my siblings. But in Nairus I finally recognized a familiar face I had not seen since my early childhood, my cousin James Mum. He had been missing since the time I was lost with my mother and my aunt and found the big lizard. We had much to talk about as we compared our journeys, which turned out to be very similar—days without food and the loss of many friends along the way.

My cousin James had fled with a group of boys during the previous raid, so he was not among those traveling with me. But when I found him later in a refugee camp, he told me this story: They too had fled from Ethiopia in hopes of finding safety across the border in Kenya. Again, they had nothing to eat, so he and some of his friends decided to go back to get some food that had been left at the camp in Ethiopia. They had fled in such a hurry that they were unable to gather up and take the meager supplies with them, and now hunger drove them to take the risk of retrieving them.

James and the boys made it back to the camp and found the abandoned food. They rolled it in their shirts and began the long walk back to Pachala. They had been traveling for two days when they heard a strange noise behind them and turned around to see what it was. There they saw Mr. Lion King bounding towards them, mouth wide open, ready to devour them. The sight of the ferocious animal caused the boys to forget about the food they had carried for two days. They quickly tossed it and plunged into the river and crossed back safely to Pachala. They returned without food, but they were thankful to have escaped the lion, who had almost taken their lives. James told me that they barely slept for the next two nights because of visions of the beastly encounter.

It was 1992 or shortly after when we finally crossed over into Kenya and settled just inside the border at Lokichogio. There we faced hunger again and many other hardships. United Nations water truckers, or water buffaloes, would bring water for us, but the line to get it was extremely long. You could stand in the line for nearly a day to get just enough water for drinking, but nothing to use for cooking food. The water lines became a battleground of sorts, with the stronger people getting water first. The weaker ones like me would get water only after the stronger ones had gotten theirs.

While I was in the camp at Lokichogio, I became deathly ill from a tapeworm inside me, and I couldn't keep any food down. Every time I tried to eat, I would throw the food back up. I was also passing a great amount of blood, so I became terribly weak. But thank God, by the help of the UN, I was admitted to the portable hospital they had set up for us in Kenya. It was July when I was admitted, and in August almost everyone in the Lokichogio camp was moved to Kakuma camp, which was just inside the Kenyan border in what was called the Turkana District. Since I was still in the hospital, I was kept behind along with the other patients until everyone else had moved.

The hospital was a large tent where between thirty and forty patients were receiving care. One night I heard a loud commotion and learned that we were being attacked by one of the Turkana gangs from Kenya. These gangs were notorious for their thievery and were a constant threat in Kenya. Although some of the patients were injured, we all survived the raid, but the gangs succeeded in stripping the hospital of most of its supplies of bedding and food.

I was thankful that I had cousins who had thus far survived the journey along with me. My cousin Majok Nyol Kuol was with me in the hospital, taking care of me and tending to me the way a mother would. He used to wash me like a little baby, and he would feed me my food because I was not strong enough to feed myself. I had become so weak that I was given ten units of blood to replace the blood and fluids my body had lost.

An interesting thing happened while I was recovering in the hospital: I would talk in different tongues while singing the church songs I had heard in the camp church services. I hadn't attended the services, but I would walk by outside and hear the singing. The words of the songs and the message they conveyed drew me like a magnet. My faith in God is what encouraged me throughout this time of illness.

A few days later in August, those of us who had been left at the hospital were taken to the Kakuma camp to join those who had been moved there earlier. This marked the end of our walking; we had at last reached the "final place." The camp was a vast expanse of desert, and the temperature was brutally hot, with few trees to bring shelter from the sun. The United Nations had dropped off materials for us to begin building shelters, which would consist of simple wooden frames covered with banana leaves or whatever materials could be found. The name of the camp, Kakuma, is a Swahili word meaning "nowhere," which proved to be a very fitting name.

I thought by this time that I was free from Mr. Tapeworm, but he was still hiding inside my body. He started his campaign again in my stomach and wanted to *kill* me. On the other hand, God said *no* to Mr. Tapeworm. I went to see the doctor at the hospital and told him that the tapeworm was still in my stomach, and he asked me how I *knew* that. So I told him that I went to the wood lines to use the bathroom, and when I was through, I saw small pieces that were the tapeworm's soldiers.

I explained to the doctor that I had been admitted to the hospital for a whole month because of the tapeworm before we came to the Kakuma camp. He then gave me some small pills and told me to take them as soon as I got home. The pills were pink and tasted sweet like candy, but they were deadly to the tapeworm's body. In a matter of hours, I retrieved my offender. I quickly put it in a trash bag and took it to the hospital for the doctor to see. He was astounded to see that I had been carrying around a tapeworm that was more than *three times* the length of my body! He told me that I was very fortunate, because I had been just a few days away from death. God had refused to let the tapeworm destroy me. From that day, I began to regain my strength, and my life was soon back to normal.

There at Kakuma, we began having school under the trees again. We didn't have many supplies, but because the ground was dry, we could do our lessons by writing with sticks in the sand. The important thing was, we were getting an *education,* and that would be our key to survival in the future.

At the same time our food supply was *decreasing* in the camp, the refugee population was *increasing.* We had refugees from Ethiopia, Uganda, Congo, Somalia, and a large number from Sudan and other places. The camp had become extremely overcrowded, and there was never enough food. We would each get a small ration of food that was intended to last for seven days. In the Lost Villages, or Minors—called that because we were all minors—we found that putting our rations together helped to stretch our food until the next cycle came. But sometimes we ran out of food entirely and had nothing to eat for days.

When we didn't have food, we called those days "Black Entertainment Days," or BED. It was our way of coping with the unthinkable. We had small areas in the camp where we came together to entertain ourselves and try to get our minds off our hunger. We called those places "Minors Problem Church," or MPC. In the MPCs, we used to discuss our problems—what would come *next*, the *solution* to the problems, and what could be done to *minimize* those problems that faced us daily in the camp.

We were bonded like family—the older Lost Boys taking care of younger ones. We played soccer and basketball and competed in comedy shows for our own entertainment. For example, some Lost Boys would make jokes about themselves. We made fun of those who had been lost running after rabbits like I had … and my cousin Deng Malual, who had called my cousin Malual Ajak "Uncle Hammer." We made fun of other guys too. For example, some boys used to cry because of hunger, and it was easy to make fun of them because we *all* had the same problem. I ran after the rabbits and got *lost* because of the hunger. My cousin Deng got *beaten up* by the owner of the cornfield because he was hunting rats, hoping to have meat for one more meal.

Next to survival itself, education remained our *number one priority*; we knew there was no way out of the camp without it.

Because we were away from our own families, we used to say that education was "our parents." During the days, we continued to have classes under the trees while waiting for schools to be built. Then after our regular classes, from four o'clock to six every day, we had Bible study.

I looked forward to the daily Bible classes. I was learning a lot of things about God that I hadn't known before. The more I studied the Bible, the more my personal faith grew. Then came one of the most important days of my life—the day I was confirmed by the Catholic Church and afterward baptized. At my baptism, I took the name Dominic as my Christian name. There were several names I could choose from, but I chose the name of one of the priests who had been instrumental in our education. Unfortunately, Father Dominic died before I had a chance to meet him, but I know I was named in honor of a very special man.

We had finally built a crude schoolhouse from tree limbs and leaves and had furnished it with benches made from mud brick. This was a big improvement over sitting under a tree and writing in the sand. Then the UN sent plywood and other building materials for a simple school to be constructed. It was a happy day when we actually moved into a wooden structure, complete with wooden benches to sit on during our classes.

In the evening hours, we studied hard for our examinations, and when we had our finals, I was one of the top three students in our classroom by grade points. Most of our teachers were from Kenya, Ethiopia, and Sudan, but there were also teachers from various other countries. We started learning Swahili in the school, and that helped us later in our final examinations in the eighth and twelfth grades.

Learning Swahili also helped Sudanese and Kenyan women in the shopping centers because of subtle differences in important words. For example, the Arabic word for bedsheet is *milaya*, while the Swahili word *malaya* means "prostitute." Misunderstandings in the use of these words caused fights to break out among the women when Sudanese women went to purchase bedsheets from women who spoke Swahili. The Kenyan shopkeepers, who understood only Swahili, thought the women were calling them *prostitutes*, and they did not take it very well. These language disputes would finally be settled once someone who knew *both* languages intervened.

Back to the food problem ... tribalism was there—the strong overpowering the weak—with food being the objective. Members of the Kenyan tribe known as the Turkana gangs, the same gangs who had raided the UN hospital while I was a patient there, were notorious around the camp, and they were dealing with hunger the same as *we* were. They used to enter the camps at night and take people's belongings by force. They were to be feared because they always carried weapons and didn't hesitate to behead anyone who dared challenge them.

The United Nations had built a storehouse within the Sudanese camp and had stocked it well with building materials, medicines, kitchen and school supplies, and bicycles. The storehouse was robbed once during the day by the Turkana gangs. After the storehouse was raided, the people in the camp followed the gangs in the plunder, resulting in a free-for-all that left the place in shambles. The stolen goods were worth about five million dollars, because the storehouse held supplies intended for *thousands* of people throughout the refugee camp.

The intruders had come armed with knives, and the raid left two people dead and many refugees suffering stab wounds. Two large snakes that had somehow entered the building were also found dead. Such raids were possible because the Kenyan government failed to provide security for the refugees in the camp. It was an extremely frustrating and frightening time for us, and there was nothing we could do about it. We either *died* or we *survived*—there were no other alternatives. We just clung to our faith in God. That was the only way we could endure the challenges we faced.

It was 1993, and a big bus pulled into the camp at Kakuma. Men began spilling out of the bus and spreading about in our area. We were all curious as to who the visitors might be. Then we saw cameramen and other members of the media and assumed it was something the UN was doing. But then a tall figure emerged from the group—*very* tall. I recognized him at once as my uncle Manute Bol. I'm not sure if it was from seeing lost family again, or if he was reacting to the misery of our existence in the camp, but he began to cry. He gathered with a group of us under a large tree and began to speak. He told us that he was now living in America and playing basketball with the NBA. We'd had no idea that he had become a famous athlete—but after hearing his story, we felt very humbled that he would travel halfway around the world to see us. He spent some time with us individually, giving us each a little money for food. He also gave a large sum of money to the UN at that time to help make sure we were fed. I wonder if he even realized the effect his acts of compassion had on us. His visit was truly a blessing from Almighty God.

Time dragged on, but my life stood still. We had long ago reached the "final place" we had dreamed about—but was *this* all there was to it? I was twelve years old, and I couldn't fathom spending the rest of my life in such an existence. Then an unexpected visit from a stranger set the wheels of change into motion.

It was midafternoon one day in May and I was out playing soccer with my friends, when a taxi paused in front of the shelter I shared with half a dozen boys. Vehicles came through every day, but they were usually headed toward the United Nations center on business. Then the taxi came to a complete halt, and a woman stepped out. I wondered who she was and why she was stopping in *our* area. She looked to be about thirty years old and had a pleasant face. She glanced around a moment, and then she spotted me and spoke as if she *knew* me.

"Just *look* at you!" she said. "You've got some *height* on you!" She could see that I didn't recognize her, so she continued, "You don't remember me, do you? I'm Nyanaguek Anyel—your aunt Anoon's daughter."

Suddenly it began to come back to me. Our mothers were sisters, and they had managed to keep a close relationship despite the eight-hour distance that separated them in the villages. I remembered walking to my aunt's home with my mother when I was very young. We would stay with her for a day or two to visit, and then we would set out on foot to return home again. Mother never minded the long walk, because family relationships were vitally important to us.

Nyanaguek too had fled from home when her village was raided, but she had gone with a group to Egypt. There she had met and married Maluak Ayuel, a Dinka refugee who had graduated from the University of Alexandria. They later moved to the West Pokot District in Kenya and had five young children. Her husband was now serving in the military and was stationed in Sudan, but not in the area we had come from.

I wondered how my cousin had found me among the many thousands of refugees. Then she explained that someone who had left the camp told her I was there and told her which zone I was in so she could locate me. We talked at length, and then before she left she told me she would be back in a few months to take me home with her and put me in a Kenyan school. For me, reuniting with Nyanaguek was nothing short of a miracle!

I didn't hear from my cousin during the following months, so I tried to put the idea out of my mind because I didn't want to be disappointed. Then seven months later, in December 1994, she came back, keeping her promise to take me home with her.

When Nyanaguek's taxi pulled up, I was outside playing soccer with my friend John Bol and some other boys. I had told them about her promise to take me home, so they were not all that surprised to see her. "You are so *lucky*," John Bol told me. "You are really lucky to have someone come and take you out of this place and put you in *school*!" I knew what John said was true, and I hoped he too would someday have the same good fortune.

"Go and grab your things," Nyanaguek said. "And put a *shirt* on!" I was so used to going shirtless that it hadn't occurred to me that

I even *needed* one. So I grabbed the only shirt I owned, along with the small backpack that held my writing materials and report card, and got into the waiting cab. Then I said good-bye to my friends and waved to them as the driver pulled away.

I leaned back in the seat of the taxi, savoring the experience of my first ride in such a vehicle. Not that it was *luxurious* in any way—but for someone who had trod barefoot for hundreds of miles, it was no less than *heavenly*! The UN had brought equipment into the refugee camp in the past—equipment to be used for clearing and digging. And I had perched atop some of these vehicles next to the driver on a few occasions, but that had been the extent of my motorized travel.

The only form of identification I had was my school report card, and when we were stopped at the checkpoint on our way to West Pokot, the Kenyan police tried to give my cousin and me a difficult time about it. He refused to accept it as valid identification and told my cousin to "support" my report card, which was his way of asking her to give him money so that he would let me go.

He knew that since I was just a student, I wasn't apt to have any cash on me, so my cousin handed him some money. They referred to that as *towa kitu kidogo*, or TKK, which literally means, "Bring out something small," meaning a small amount of *money*. In the United States, we would call it a bribe. But we didn't let it bother us, because that seemed to be standard procedure in Kenya.

After I arrived at my cousin's place and had settled in, she took me to the West Pokot School to register me for the fourth grade. The headmaster looked at my school records and wanted to place me in the fifth grade because of my high grades. I had just turned twelve, although at the time I had not yet learned my *true* age. I was actually two to three years older than most of the students. But I asked to be allowed to stay in fourth grade because I was weak in the Swahili language and would need to be able to keep up with the other students. He understood my request and granted it.

One day one of the students took advantage of my weakness in the language. The teacher had asked me to greet another classmate by saying, "How are you?" in Swahili. The correct word was *hujambo*, but I wasn't sure if I had remembered it. Then the teacher stepped out of the room for a moment, and another student told me that the correct word to say was *ninakupend*. I looked at the girl I was to greet and said, "Ninakupend," and all the students in the room began to laugh. I wondered why they were laughing, and then I found out that instead of *greeting* her, I had said, "I love you."

When the teacher returned and found out what I had said, she was quite upset with me, so I explained what had happened. She then took me to the teachers' conference room, along with the boy who had set me up, so the headmaster, or principal, could handle the situation. At first, he was going to whip me, but when he found out that the other student had tricked me into saying the forbidden word in front of the class, he whipped *him* instead. Some of teachers were amused and were chuckling, but others felt sorry for me because they knew Swahili was my third language and that I was still struggling with it. In Africa, it was considered shameful for someone as young as we were to say, "I love you" to a person of the opposite sex. But they told me I was not in trouble, and I was allowed to return to the classroom and continue my studies.

Swahili was still somewhat difficult for me, and I got a C in it on my exam—but the student who had told me to say the "love" word ended up with a D, and I couldn't help but feel somewhat smug about it.

I came in fifth out of seventy students in the final exam and felt satisfied, even though it was a little lower than I had placed in the past. I had usually been among the top three students in our school, but I had been sick a few months before the exams and was unable to study as much as I liked. My eyes had become swollen and sensitive to light, and I thought for a while that I wouldn't be able to complete my finals. I thank God, because it was by his mercy that I passed my exams. As a result, I was selected to attend Ortum High School, considered the best school in that district.

I enjoyed my home life at my cousin's house, and I assumed the role of "big brother" to her children. Her boys—Atem Maluak, Aluel, and Roor—wanted to know *everything* about my journey with the Lost Boys. "Tell us a story," they would beg. "Tell us about crossing the rivers where there were crocodiles!" When I was not studying or playing sports, I regaled them with stories of my adventures of survival in Ethiopia and Sudan. Who would have thought that the intense suffering we had endured would provide *entertainment* to curious children?

I had been used to looking out for myself, as well as for younger boys in my group in the camp, so I was happy to help out at home. My cousin's girls, Nyankiir and Abuk, were too young to help much with the meals, but I was quite comfortable in the kitchen.

Nyanaguek would occasionally travel to Sudan to visit her husband at the military base, and she had a maid who was there to oversee things in her abence. The maid was surprised at the way I would take over in the kitchen and do the cooking. "You think that because I'm *young* I don't know how to prepare meals," I said. "You forget that I've been cooking my own food for years."

My domestic skills came in handy when the maid picked up and left while Nyanaguek was away for two weeks. During that time, I got up at six o'clock every morning and fixed breakfast for my cousins, and I prepared dinner for them after we came home from school in the evening. I also made sure the laundry was done and the house was kept clean. Things actually went smoothly, but Nyanaguek was quite disturbed when she returned and found the lady *gone*.

"What happened?" she wanted to know. "Why did she leave?"

"She told me she couldn't stay, because you hadn't *paid* her," I said.

Nyanaguek was in disbelief. "I don't know why she would say that—I paid her in *advance* before I left!" I didn't know what to make of the situation, but I *did* know that my cousin was an honest person. Then before long the girl returned, expecting to still have her job. Nyanaguek confronted her about the pay, and she held to her story. Then Nyanaguek took out the ledger, where she had kept a careful record of her weekly payments along with the girl's signature as proof that she had received the money. The girl apparently had some personal problems she was trying to deal with and, in my cousin's absence, had walked off the job.

Just because I was out of the refugee camp didn't mean that schooling was without effort. The school was a good distance from home, and I would walk with my young cousins for nearly two hours each way. Whenever money allowed, Nyanaguek would give us bus fare so we could ride—but most of the time we were content to walk.

As if I didn't have enough nicknames *already*, the students in Kenya gave me still *more*. My close friends called me "Rafiki," Swahili for friend. Others liked to call me "Babu," which means "grandfather." I didn't mind it, because I *was* older than the other students in my class.

Language skills took priority in the schools, but our regular curriculum included other subjects such as math, science, and geography. We learned about the other continents and countries of the world, including the United States of America, but I saw it as just another place on the map—a place far across the ocean.

I was happy that our school had an athletic program and I got to play soccer and volleyball in the eighth grade. This was fun because I had enjoyed soccer while I was in the refugee camp. I also joined the school's track team and competed in the four hundred by four, a four hundred meter relay with four runners, for eighth graders, I placed number one in our district. Our track team then went to the province finals, and things were tougher there, but our district was still in the top ten districts of Rift Valley Province in Kenya.

When I entered high school, I again joined the soccer team, and our school's team was very good. We beat the other teams in our district and went to the finals again. There at the finals, our school came in number four out of several high schools. I also got to be on the high school track team, which made me happy because I had always been a good runner.

In the spring of 1997, an announcement was made saying that *all* refugees had to go back to the camp for a head count, so I returned to the camp for about two months. Afterward, I came back to my cousin's home and continued going to school. Then when the school break came, I received a letter from my cousins James Mum and Ajuong Majok Malual saying that the boys there were being processed for going to the United States of America. They said if I was interested, I needed to come back to the camp again.

I had never been in the same camp as James and Ajuong, but they had found out that I was living with our cousin in West Pokot and had gotten her address so they could write and give me the good news. I thought it sounded like a great adventure, but with my limited knowledge of this place called the United States, I thought perhaps they were just moving us to a better *refugee* camp. Yet as always, my main concern was for my education. I hoped I would have the opportunity to continue my schooling, should I be among those selected to go. I showed the letter to my cousin Nyanaguek to see what she thought about it, because I trusted her opinion. She said it was a rare opportunity for someone like me—one that could change my entire life. But she urged me to make my own decision.

Before I left the Kenyan camp, I received some devastating news from one of my countrymen. The man informed me that our village had suffered a major raid again in 1996. My daddy had been killed during the conflict, and all the cattle had been taken from the camps. By that time, the herds in the camps my daddy oversaw numbered about five thousand head, but the number of cattle he personally owned was around five hundred.

Thousands of people resided in the Kenyan refugee camp, but the directors tried to group the people together based on the country and county they had come from. That way, people often found lost relatives or neighbors simply by knowing which zone they were in. That was how my cousin had managed to find me years earlier.

I asked the man how he had recognized me. "You resemble your father," he told me. "Besides, I remember you from the village when you were just a little boy. I worked in your father's cattle camp." There is the saying "Like father, like son," and I was proud to have my father's blood living on in me. I had been very close to my dad as a child, and it pained me to think how tormented he must have been after I left, not knowing whether I was dead or alive. But he was aware of the dangers I might someday face, and he had trained me to be a *survivor*—so I like to think he knew I was okay.

The man told me how much the people of our village mourned and wept because my daddy was gone. They had all admired his leadership and kind devotion to his people. The enemies took all the cows from the camp, the man said, and killed a lot of people in the process. But my daddy had *refused* to run for safety. He guarded the cattle camp with his life, the way a captain guards his ship. The man didn't give me any further details of my father's death, but I hoped someday to find out exactly what had happened. My daddy will always be remembered as a brave leader, not just in *my* memory, but in the memories of all the people of our village.

I was greatly saddened to learn of my father's death—but the man brought me *good* news as well. My futile searching of the refugee camps over the years had left me wondering if my parents and siblings had all been killed at the time I fled. But the man told me that my mother was still living. My mother—the woman who had daily occupied my thoughts—was still *alive*! How I wished I could let her know I too was alive and living in Kenya.

"You can arrange to speak with your mother by radio," the man said. "Some men from Somalia have set up a radio station where people from the camp are making calls to southern Sudan, Somalia, and even America." He gave me the information I would need to arrange my call, and I was soon on my way.

The Somalian men wanted one hundred Kenyan shillings for

thirty minutes' radio time. It was not a bad price to be able to connect again with my mother, yet an enormous amount for a boy with no money. Fortunately, my cousin James Mum was with me in the camp at that time, and he agreed to share his food rations with me for a week so I could sell my own food to pay for the call. After arranging for the call, James walked with me the six miles to the radio location, where we stood in line for two hours awaiting my turn to talk.

My brother Garang had helped get my mother to a place where she could receive my call when it came. I was almost in shock at hearing my mother's voice. Speaking to her seemed unreal—almost like the whole thing was a joke. She had her doubts too, because my voice was no longer that of a child. Then she thought of a question that only I could answer.

"Who is Achel Anguam?"

"That was my *mother* cow—the one you nicknamed me after." I could feel it over the radio—her tears of joy as she realized she was actually speaking again to me, her lost son. We talked for perhaps fifteen minutes—conversing in the Dinka language, which is what my mother understood. My brother Garang, too, was amazed to hear my voice. He wanted to come and take me back home to the village, because he had heard of the violence and killings occurring in the camp where I was. He didn't want me to be killed like our father had been.

"No, my brother, "I said. "It would take you many months to come by foot to this camp." He wanted to know how my life in the camp *really* was, and I told him the place was neither bad nor good—it was just a place to *survive* until my day would come. He was still asking me questions when my radio time ran out.

I knew it was not realistic to go back home, but hearing my mother's voice again brought back many childhood memories. I envisioned life back in our village, and I wondered if I would still recognize Garang and my other brothers and sisters when I saw them. My mother's face was the only one that was still clear in my mind.

The news that some of us would be leaving Kenya to come to the United States brought a ray of hope after many years of suffering. We had teachers who worked patiently with us helping prepare our "stories," or biographies. It was challenging for us because we had to look back over several years and try to recall just where we had been at various times in our travels.

The teachers also briefed us on American culture and showed us pictures from places such as New York City, with its tall skyscrapers and the famed Statue of Liberty.

It came as a surprise to all of us when we encountered the judges who would be questioning us during the processing. We had never expected to be interviewed by *white* judges from the United States. This scared a lot of the boys. Some of the judges wanted to know why we had left Sudan at such a young age without our parents. Because of the clever way northern Sudan controlled the news media, the judges were unaware of the terrible genocide that had been taking place. They were being told different things by the Sudanese government. One common explanation was that we had been captured by southern Sudanese rebels and taken from our families by force. This, of course, *never* happened to us. Why would rebels take us away from our parents when the rebels were the ones *protecting* us from the Sudanese government? All of the rebels in southern Sudan were from among our own people.

From the time I left my village to flee to Ethiopia, I'd had no way of knowing whether my daddy was dead or alive. I had failed to find him during my search of the refugee camps, so I thought he may very well have been killed in the raid the day I left. But now that I had learned the *truth* about his death, I told one of the judges that my daddy was no longer alive. And when she asked me *how* he had died, I just said he had died of natural causes. I didn't want her to start quizzing me about *when* and *how* I had become separated from my family.

We had to tolerate a lot from the judges who had been sent for our interviews. First, they looked at our life stories, and then they quizzed us on everything that was written down to make sure our facts matched up. This required us to remember all the details of our travels from Sudan to Ethiopia, back again to Sudan, and finally to Kenya in 1992. The interviews were very intimidating to the boys. With all the walking and moving about we had done, it was difficult to remember all the details, and this caused some of the Lost Boys to fail their interviews.

The prospect of leaving the refugee camp to come to America was causing excitement in the camp. Sadly, only a select group would make it—only those who successfully passed their interviews. If they had passed, their names were put on a large board for everyone to see, so people would go to the UN compound daily to search the board to see if their names appeared.

Yet as significant and life-changing as the move would be, we hadn't taken it seriously in the beginning. We had thought it was a joke—like being told you've won something when it was just a gimmick. Because of this, some of us—my cousins and I included—made up *nicknames* to use during our processing. Then when we were asked for the *correct* names in our interviews, some names failed to match with the stories. The judges were not aware of our using nicknames and thought we were lying to them, so they were not pleased. My cousins and I avoided that problem by *keeping* those nicknames during the interviews and changing them to our correct names later when we came to America.

Another factor that caused some of the boys to fail their interviews was the language barrier. Some of the translators had trouble translating the stories the Lost Boys had told the judges. The translator who was working with me and my cousins Deng Makuac and Kiir Akol was having a lot of difficulty with the language. She tried very hard, but I caught her translating something to the judge incorrectly, and I said, "No" to her in English.

"You speak *English*?" the judge asked, sounding surprised.

"Yes, I do," I told him. "I know a little bit." And from there I went on to explain everything to him, answering any questions he had.

"Good job!" he said when we were through. "You did very well—but since you can speak English, why did you let the lady *translate* for you?"

"I didn't want to interrupt her from her job," I told him politely. "And I knew she was being *paid* to translate."

After my cousins and I had gone through the interviews successfully, we were excited to learn that we were among the Lost Boys who would indeed be going to America. Still it was a bittersweet experience. When we left the camp, friends and families were crying because we knew there was a good chance we would never see each other again.

Life in the camp changed for our friends who had failed their interviews and were left behind. They felt as though the world was ending for them, because we were leaving them in a place they called "the hell of the world," while *we* were going to the land of opportunity, where we would become educated and lead a good life. They were concerned that living in America would change us and make us forget our Sudanese heritage. Some of the Lost Boys said that while they *did* believe we had spent time in the camp for a reason, they did not think we were meant to live there *forever*. A total of thirty-eight hundred Lost Boys made their way to the United States that year, settling in various cities across the country.

On January 31, 2001, I left Kenya along with my cousins Deng Makuac and Kiir Akol, to go to Richmond, Virginia, in the United States. Deng Makuac was only seventeen, and I had agreed to take responsibility for him and had also borrowed money to pay for his travel documents. Many of the Lost Boys had already gone to the United States ahead of us and were now enjoying a new life. Among those boys were my cousins James Mum and Mayom Ajuong Majok Malual—the ones who had written the letter telling me to return to the camp for processing.

About one hundred Lost Boys were on the plane leaving Kenya that day. They were actually young *adults*, ranging from fifteen to twenty-five years of age, but they had been given the label of "Lost Boys" and it had stuck. The number was broken down into small groups who made the trip sticking together as families. My group consisted of my two cousins, myself, and four other boys. It was easy to identify us at the airport because all us wore pale gray sweaters with the letters "IOM" on the front, and we carried small tote bags with a few personal belongings. From our appearance, we might have been members of an athletic team, but the initials stood for International Organization for Migration— the organization that had handled our interviews and processing at the Kenyan camp.

The flight from Kenya was quite an experience for all of us because most of the boys, including myself, had never been on an airplane before. In my head, there was still the image of the first motor vehicle I had ever seen—the one I had thought was an *animal*. You can imagine the culture shock of boarding not just a *motor vehicle*, but one that would actually travel across the *sky!* Some of the boys had trouble with motion sickness and threw up on the plane, and others were frightened by the jolt they felt whenever the plane took off or landed.

Traveling from Nairobi, Kenya, to Belgium was amusing at times—like when one of the boys walked into the glass doors at the airport because he was not familiar with such things as clear glass. Automatic doors and flush toilets in the airport were a little frightening too. It was the beginning of *new things* and a *new life* for all of us.

Nobody could blame us for our ignorance of these things. The bloody government of Sudan was cruel. They developed their *own* part of the country while refusing to provide schools for the kids in southern Sudan so that they could learn about and maybe tour places that had automatic doors and modern conveniences. Clearly the government cared only about seizing the wealth and resources of our land.

Dominic taking the eighth-grade national exam, Kenya Certificate of Primary Education, required to pass to attend high school (Kapenguria, West Pakot District, 1999).

Makutano Primary School,- Kenya (2000). (Left to right) Cousin Atem Maluak Ayuel, Dominic, principal Mr. Sango, Makuie Deng Mabior (nephew to John Garang de Mabior, former leader of the South Sudan Movement).

CHAPTER 3

Hello, America!

I was designated as the leader, or "captain," of our group of seven boys as we traveled. I didn't mind, because the years I had attended school in Kenya while staying with Nyanaguek had given me a definite advantage the others didn't have. I could read and understand both English and Swahili, although I was not fluent in either. So from airport to airport, my cousins and friends would sleep while I watched the screens for flights. And if I wasn't sure of something, I was not afraid to ask. Then after a very long flight, I looked out the plane's window and saw in the distance a giant figure with skyscrapers in the background. As we came a little closer, I recognized it as the Statue of Liberty. We were landing at the airport in New York City—we were in *America* at last!

After we had been in the air for more than thirty hours, traveling from Africa to Europe to America, our legs were stiff and our bodies were weary—but we weren't *home* yet. We still had to fly from New York to Washington, DC, and on to Richmond, Virginia, where we had been told we would be living.

At the airport in Richmond, we were welcomed by a young man who introduced himself as Michael and told us he had been assigned to be our caseworker. He had come from Somalia, but he was a Christian follower. He took us to the apartment that had been rented for us by a local church for four months. Once we got inside with our bags, all we wanted to do was sleep, so we went directly to bed and slept nearly all day.

It felt strange getting up during the next few mornings, because things somehow didn't seem right. The sun *rose* from the wrong direction and *set* in the wrong direction. It was the first week of February, and the sun was not over us in the same place as it would have been in Africa. Friends of ours who had recently arrived told us that they were confused by the sun's direction too. Another thing was the trees: they looked like they were *dead*, because they had no leaves. In Africa, trees do not lose their leaves in winter. And the weather ... we had arrived in America during the most *frigid* time of year, and we had never experienced such cold!

Volunteers from churches in the area helped the three of us settle in. They had furnished our rooms with beds and blankets before we arrived, and now they came with warm clothing, books, a TV, and a radio. They also took us out and showed us the different places we would need to become familiar with, such as the post office, bank, and shopping centers. I was thankful for the time I had spent attending school in West Pokot, Kenya. It made for easy communication with the volunteers. My cousins were also fortunate to have gotten a little background in English at school in the camp before we left Kenya.

Our sponsors and volunteers were a tremendous help. Some of them paid our rent until we found jobs and could pay it ourselves, and the organization that helped us settle in paid our utilities. But we did have a surprise one day when we found that our power had been cut off. It was an oversight, of course. Someone had forgotten to pay the electric bill. We called and got it straightened out, but in the meantime, we had no lights and the food in our refrigerator went bad. The boss came to our apartment later to make sure everything had been properly taken care of, and he apologized for the slipup. We realized it was all a part of adjusting to life in America, but it was a hard thing for us as newcomers to the country.

Month by month in Virginia, we moved forward with our new lives. Before I got a job, I met a very kind lady named Sally Bolte who attended the Presbyterian church. She and her husband knew we needed better transportation than the used bicycle I was riding, and they promised to give me a car if I could pass the driver's test at the DMV. I knew it would cost money to drive a car, so I began looking for work right away.

I soon got a job washing dishes at Popeye's, plus a second job as a host at the Great American Restaurant. I was so eager to drive that I would study for my driver's test while riding my bike to work. After just a week, I went to the DMV and took the test, but I failed it because I didn't know how to use the computer touch screen. But when I went back a second time and took the written test, I passed it.

When Mr. and Mrs. Bolte learned that I had passed my driving test, they brought the car—a Honda—and explained everything about it from the inside out. With good transportation, the world would definitely begin to open up for my cousins and me—once I actually learned to *drive*.

My cousin Mum, now called "James," was living with his brother Mayom in Grand Rapids, Michigan, with their foster parents, Rita and Gary VanderVen. James and Mayom told Rita about us, and she gave us a call, and we got acquainted by telephone. A short time later she had a business appointment in Washington, DC. So she flew there bringing Mayom and James with her, and then she sent them on by train to visit us in Richmond.

Rita was amazed when she heard our life stories, and she quickly became close to me like a foster mother, although she lived at a distance. She had a college friend named Penny who lived in the Richmond area, and she told Penny we might need some assistance. Unlike many of the Lost Boys, my cousins and I did not have foster parents to help us. We had a caseworker and sponsors who helped us, but we had moved directly into our own apartment. So Penny got in touch with us and made herself available should we need help with anything.

There *was* something I needed help with; I needed someone to teach me how to *drive*. I told Penny that I had passed my written driving test and now had a car, but I had never actually driven. One of the first things she did to help was give me driving lessons using her own car.

We got to know Penny's family—her husband, Vince, and their two children—and we looked up to her as our "American mother." We were a little shy at first about calling her "Mommy," but she accepted the title with no problem. Penny was such a caring person that when she heard about my cousins having younger brothers back in Kenya, she began sponsoring them—providing the funds for them to complete their primary and high school education.

Penny was a great teacher and had a lot of patience while teaching me to drive. She was instructing me on how to parallel park one day, when I bumped the car in front of me while I was pulling out from my parking spot. Fortunately, there was no damage to either vehicle, but I was still scared. Penny told me not to be afraid, because it was normal in America for first-time drivers to hit something in the process of learning. Still, as a matter of courtesy, she left a note with her phone number tucked under the wiper blade of the car I had bumped.

Penny's reassurance gave me confidence. I was eager to keep going. "Let's go and practice driving *my* car," I said. But she told me we would have to call the Boltes and let them know about it first. We then drove Penny's car to an open parking lot and practiced for a whole hour. By then I was exhausted and ready to call it quits for the day.

Penny also taught me something about accidents in America—that when you hit someone else's car, you should never leave the scene, because it would be considered hit-and-run. Then the police could take you to jail. Later on, that actually happened to my friend Ring Deng. He had been placed in a foster home in California when he arrived in the United States, but Mommy Penny flew there and brought him back to stay with us, because he was my cousin Kiir Akol's best friend.

Later, when Ring was learning to drive in the neighborhood in Richmond, he hit another car. He thought it was only a minor problem and decided to drive off. But somebody was watching him and reported it to the police, and they caught him and charged him with hit-and-run. Ring was taken to jail for two days, but Mommy Penny went and bailed him out. My cousins and I went to court with her, and we watched on the TV monitor as Ring talked to the judge. Seeing my friend going through that incident was my first experience in court. I was very grateful to Mommy Penny for her extraordinary help to our friend, who didn't understand American traffic laws of hit-and-run.

After Mommy Penny taught me how to drive, our sponsor paid for me to take three days of driver's training from a professional driving school. It took me a couple tries before I passed my road test, but I was very excited when I did, because I could now enjoy the Honda gift from Sally Bolte. The ability to drive was important to *all* of us, so once I felt confident with my *own* driving, I taught my nineteen-year-old cousin Kiir Akol to drive.

The timing for getting my license was perfect, because I had just learned that there was going to be a Lost Boys' conference and dance in Tennessee. I drove there in my Honda and took my cousins Deng and Kiir with me. I was proud of having a driver's license, because there were Lost Boys from Michigan who had made the trip with their caseworkers, while my cousins and I had driven to Tennessee by *ourselves*. The other boys were surprised to see me driving such a long distance in light of the very short time I had been in the States.

I was adjusting well to my new environment and feeling more and more confident, but I was still in charge of my cousin Deng Makuac because he was underage. I had gone to court and signed papers making me his legal guardian until he finished high school. I was only nineteen at the time—but because I didn't know my actual birth date, they had *estimated* my age during processing in Kenya and listed me as being twenty-three. Without knowledge of their *true* birth dates, most of the Lost Boys were given January 1 as their date of birth. January 1 was also the date of Sudan's independence from the British.

I was eager to continue my education, so I enrolled at the Richmond Community College when the next semester began. I also quit my two restaurant jobs and took a full-time job operating a box-gluing machine at Tyson Foods, a company that killed and processed many thousand chickens daily for consumption in the United States and other countries. I liked my job because, unlike most of the employees, I was not stuck in a cold room for eight hours a day cutting chicken with sharp knives. Balancing work and school was tough for me, but I had financial responsibilities to meet. I reported to work at 5 p.m. daily and got out at 2 a.m. My first class was at 7 a.m. in the morning, so I had very little time for sleeping.

Things went well at work, and I felt honored when I was chosen as "employee of the month" out of several thousand third-shift workers. My boss was aware of my schedule and my early morning classes, so it took me by surprise when she *ordered* me one night to stay and work overtime. I told her politely that I wouldn't be able to stay because of my early class. But she told me I had to stay whether I liked it or not. I explained to her that education was my mother and father and that it was because I was attending school that I had gotten my job in the first place. I reminded her that if I hadn't gone to school and learned how to read and write English, and then *speak* it, I would not have been hired by the company. Then I said, "Please, ma'am—I'm going home."

"It's *your* choice," she said. "But if you leave, I'll see you when you come back in to work for not listening to me." As I turned to leave, she called to me and said, "You're getting *fired* tomorrow!" I hadn't meant to be disrespectful to someone in authority, but I wondered why she didn't understand the importance I placed on my education.

When I reported for work in the evening, my boss took me straight to the manager's office. It was an uncomfortable situation—I had *always* gotten along well at work. My boss then left me alone with the manager, and I explained to him why my education was my first priority. Had they known about my background, they might have understood why I had chosen to leave. "Why did *you* go to school?" I asked the manager. "Wasn't it to improve your life and then help your family?"

The manager was patient and heard me out, and I think

he understood. But he told me that I should have accepted my supervisor's request—and then come to *him* the next day to request that she not ask me to work overtime anymore. He acknowledged the fact that I had been selected as employee of the month, and he said he'd heard what a good job I had been doing for the company. But he still gave me a three-day suspension from work for not handling the problem correctly. In the end, it had been a growing experience for me, and I learned some difficult lessons about the workplace at that time. I stayed and worked at Tyson for two years and then quit my job and moved to Grand Rapids, Michigan.

My cousins James Mum and Mayom had moved to their own apartment after living with the VanderVens for two and a half years, and Angelo, another one of our cousins, had moved in with them. They contacted me and asked what I thought of moving to Michigan and sharing their apartment. I didn't want to abandon Deng Makuac and Kiir Akol after living with them for so long, so I asked them if they would like to move with me. They said they liked Richmond and wanted to stay, but for me to go ahead if I wanted to. By this time, Deng Makuac had completed high school and was on his own, so nothing was preventing me from moving.

After many miles on the road, the Honda I had gotten from the Boltes had worn out, so I packed the few belongings I had and boarded a bus to Grand Rapids. It was late August 2003 when I moved in with my cousins in Kentwood, not far from the Gerald R. Ford International Airport. Within a month, I had gotten a job at the airport with Alamo and National car rentals servicing their vehicles. Then I enrolled at the Grand Rapids Community College to continue my education.

Later, I was hired to shuttle cars between the service area at the airport to the rental parking lot. The job didn't pay a lot, but it covered my bills so I could continue to attend school at GRCC. I was taking several classes, including English as a second language, which I did well in. I had been speaking English for several years by then but still needed improvement in some areas. I had no problem keeping up with my regular living expenses, but my classes were costing me more than I could handle. My income level should have allowed me to get financial aid, but it was denied.

Then Almighty God brought *another* helper to my cousins and me—Mr. Duffy, a businessman from Holland, Michigan. He had heard about the Lost Boys from Sudan and about the way we had suffered because of the war. He met with the four of us, and after hearing what our plans were, he promised to pay our rent and school fees if we were ready to do well at school. We agreed to his terms, and he paid those expenses for a full year. The biggest problem we were having was with transportation, as we had no car. Then my cousins' foster mother, Mama Rita, bought a new car and gave her used Dodge van to the four of us. That made our lives so much easier.

Mr. Duffy's daughter Colleen, who also lived in Holland, had been keeping tabs on us for her father—but that was hard for her with our living in Grand Rapids. In January 2005, we moved to Holland, where Colleen and Mr. Duffy's brother Pat were able to come and see us regularly and monitor how we were doing in school. This arrangement required that we drive from Holland to GRCC every day, but it made things a lot easier for Mr. Duffy and we appreciated his generosity. He kept his promise and continued to send monthly checks until the end of the school year. I stayed with my cousins in Holland until the middle of September 2005; then I left both them and GRCC for the only thing important enough to interrupt my education. I joined the US Army.

I joined the army for two reasons: to *serve* and to *protect* this country. It was *this* country that rescued us from the refugee camp in Kenya, and it brought us here to change our lives. So anyone who attacks America attacks *us* too. I had watched the news in 1998 when the American embassies in Kenya and Tanzania were attacked, and I wept when the Twin Towers went down three years later, taking the lives of nearly three thousand people. The September 11 attack stayed on my mind and was eventually what compelled me to join the US Army. But while I was still living in Holland, something else happened that would change my life *forever*.

One Saturday night I gave one of my friends a ride to my cousin's apartment in Lansing, where we were going to "hang out," as they say. My cousin Nyanayai Dau Deng had invited a girl from her school over for the evening. They had met one day as the girl waited to be picked up after school, and my cousin offered her a ride home. My cousin was surprised to see that she was taking the girl to her *own* previous address. It turned out that Ann Dennis, who had been my cousin's foster mother, was now *this* girl's foster mom.

The moment I stepped inside my cousin's apartment that evening and *saw* the girl, my heart almost stopped. *I know her*, I thought. I had had a *dream* in the past of a beautiful light-skinned lady—and here she *was!* "Dominic," Nyanayai said, "I'd like you to meet my friend Felisan. She's from Ethiopia. She goes to my school."

"*Dinanish*," I said, speaking the word for "hello" in her native language of Amharic. Her eyes lit up, and she responded with a smile and motioned for me to sit down where we could visit.

"Are *you* from Ethiopia?" she asked. I told her no, I was from Sudan, but I had spent time in Ethiopia. Our conversation led to both of us sharing our incredible stories, and we talked until early the next morning. Then before I left, we exchanged phone numbers. Day by day, we called each other and talked; and my heart told me to go ahead and ask her out. When I finally got up the courage to ask her, she at first played "hard to get." But I refused to give up, because I *knew* without question that she was the one for me. My persistence eventually won out, and she soon became my steady girlfriend.

Before I left for my basic training in Atlanta, Georgia, my beautiful girlfriend, Felisan—who is now my wife, Mahalet—told me she'd just found out she was pregnant. I was happy and sad at the same time. I was happy because I was going to be a father, but sad because I would be stationed far away during basic training. When the time came for me to leave for camp, Mahalet cried. It was hard for her because she had already experienced separation from family and too much loneliness in her life, but she was a very brave woman.

Mahalet's story was like mine in some ways—yet very different in others. This is her story as she told it to me on the night we first met at the home of my cousin:

Mahalet was born in the Ethiopian city of Dire Dawa. Her father was a wealthy sheik—an Islamic priest—and her mother was one of his four wives. Her family had fled to Somalia in 1991 because of the civil war being waged in Ethiopia. She was a small child at the time—too young to remember much about the move. She had lived in Somalia just two years when civil war also broke out there and she became separated from her family, and she never saw them again. She was perhaps six or seven years old at the time.

The evening had started out innocently enough. Her mother had sent her to a place about half a mile away to get drinking water for the family. But as Mahalet neared the house where the water was, she heard a woman screaming. She looked toward the open door and saw someone holding a knife to a woman's throat. Mahalet was terrified and ran back home where she would be safe; but when she got there, she saw her mother being attacked in the same way, with a knife held to her throat. During enemy attacks, beheading was a common means of killing.

A neighbor woman, who was a friend of Mahalet's mother, shouted to the girl to run, because the gangs would kill her if she stayed. Some of the raiders were already filling bags with gold and valuable jewels from her mother's house, while others were attacking and killing her neighbors, tossing their heads into a lake next to her home.

She fled on foot with the neighbor woman to the nearest train station—about a two-hour walk. There the two of them boarded a train and traveled to a small town across the border inside Djibouti. The neighbor woman looked after Mahalet for about a month and then left to go to Addis Ababa, the capital of Ethiopia. The woman didn't like having to leave the little girl alone, but it was all she could do to care for herself. She told Mahalet she should be able to make it on her own and suggested that she look for work babysitting for one of the women in town.

Mahalet wasted no time and soon had a job caring for the small children of an amiable lady. But after only a month, the lady moved away, leaving Mahalet to hunt for another family needing child care. It didn't take her long to find another woman who needed help with her family, and the woman promised to pay Mahalet a small amount of money in addition to her room and board.

Things changed, however, during the following weeks, and the woman became mean and abusive and allowed her very little food. Mahalet had tried her best to help the family, but the woman insulted her and refused to give her the money she had promised. "Why should I pay you?" the woman screamed. "You're just a homeless baby in town! In fact, you owe me money. You need to pay me for the food you've been eating for the past two months!" Mahalet was heartbroken by the woman's cruel words. Homeless again and hungry, she left the house in tears and began walking the streets hoping to find some means of support.

She soon found herself a home with another woman who had small children, and again she was promised a small amount of pay in addition to her meals. She hoped this woman would treat her kindly, the way the first one had. She stayed and helped in the home for a few weeks—until she could save enough money for a train ticket to Addis Ababa, where her neighbor had gone. But when it came time to get her money, the woman told her that she couldn't pay her, because her husband was out of town and she had no money at home.

"But I can't wait for him to come home," she said. "I need my money now!"

At that, the woman flew into a rage. She yanked the tiny girl up like a rag doll and began banging her head against the wall.

"Mama," she sobbed. "Mama, help me!"

"You want your mother?" the woman screamed. "Then let her

fall from the sky and come and rescue you! Get out of my house—and if you don't go now, you will face serious consequences!"

Mahalet left the angry woman's house and set out walking to the train station, even though she had no money for a ticket. If she could just get to Addis Ababa, maybe she would run into her mother's friend and things would be all right. It was even possible that her parents were still alive and had sought refuge in Addis Ababa. Whatever the case, she had to move on.

Mahalet reached the station and saw other refugees getting on a train to Ethiopia, and she joined them in line. She couldn't let her lack of train fare stop her from doing what she needed to do. Little as she was, she managed to slip between other passengers unnoticed and board the crowded train. She was exhausted from the long walk and was weak from hunger as she lay down on the floor just inside the door of the passenger car. Soon she drifted off to sleep.

It was nighttime, and as the train jostled along the track, the sleeping girl rolled out the open door and landed on the ground beside the tracks at the border just inside Ethiopia. It was probably a couple hours later when she woke up in terrible pain and found herself all alone in pitch-darkness in the middle of nowhere. Her left arm had been broken in the fall from the train, and she was covered with scrapes, bruises, and blood. She sobbed and cried out in pain.

Luckily, some game hunters were passing by that night and heard what sounded like a little child crying. With flashlights in hand they walked over to the track to investigate, and they found Mahalet alone beside the train tracks, smeared with blood. They asked her what had happened to her. She told them that she had been on a train, had fallen asleep by an open door, and had rolled out.

They picked her up and took her home with them, where they cleaned her up and gave her something to eat and put her to bed. The next morning, they took her to an old lady who knew how to treat the wounds of injured people in the traditional tribal way. The old lady was good to Mahalet and took care of her until she had recovered enough to travel. Then she took her to the train station so that she could go to Addis Ababa to seek help at the refugee center.

There was a nice-appearing young man aboard the train, and Mahalet noticed that he was staring at her. After a while, he came over and struck up a conversation with her. He asked a lot of questions and wanted to know her name and who her parents were. He noticed the traditional bandage on her arm and the bruises on her face from her fall, and he asked what had happened. She opened up and told the man her whole story. He appeared very sympathetic and said he would like to help her. He told her if she would come home with him, he would care for her and be like a father to her.

After the man had returned to his seat, a policeman and his wife who had overheard the conversation came over to talk to Mahalet. They told her they had heard what the man had said and had come to warn her about people like him. What they told her was the same thing her mother had once said to her when she had asked about the little children with no eyes who sat along the streets in Djibouti begging money from strangers. "If you are ever alone," her mother had said, "don't listen to strange men who talk nice and want to help you. These men are very bad! They will take you home, pull your teeth, and put your eyes out so you can't see. Then they will set you along the street to beg all day, and they will keep all the money for themselves."

The policeman and his wife took Mahalet home with them, where they fed her and let her sleep for the night. The next day they helped her get to the refugee center, because they assumed that she was a Somalian citizen. Had they had known she was actually Ethiopian but had moved to Somalia as a small child, she might not have been accepted at the center.

From the time Mahalet left the homes of the women who had mistreated her until she was placed in the refugee center, God had been protecting her. He had directed the game hunters to where she had fallen from the train and had placed the policeman and his wife on the train to rescue her from the man who had wanted to take her home. Then a lady from the Christian Orthodox church in Addis Ababa got her from the refugee center and took her in as her foster child. She was now safe and in good hands. Her foster mother, Wide Jote, attended church, and Mahalet was taught from the Bible. Later, Mahalet was baptized, and Wide Jote became her godmother. Mahalet attended school in Ethiopia, and after ten years of living with Wide Jote, Mahalet, along with other refugees, was processed to come to the United States.

She arrived in the United States on September 12, 2004, and she was initially placed by Lutheran Services in the home of an Iranian woman in Michigan. When that arrangement didn't work out, they moved Mahalet to Portland, Michigan, to the home of Ann Dennis, where she lived until she became my wife. Ann Dennis is still her American mom and the grandma to our children.

Mahalet'godmother, Wide Jote (top right) with Mahalet, age twelve (bottom right), at a family wedding in Addis Ababa, Ethiopia.

The VanderVens meet my cousins James Mum and Mayom
Ajuong for the first time! They were with the first Lost Boys to
arrive in Grand Rapids, Michigan, from the Kakuma refugee
camp in November 2000. (Left to right) Gary VanderVen, James
Mum, Tyler V., Mayom, Mama Rita, Kerstin V., and Quinn V.

My cousins visit me in Virginia in 2001 (Left to right) Mama Penny,
James Mum, Deng Makuac, Mayom Ajuong, and Dominic.

Dominic adjusts to the Michigan winters.

CHAPTER 4

In the Boot

The Lord is your protection: you have made God Most High your place of Safety.

—Psalm 91:9 (NCV)

I never will forget that day in September 2001. I had been in the United States just over seven months, and I was working at the Tyson chicken processing plant while attending Richmond Community College in Virginia. I had just gotten home from my morning classes and had reached to turn on the TV to catch the latest news before going to bed. It was Breaking News—the Twin Towers in New York City had just been struck by planes believed to have been piloted by terrorists. I stood there in disbelief and wept.

When terrorists raided my village back in Sudan, I fled for my life. I couldn't understand why people wanted to hurt my family and destroy our property. If I had been older, I might have tried to fight back—but I would surely have been killed like so many in my village had been. But I was only seven, so what could *I* do? But that was *then*.

As I continued to watch the newscasts during the days and months following the attacks of 9-11, anger at the terrorists began to build inside me. Terrorists had brutally attacked and killed my own people in Sudan and had pursued us relentlessly along the way as we fled. Now terrorists had dared to attack us *here* in America. This was now *my* country, and I was no longer a helpless seven-year-old boy. But because my education was so critical to me, I continued with my classes, along with my job, until 2005, when I quit both and enlisted in the US Army.

I flew with a group of recruits from the airport in Lansing, Michigan, to Atlanta, Georgia—my first flight since I arrived in Richmond a few years earlier. We spent a whole month in Atlanta getting prepared for boot camp. We were given the required vaccinations, divided into groups and platoons, and taught some of the basics of military life, including marching. When our training there was finished, we were taken by bus to the actual basic training camp.

When we arrived, drill sergeants were waiting for us, and they welcomed us with something called "shark attacks." The moment our feet stepped down from the bus, they came running toward us with angry expressions on their faces and began barking commands at us.

Anyway, we got the message that from that moment on, *everything* we did was subject to the approval of those in charge! We were then put through more than two hours of exercise so rigorous that it actually had some of the recruits in tears.

There were two hundred men in our company and sixteen drill sergeants—four assigned to each company of fifty men. Early every morning we were awakened by a loud blast from the horn of the drill sergeant. This was the daily routine until we fit into the system, responding to it as being *urgent*. That was to prepare us for war.

I enjoyed the challenges of basic training, but all the time I was missing my girlfriend. I hadn't realized how hard it would be to be separated from her. And if it was tough for *me*, it was even tougher for Mahalet because she was pregnant. I called her whenever I got the chance, and she would cry because she missed me. We discussed a lot of things over the phone, but we usually focused on our baby and how we were going to raise it.

Mahalet told me that some ladies had come to see her, urging her to *adopt* the baby out if I was not able to take care of it. Somehow that didn't surprise me, because other people didn't know me that well. They didn't know that I was a responsible person who would take care of this child and any *more* that we might have. I had seen many bad things and had lived a hard life during my childhood, and I would never want *my* children's lives to be like mine had been. Like most parents, I want my children to have a better life than my own.

Christmas was approaching, and I was elated when they gave us all a two-week leave so we could go home and spend the holidays with our families. I could hardly wait to see Mahalet and see how our baby she was carrying was doing.

When I arrived, Mahalet was so glad to have me home, and we treasured the time we shared as we celebrated our first Christmas together. She was far enough along in her pregnancy that she could feel the baby moving. It was very active and seemed to be jumping all around in her belly. We had long talks about our future together, but I knew that in a matter of months I would be deployed to Iraq. The life of every soldier is in danger during war, and I didn't want Mahalet to risk being left as a single mother with no benefits. We made plans to get married before my deployment.

Mahalet had never driven a car, so while I was still in basic training, she enrolled in driver's training. It was a crash course, working with an instructor for one day, at a cost of one hundred dollars. But when Mahalet went to take her road test, she failed it. While I was home for Christmas, I took her driving and had her practice parking and making turns in a parking lot, the way Penny had done with me.

After I returned to camp, I called Mahalet and learned that she had passed the road test and had gotten her Michigan driver's license. I was so proud of her! She was very excited about it, and she called the instructor who had been paid to teach her and told her the news. The lady said, "How is it that when *I* taught you, you failed the test—but when your *boyfriend* taught you, you passed?"

Also, while I was home, I was able to reach my mother by telephone. That sounds simple enough here in America—you just pick up the phone, dial the number, and Mom answers. But for me to reach my mother in South Sudan, it meant calling a relative or neighbor of hers who had a cell phone, and then arranging a time for Mother to speak with me. This is because she lives in an area so remote that getting reception is extremely difficult. For the men, it's a little easier; they simply climb a tall tree and talk—much like in the old television program *Green Acres*, where Oliver had to climb the telephone pole whenever he needed to make a call. But for my mother to talk on the phone, they have to help her climb a rope ladder to the correct height to get reception. And after I reach her, it is very expensive for us to speak for even a few minutes.

It was the second time I had spoken with my mother since we were separated by war in 1989, and we had so much to talk about. I had first spoken with her while I was still in the refugee camp and reached her by radio, so she knew I was alive and living in America. When we talked *this* time, she was happy when I told her she was going to have a grandchild, and that I had joined the US Army here in my new homeland.

"I don't worry about you in the war, my son," she said. "Men are *born* to challenges, and they have to face them wherever they are. Your daddy is in your body, and you are strong like he was." She mentioned how all the wealth that was once in our family had vanished overnight with his death. "You will bring back all of your daddy's wealth to me," she said, "no matter how long it takes or what you must do in the future to make it happen."

She said this because in Sudanese culture, it is the duty of a mother's *youngest* son to see that she is always cared for. She told me she would see me with my children—both girls and boys—in the future after the war was over. I then told her much of what I had been through during the years since we were separated by the Sudan war.

After the phone call, I went to bed and tried to sleep. I eventually drifted off, but I woke up suddenly as thoughts of my mother and her hardships struck me to the core. I broke down and cried until I was exhausted and fell asleep again. "Are you *okay*?" Mahalet asked when I awoke the next morning.

"Yes," I lied. "I'm doing just *fine*." But she could see that my eyes were red and puffy from crying.

Imagine anyone in my situation—how would he or she handle everything that I went through? I can't speak for other people, but I know I will be telling my experiences to my own children someday. And I will pass on to them my mother's wisdom, telling them to be *strong* and to stand up for every challenge that they come across. They cannot be afraid of war, hunger, thirst, diseases, and whatever other kinds of challenges they may encounter. I will tell them to be strong and smart and to stand up for *others* as well as for themselves. When people do that, they can overcome the rest of the world at any time.

When my two weeks' leave was over, I flew back to Fort Benning, Georgia, to get ready for graduation. We were given various army physical fitness tests, including the two-mile run, in which I came in number one in the entire company, making it in ten minutes and fifty-five seconds. Some of the soldiers made fun of me, saying that I used to run after lions and all kinds of wild animals in Africa. Even the drill sergeants joked with me about my running.

Some of the soldiers began calling me "African Cheetah," but one of them, Raymond Spencer, who became my good buddy, used to call me "Gazelle." Raymond was a super guy. He was from California and had been a volunteer firefighter before he joined the army. He loved to hear my stories about Africa—especially the ones about all the wild animals. We talked about someday going to visit Africa together, and that became Raymond's dream.

When it came to my last name, people couldn't pronounce Malual, so they just gave up on it and nicknamed me "Sudan" because that's where I'm from. *Everyone* called me Sudan—even our company commander, LTC Burns. He remembered me because of my locker. He said that during inspection, it was the *neatest* and most *squared away* of all those in our platoon. I would meet him again in Iraq in 2007 as one of the commanders who were training Iraqi soldiers.

After graduation in January 2006, the other soldiers and I were sent to Fort Bliss, Texas, where we were trained to drive Bradley Fighting Vehicles and qualify with weapons. There was so much to learn—especially when it came to dealing with IEDs (improvised explosive devices), because they were responsible for most of the war casualties.

I may have been quick to acquire military skills, but I still had much to learn about the way business is done in everyday life. I was trusting of people—always willing to do someone a favor. I remember the time when a man asked me for help when he bought a used car. He told me he needed a "reference," so I agreed to help. I didn't know the man all that well, but I knew him well enough that I felt I could sign as a character reference to help him out. Big mistake! I didn't realize until later that what I actually did was *cosign* for the man's car loan! If the dealership had done any checking, they would have seen that my credit wasn't established enough at that time for me to even *qualify* as a cosigner.

Things turned bad sometime later when I learned that payments were not being made on the vehicle. As cosigner, I became liable for the debt, and the charges—which amounted to several hundred dollars—were drafted from my bank account. I went to the man who had bought the car and told him what had happened, and he apologized and promised to take care of the matter. I was still a fairly new US citizen and was naive—but I was beginning to realize how careful a person has to be in doing business. I was just glad the ordeal was finally over!

On Friday, April 14, 2008 I flew from Fort Bliss, Texas, to Lansing, Michigan, to see Mahalet. It was Easter weekend, and it had been close to four months since I'd been home. My cousin met me at the airport, and we drove to Portland to pick Mahalet up from her foster mom's. Then we drove back to Lansing so we could spend the weekend together at my cousins' apartment.

The next morning, Mahalet went into labor. I took her to Sparrow Hospital in Lansing, where we spent twenty-four hours waiting for our baby to come into the world. Then on Easter Sunday, my first daughter was born. Thank God for the gift of my daughter who was born on Easter Sunday!

The baby's due date was April 13th, but she had held off her arrival until I could get home. It really amazed my cousins how the timing of her birth had worked out. At the hospital, I never left Mahalet's side but remained with her all through her labor and delivery, encouraging her to be strong. When the nurse handed me my daughter, I couldn't believe how beautiful she was. She was perfect and had light skin just like her mommy. She weighed eight pounds and six ounces, and we named her Achuei after a very special lady in my family's lineage.

Many years ago, my great, great, great, great-grandmother on my father's side became a single mother of one son after her husband was killed by the government militia during one of the many raids on the cattle camps. In Dinka culture, when a woman is widowed, she is still *owned* by her husband's family because she has been *paid* for with his family's dowry. For this reason, she is never allowed to remarry outside his family—but if she wants to have more children, one of his brothers, or another family member, would have to father the children. She would not, however, become a *wife* of that brother, and no further dowry would have to be paid, because she is already considered a *family wife*. Any children she then has by that brother or other relative are considered to be children of her deceased husband.

Achuei longed for more children and went to her husband's brothers—but they *all* refused to father children for her. The reason, they said, was because her father was a spiritual leader and they didn't want his spirit to control them. This rejection was very sad for Achuei because she had hoped to have a large family like the other women around her. But she worked very hard and raised that one son and told people, "One day my son will have a *big* family with lots of children and will have much wealth."

Achuei's prophecy came true, and her son became the father and grandfather to many children. Ever since then, the families of my grandfathers have shown their pride and respect for her by naming their first daughter Achuei.

It had been a wonderful surprise for me to have our baby girl born before I went back to Fort Bliss, Texas, but my four-day leave had gone by much too fast. It was painful to leave Mahalet when she'd just had a baby, but she was very strong and we agreed that the *next* time I came home, we would be getting married.

Three months later I went back to Michigan for our wedding, which took place on Saturday, July 8, 2006. A local pastor named Yohaness, who had come from Ethiopia, agreed to perform our wedding ceremony. The day before the wedding, my cousin James Mum and I went to East Lansing to rent a limousine. We found one greedy man who charged us a thousand dollars just to come and take us to the church—a distance of about two miles. The man was clearly trying to run away with our money!

When it came to business dealings, I had learned my lesson the *hard* way with the car incident. So I asked this man to show me his business license and his driver's license. He refused to show me his IDs, so I called the police to come and deal with the problem. When the police came, they didn't do anything to the limousine driver. They let him leave without even giving him a ticket. I couldn't believe it, but my cousin and I were definitely *not* happy about it.

The next day was our wedding day. My aunt Ayak drove up from Ohio with her daughter Tisier, my cousin Yoahnes, and my aunt's friend Nyanamiek. The ladies put beautiful temporary tattoos on Mahalet's hands, and they lasted almost a month before fading away. She had her hair done up with beautiful braids and curls, and she wore a lovely white sleeveless wedding gown. She looked stunning! She was definitely the woman I had dreamed about long before we ever met.

Many friends, relatives, and other people attended the ceremony—several from out of state. Mahalet's foster mom, Ann Dennis, and her boyfriend were there, and Ann's daughter and her husband stood up for us in the wedding. My cousin Mum Ajuong Majok also stood up for me. Gum Ring Gum was there and witnessed the signing of the wedding certificate. My friends Deng Mtoto, Lual Juach, and Akot Yuot were my best men. Dau Deng, Ayan Kuanyin, and Birukitawi from Ethiopia were Mahalet's bridesmaids.

After the ceremony, my friend Nhail Deng drove us back to Mahalet's foster mom's house, where we had our wedding reception. We nicknamed Nhail "Limo Driver," because he took over when the actual limousine driver left us at the church, and then later on asked us for even *more* money. But we told him to *leave* because he was as greedy as a hyena!

Our wedding was more of a traditional American wedding, unlike the ones in Sudan, but the way Mahalet and I had *met* was more American also. In Sudan, couples don't usually date like American couples do. In our village, a young man might see a girl he likes, and she might be as young as fourteen or fifteen—not old enough yet for marriage. So he will walk over and stand by the fence bordering her property and snap his fingers to catch her attention. If she doesn't go willingly to meet him, her father might tell her, "Go!" This is how the two get to know each other and learn about each other's families.

These meetings continue until she is at least sixteen; then she is old enough to be *promised* to a man. The man then talks to the girl's father and explains his intentions. If the girl's father and family *approve*, forty cows will be brought to her father as the first part of her dowry. And when the girl reaches age eighteen, she is free to marry and her suitor then brings the remaining cows to her family as full payment for her.

Daughters are very valuable to a family for this reason. An eighteen-year-old woman who is a virgin and a hard worker is generally worth one hundred cows—but if she is also *educated*, she might bring 120 head of cattle. Because daughters are a valuable asset, if one reaches her teens without being promised to a man, her father can *negotiate* a deal for her. The cattle received for her are vital to her family's existence. Weddings in Sudan are a cause for great celebration and last for a full week. Throughout this time there are feasting, singing, dancing, and much merrymaking.

After the wedding, I took Mahalet and Achuei with me to Texas, where I was stationed, so they could be near me. I was being sent to California for a short time for further training and had planned to rent an apartment for them in El Paso. Then one of my army buddies, who was also leaving for training, asked if they could stay with his wife, Angie, until we got back from California. Then we could get our own place. That plan worked out well, because Angie also had a young baby to care for but didn't know how to drive, and Mahalet was able to teach her to drive while we were gone.

It was September—two months before I would be deployed to Iraq. I didn't want to leave Mahalet and Achuei there alone in El Paso, so I took them to Dayton to stay with my aunt Ayak and her children. We made the trip in a Pontiac Sunfire that I had bought from my platoon officer. It took about thirty hours for us to drive from El Paso, Texas, to Dayton, Ohio, because we had to stop and feed the baby on the way and also needed breaks to rest. It was a hurried trip—I couldn't stay. After getting my wife and baby settled at my aunt Ayak's, I drove back to Fort Bliss.

Vietnam Veterans were at the base and had a party for us in preparation for our deployment. They had been through a difficult war themselves and wanted to offer encouragement. They gave us wristbands with heroes' words on them. My wristband said, "Here's to the Heroes," and I wore that band for almost three years. I went to war with it on my arm, and I came back with it still intact. That was a miracle to me; then it just broke into two pieces in 2009 after I got out of the military and moved back to Michigan.

We left Fort Bliss at the end of October 2006 to go to Kuwait, and there we were given orientation for the Iraq war. We were briefed about deadly roadside bombs, sniper attacks, IEDs, and other dangers we would be dealing with. Now that we were ready to face actual combat, everyone's thoughts were on their families back in the States. I thought of Mahalet and Achuei too—but as much as I missed them, I knew that at *this* moment, I was called to be a *soldier.*

In Kuwait, I was selected to be at the battalion headquarters as one of the personal security detachments for the battalion commander. Our company commander had wanted me to stay with Alpha Company because I know a little bit of Arabic, but the battalion commander had the higher rank, so the choice was his. But I was still *attached* to Alpha Company.

We were outfitted with what we needed for use in the war, and we were given additional training on how to protect the commanders and the VIPs when they came to our sections in Iraq. Then after three weeks in Kuwait, we flew to Baghdad and landed at Baghdad International Airport. After many weeks of training, we were now ready for the *real* war.

When I had arrived at Fort Benning for my basic training, I had been welcomed with "shark attacks," which were staged to get us used to danger. But when I landed in Baghdad, I was welcomed by the scent of *sweat* and *death.* This was a smell that I knew all too well, because I had been in the war before as a child—but the experience was foreign to many of the other soldiers.

The moment I touched the tent floor, I tested the clay and then prayed. "Almighty God, I've come here, not to kill, but to bring peace. I would bring down those who don't like peace, when they don't agree with me, and then bring peace to those who need it and to the innocent children of this country." After that, I never worried about anything in Baghdad.

We were given our sector in the northwest side of the city, the worst in Baghdad—a sector called Ghazaliyah. We nicknamed that place, "Ghost Town in Baghdad." We called it that because of the death of the people who had once lived there. It was now all but deserted, and when we *did* see people, they looked like ghosts to us.

The enemy didn't want us there in Ghazaliyah, and to *prove* it, they continually planted roadside bombs between there and our forward operating base. Every time we went to patrol the area, we had to fight our way out and back to our FOB. My fellow soldiers soon began calling me "Mayor of Baghdad" and "King Kong." Everything was a nightmare to us in Ghazaliyah. Dogs roamed the area like hyenas, searching for dead bodies, adding further to the already grisly atmosphere. The enemy *knew* our sectors, locations, where we slept, and where we ate our food. We fought with them about fifty times a week, every week.

There were twenty of us in the Battalion PSD Team Alpha Company, and we were like a close-knit family. Before going on our assigned missions each day, we had prayer together. I sometimes led the prayers, but we all took our turns. The Bible was always an important part of my daily routine, and I read Psalm 91 every single morning before leaving our FOB for the day's mission. Sometimes I read it aloud for the others to hear. It was my favorite passage because it spoke of God's constant protection, which I counted on him for *every day.*

If we were to succeed in our mission, we needed a good rapport in the community. We developed a good relationship with Sheik Mohammed, the local spiritual leader. Our officers would stop at his house two or three times each week and spend a couple of hours with him. This helped build good relations in the community, and we provided the sheik with needed security. This was important to him because he was constantly being watched by the enemy to make sure he wasn't giving us information—they threatened to *kill* him if he ever did. Of course, *we* were being watched too, and the enemy would try to ambush us as we came from the sheik's house. But Sheik Mohammed was very friendly with our officers, and he sometimes got into their vehicles and rode with them to the mosque and other places they had to go.

During my very first mission in Iraq, our convoy was hit by an IED. One of our soldiers lost both of his legs, and two other men had less serious injuries. I knew war was brutal, but now I was seeing it up close for the first time since my childhood. The next day we were hit by a smaller IED, and this time it was *my* vehicle that got hit. The damage to the vehicle was only minor, but we all suffered tremendous headaches from it. IEDs were always our biggest threat because there was no way to control them. The enemy concealed them in the trash, which was *everywhere* in Baghdad. They hid them inside soda cans, in manholes, and just about anyplace else where they would not be seen.

Christmas was approaching, and thoughts of Mahalet and Achuei filled my mind, but being away from family is something soldiers must deal with. Four days before the holiday we ran our mission, which took us past the mosque, so we stopped to give out treats to the kids who were waiting outside for us. They knew we *always* carried candy and soccer balls with us, and we made friends with them that way. I don't know if they were even aware of its being Christmas.

As we crossed a bridge on our way back to the base that day, we struck a deadly IED. The explosion was very loud and sent a huge cloud of smoke and dust into the sky, but instead of stopping we drove straight through and got out of the kill zone. The enemy would sometimes use roadside bombs to disable vehicles in order to ambush us when we returned to recover the damaged vehicles.

Two vehicles were seriously damaged, and one of the gunners was wounded in the arm by shrapnel. I was also gunning at the time, but I was far enough away my vehicle had nothing more than a small piece of shrapnel. Luckily, we didn't stop and give them the opportunity to attack us, but went directly to our base, which was just a couple miles away.

Back at the base, the injured soldier was treated at the troop medical clinic, and the rest of us were given painkillers for the horrendous headaches caused by the blast. I thanked God that the damage was mostly limited to our vehicles and no lives were lost.

Aside from the severe headache, I had felt fine—but three days later I woke up with a stabbing pain in my back. The doctor gave me some strong pain medication, which helped at the time. But since I was feeling good, I went to the motor pool to help my guys who were fixing the track shoe for the Bradley, and the strain of pulling and carrying the track shoes close to the vehicle caused the pain in my back to return. I ended the day by going to the church for Sunday prayers—it was Christmas Eve.

I woke up the next morning in a lot of pain and went back to the clinic, where they popped my back. That finally brought relief. Because it was Christmas, we had the day off to rest, but they did serve a special lunch for us in the chow hall. After we ate, we went back to our trailers, and we called it a *great* Christmas in the war zone—but without our families to celebrate with us. That was how we celebrated Christmas in Iraq. I thought of the true meaning of the holiday, and I thanked Almighty God for the gift of his son to the world. And I prayed that God would bring peace to the people of this war-torn country and around the world.

Five days later was a bloody day in Iraq. The big news of the day was the death by hanging of the country's former president, Saddam Hussein. The execution had taken place at Camp Justice, a joint security station that was often included in our daily missions. Within hours of the leader's death, rioting had erupted, and close to seventy people were killed by bombs. We heard a lot of mortars landing around our FOB, and the wail of a siren gave warning to everyone in the area.

That same day, I received word that my uncle had been killed in a car accident in southern Sudan. He was riding with other passengers when their car lost control while descending a hill, killing everyone in the vehicle. I thought back to the accident my family had been in when they were taking my mother to Wau and so many passengers had been killed. After all those years, the government *still* had no concern for making the roads safe for the people of South Sudan.

For fifteen years, my uncle had served as wingman, or bodyguard, for the late leader of South Sudan, John Garang de Mabior, who died in a helicopter crash in 2005, after the peace agreement with the northern Sudanese government. The crash was called an *accident*, but I've never been willing to accept that, because a lot of mystery has surrounded John Garang's death. I think the Sudanese government may have played a role in his demise because of his dedication to his people in South Sudan. I believe the truth will eventually come out.

I was given leave to attend my uncle's funeral and left before dawn on January 1 to return to the States. There was a long line of soldiers standing in the cold outside the Baghdad airport when we arrived there, and I joined them. After our IDs had been checked, we went inside the terminal and waited. We found that our plane to Kuwait wouldn't be leaving until 6 p.m., and many of the soldiers slept on the floor during the wait. Then after a one-hour flight on a C-130 cargo plane, we were in for an even *longer* wait. Our plane would not be leaving Kuwait until the next day, so we were given tents to sleep in. But because of the cold weather, we stayed inside the terminal as long as possible and watched football.

It was the Rose Bowl game—the University of Michigan Wolverines versus the University of Southern California Trojans. I was cheering for Michigan and was mad at them for losing. There had been a moment of silence just before the National Anthem. This was because they had lost two very important men in Michigan's history—their great coach Bo Schembechler, who had passed away in November, and the nation's thirty-eighth president, Gerald R. Ford, who had died December 26th. I believe the hearts of the players were touched by the loss of these men. I know it touched me, because I was on my way to the funeral of my uncle.

The next morning, we woke up at 5:30 for roll call again. Our bags were checked for illegal stuff that cannot be transported back to the States—bad magazines, weapons, and ammo—and I boarded the plane taking a window seat. I watched as we crossed the border between Iraq and Syria, and then the Black Sea, until nothing but clouds were visible. In the seats around me, weary soldiers slept.

It was raining when we finally landed at the Cologne airport in Germany. After a two-hour wait, we were on the plane for the nine-and-a-half-hour flight to the States. I made notes in my journal as they announced our various locations—when we passed over London, the Atlantic Ocean, and Philadelphia before finally landing at the airport in Atlanta. While I was waiting for my final flight, I called Mahalet to let her know where we were and what time I would be arriving in Dayton.

It was so good to see my wife and baby again! We spent the night in Dayton and left the next morning for Grand Rapids to attend the funeral. The body of my uncle had been buried in Sudan, but it is our custom to have a service with family members who cannot be present at the actual burial. The service was held at the apartment of my cousins James and Mayom, and close to forty people attended. We were able to get a Sudanese Presbyterian minister to officiate.

In Sudan, funerals are very long, lasting forty days. During the first thirty days, we wear black or dark clothing as a sign of mourning, and then we change to *bright* colors for the last ten days. I was in uniform, so I didn't follow that tradition.

During the rest of my leave, Mahalet and I spent time with family members and also had a lot of time to ourselves. We talked of plans for the future and about having more children. I couldn't believe how much Achuei had grown in the few weeks since I'd last seen her. She was looking more and more like her mommy, and I enjoyed every minute I could spend with my baby girl. Then all too soon, it was time for me to leave.

My friend Mario drove me, along with my wife and my daughter, to Dayton International Airport to catch my flight to Atlanta. There I told Mahalet good-bye and told her to keep praying to God and to *never lose hope* if something bad should happen to me. We landed in Atlanta and were soon boarding the Omni Air International to Germany—an eight-hour flight. We passed the time by watching an in-flight movie called *Model Behavior.*

We arrived in Germany around two o'clock the following afternoon and had an hour's layover before leaving for Kuwait, a distance of twenty-two hundred miles. After we landed, buses came to pick us up and take us from the airport in Kuwait to Ali Al Salem Air Base. There we waited in tents again as we had on our way to the States. The next morning, we left the same way we had come—by C-130 cargo plane.

When I got back to my base, I was welcomed by my team and I was glad to see everyone safe. It made me realized how, in just a matter of months, we had truly bonded as a family.

It was January 23, 2008 and I was sleeping in my room when I had a strange dream. As I slept, I saw a huge animal that looked like a lion, only bigger, and it had two humps on its back like a camel. Then I saw another animal that looked like a monkey, only bigger, and it had the face of a lion and two long tails. As I was watching, the two animals got into a big fight, and the animal with two tails jumped onto the animal with two humps. As the two animals struggled, they moved close to me, and I cried out for help from my daddy, and he came to my rescue and threw spears at the animals. As I tried to run away, something snared my right leg and stopped me for a moment. I looked down on my leg and I saw it; it was a small rope thrown by a soldier. Immediately I reached down and cut the rope and ran away while my daddy was still fighting with the two animals.

Just as I woke up, my teammates were coming back from their mission, and I told my roommate about the dream I'd had. He suggested I seek *mental* help about the puzzling dream, but I didn't want to do that. My daddy was not even alive, and I was just wondering why he was in my dream. A lot of dreams *do* have special meanings, and I wished for someone who could explain the significance of my dream.

One morning later that week, we didn't have a mission and I took a midmorning nap again and had another dream. In the dream, I was talking to John Garang, the late leader of South Sudan, about the education of the youth in his country. He told me, "If anyone *hasn't* gone to school and is not currently *going* to school, that person *is not* and *will not* be part of my people and nation."

His remark disturbed me, so I asked him, "If *you* had been born with two tails, would you *deny* one tail and *accept* the other one while they are *both* part of your body?"

"No," he said.

Then I told him, "*We* are your tails—whether educated or not."

It was strange that I was dreaming of our late leader and of my daddy, who also is no longer with us. I'd never had dreams like that before. I thought, *Here I am in the war zone, and I'm having these strange dreams.* I wanted to know if there was any special *meaning* to them. John Garang is still in us today, because he told us in Washington, DC, in 2003 that we are the *living seeds* of the new Sudan. He urged us to *go to school* whether we are young or old, because we need to grow more seeds in the empty land of South Sudan. Maybe it was because of John Garang's focus on education, as well as my own desire to learn, that I had such a dream.

It's hard to be a child in a war zone, so we always tried to befriend the children. One day we went to the green zone so our officers could visit a sergeant who had been injured and was in the hospital. While we waited outside for the officers, those of us with lower ranks went inside the chow hall to get food. When we came back out, a small Iraqi boy came over to where we had parked our vehicles. "Hey, black guy!" he said. "Give me some food!" I told him I didn't have any food, although I was just teasing. But our PFC was upset with the boy for calling me "black guy" instead of "soldier." I knew the boy didn't know any better. After the men had all gotten their food, the boy came to me again and begged for something to eat, and I gave him two pieces of chicken. I couldn't ignore him, because I know all too well what it's like for a child to be hungry.

After we had finished eating, I was about to get rid of the trash when the same boy came to me again and said he would take care of it for me. He picked up the empty plates and took them to the dumpster as we prepared to leave. Then he came back to me and said, "Hey, black guy. Give me *money*, please." But I didn't give him any, because we didn't make a practice of giving kids money—only candy, food, and soccer balls.

I went with some of the officers for a meeting at Camp Justice, the Iraqi base where Saddam Hussein had been hanged just a couple months earlier. There I met LTC Burns, who had been one of the officers during my basic training at Fort Benning, Georgia. It was good to see him again. We hugged each other and visited a little, and he asked if they were treating me well. I told him they were—but I said that as a soldier I would do my job and be anywhere I was needed *regardless* of how I was treated.

A dog came running up to me there at the camp, and I thought it was going to *bite* me, so I kicked it away. Then one of the officers there told me about the dog. "That dog's not trying to hurt you," he said. "He just wants to play—but he's being *cautious* because he's been hurt."

He said the animal had been shot three times by Iraqi soldiers, and each time it had run to the American camp, where the soldiers treated its wounds. The soldiers then adopted the dog, and they had been feeding and caring for him ever since. Now he was healthy and strong. They said the dog had made his home there and never left FOB Justice. They said he always played with the American soldiers—but sometimes when he would see *Iraqi* soldiers, he would try to bite them because they had mistreated him.

After hearing the dog's story, I felt bad. I realized that he had never intended to bite me—he just wanted to *play*. I went back and played with him and took pictures of him. I felt sorry for the dog because he too was a war veteran.

Our missions often took us to interesting locations—one such place was the Unfinished Mosque. It is said to be the largest mosque in the world and was supposed to have been finished by Saddam Hussein before he was caught up in the US invasion of Iraq. The massive building looked strange because cranes were still standing around it from when the work on it had come to a halt. But it was a place our commanders would go for meetings with Iraqi officials.

We were on our way to one of those meetings at the mosque when an exploding IED hit our convoy. The blast ripped the antenna off the vehicle in which I was the gunner and sprayed the turret with shrapnel. I saw a big red flash of light surrounding my turret and saw burning metal and red pieces cutting down my antenna. Then I saw electrical lines coming down on the left side of the road. It all happened fast, and the shock waves from the IED knocked me out cold for five full minutes.

I felt whiplash and felt my back crack, but no shrapnel got into my body. However, I did have a concussion and a severe headache. I was dizzy, and I felt like throwing up. My driver, Specialist Bromely, was freaking out when he saw me—he thought for sure I had been *killed* by the IED. He told me later that he kept shaking my legs and calling to me, but he couldn't get any response. Then after five minutes I woke up and was talking very loudly, because the IED had deafened me.

That had been my *fourth* IED encounter during our missions in Iraq, but the effects of this one were much worse than those of the previous ones. Several of the men who were with me had sore arms and shoulders from the blast, and we were all given twenty-four hours of light duties. When I went back to the clinic later, they assigned me five days to recuperate in the FOB with no missions outside the wire. It was the gunners who got most of the shock waves from the roadside bombs and IEDs, and this time the blast had left me with *permanent* injuries.

Just the day before, we had lost one of our men from Delta Company—Sergeant Thrasher, a twenty-three-year-old soldier from California. He was killed by a rocket attack in the place in Baghdad we called Ghazaliyah. That night before I went to bed, I prayed for my fallen comrade. "May our soldier who lost his life yesterday rest in peace. Lord God our Father, we pray for your glory to help his family during this hard time they are facing. Thanks to Almighty God, may he bring peace to the world."

Yes, there were some difficult days—days that would haunt us for a lifetime. But there were good and even *amusing* days too … like when we would go to the motor pool to fill sandbags. We used the sandbags to make bulletproof barriers around buildings and to cover windows. I remember one day when our guys had a sand fight after filling more than three hundred bags. It reminded me of kids playing at the beach—a *silly* incident, but the kind of thing that took our minds off the war, if only for an instant. Then there was the time we took a route in northwest Baghdad and drove through the busy marketplace. We went on to the slaughterhouse, and our vehicle became stuck in deep *cow dung*. Our sergeant managed to drive the vehicle out, but it was a stinking mess as we drove back to the base.

Besides Ghazaliyah, there was another extremely dangerous area with a lot of bloodshed—a place called Shullah. It was dangerous because it lies at the border between the Shiites and the Sunnis. But it was also an area where our military worked to help the local farmers by digging deep streams for irrigation of crops and for watering livestock. The farming region was very open, with houses scattered throughout, and there were *always* children. The children loved us and would converge on us whenever they spotted our vehicles in the area. But *these* children were not asking merely for candy and cookies—they wanted pencils, pens, and books. I appreciated their thirst for learning, and after giving them some treats, I promised to bring pencils and pens the next time I came. I could well identify with them and their desire for an education.

There were two women in our unit—Privates Fifield and Fenton. They were good soldiers and were often assigned as drivers when we went on missions. But the presence of women in uniform struck some people as rather odd. One day we were waiting outside the Unfinished Mosque when a number of young people came over to talk with us. One was a boy named Nur who told us he was a twelfth-grade student. As he talked with my driver, Private Fifield, I couldn't help but be impressed with his command of the English language. He and his friends asked Private Fifield why she had joined the military, and she explained how that had been her goal ever since she was a child and told them that she enjoyed her work.

An Iraqi soldier had been watching us, and he came over and wanted to speak to Private Fifield too. He came right to the point and told her he wanted to *marry* her—but she told him she was already married, so he left her alone and went back to his convoy. This happened a lot because the Iraqis were usually surprised to see a woman with us—and to keep the men from bothering her, she would tell them she was my wife.

A few days later, we had a cameraman with us taking a lot of pictures, especially of my driver, PFC Fifield. He asked her about the mission and the war, and he wanted to know how she was handling the place as a female soldier. But her only comment to him was, "We are brothers and sisters in arms *together*." She liked driving my vehicle. She told me she always felt *safer* when I was on the gun during the missions because I didn't hesitate to return fire during firefights.

The other woman, Private Fenton, was driving for me the first time she ever witnessed an IED explosion. Because the explosions are usually followed by small-arms fire, the noise can be very frightening.

The blast took her completely by surprise, and she began screaming hysterically.

Three days earlier we had been ambushed at the same place, and she had wondered what was going on when I was the first among the PSD (personal security detachment) gunners to return fire. She thought the bad guys had overpowered us, but they hadn't. I rocked my 240 Bravo machine gun, and they felt my power when I saw the guys running between the buildings and then inside. I explained to her that I returned the fire without fear inside me—and that is what saves brave soldiers when they are on the guns. That is how I rolled out every day in that war-torn country. I never allowed fear to come close to me in the war zone.

We all had headaches from that explosion and went to the TMC afterward. Every time IEDs went off, we felt as if our blood veins were bursting inside our bodies and our heads. And they literally were, to a point—because Private Fenton's nose was bleeding from the explosion and dust.

In the middle of March, our battalion began the mission of putting up COP (combat outpost) Thrasher at what we called Ghazaliyah. This was to honor Sergeant Thrasher, who had been killed at that spot by sniper fire the previous month. Then the very day after we began the project, our platoon lost *four more* men. Five men were traveling in a vehicle when a roadside bomb that had been buried, exploded. It was a powerful blast that threw the vehicle twenty yards from the road. Only one of the men survived. Those killed were Sergeant John Allen, PFC William Davis, Sergeant Ed Santini, and John Landry Jr. Landry was only twenty years old— much too young to die. Our staff sergeant used to say, "John's a *lion boy* at heart." We would miss him because no matter how bad things were, he could always make us *laugh*—especially when he did one of his funny dances.

The following Friday we attended the funeral for the four men. Before we left for the funeral that morning, I read the newspaper account of the explosion that had claimed their lives. I also read the statistics on the war casualties. Since the war had begun four years earlier, 3,223 American soldiers had been killed and more than 24,000 others had been injured. That was far too many casualties. I prayed that Almighty God would bring *peace*!

Our two-star General Brooks was present for the funeral service. We all were shedding tears for our fallen comrades, except for the high-ranking officers. They felt the pain too, but their position required them to remain stoic. But I cried so much I got a headache. It was so painful to know that my close friends in my platoon—the ones I used to have fun and joke with—were *gone* for good. I had known them back in the States before our deployment, and we'd had good times together. The images—the *faces* of these men—would not leave my mind after the funeral. For months afterward I would see them every day while I was alone, and especially when our mission took us to the area where they had been killed.

Since we had been in the area, far too many of our soldiers had lost their lives. It seemed to me that we should have been doing more to secure areas like COP Thrasher. We *knew* the enemies placed IEDs in the road and other places at *night*—and that they watched for us to come by in the morning.

There were other casualties too—the many who suffered *injuries*. Whenever our soldiers were wounded, we would go on mission to the CASH, or combat hospital, in the Green Zone and pray for them and encourage them during their recovery. Soldiers are supposed to be *strong*, but it's still tough for them to be sick or injured without having family close by, so we tried to fill that role. Sometimes we would take something just to show the men that we were thinking of them. One time I went in with the chaplain to see one of my buddies who had been shot in the leg, and I gave him a rosary I had gotten from church. It meant a lot to him to know that we cared.

It's funny how the simplest thing can brighten your day— and I really believe that *every* good gift comes from God. It was midmorning, and I was in full gear ready for a mission when a ladybug landed on my right knee. Then one landed on my *left* knee. I was just looking at the beautiful creatures when one of my friends saw them and said, "Did you know that when a ladybug lands on you, it's a sign of good luck?" I didn't know that, so I just thanked God for whatever good he had planned for me that day.

We had to grab whatever pleasure we could to get our minds off the often grim job we faced each day. Playing with the Iraqi kids at the meeting place was always a welcome diversion. I loved talking with them. One time a little boy handed me a necklace. It was nothing of value, and I refused it at first. "But you *have* to take it," he insisted. "Last week you gave me some balls—so now you're my *friend.*" He had such a pleading look in his dark eyes. I took the necklace and thanked the boy for his gift—and then five *more* boys came begging for candy. I gave them candy and cookies, and that made their day. After that, one little boy called to me and raised his hands and said, "God *bless* you!" I reached inside my vehicle and pulled out a soccer ball and gave it to him. As we drove off, the kids were all waving to us and we waved back. The kids were very glad for our presence in their country, and they often thanked us for making things safe for them.

One day at Casino—one of the joint security stations—I danced with some Iraqi soldiers while a couple of my friends took videos. They would be fun to watch at a later date. While we were there, I decided to try one of the Iraqi sandwiches called *kabab*—ground meat seasoned and grilled on a spear and eaten with bread. It was very good, but my driver, Private Fifield, ate some and complained of an upset stomach afterward. I guess her stomach just wasn't used to the spicy sandwiches, but I always enjoyed trying the different foods.

In June, during my seventh month of deployment, things went really bad as the IEDs claimed more casualties. On one mission one of our noncommissioned officers, Sergeant Chavez, lost both of his legs—what a *tragedy* for that young man! Then four days later, another incident hit me much closer to home. My good buddy Raymond Spencer was critically wounded when an IED with explosive force penetration ripped through his Bradley Fighting Vehicle. I took a picture of the helicopter as it left the Troop Medical Center to take him to the hospital. Things looked grim, yet I prayed that he would somehow make it. But days later, we got word that he didn't survive.

His death was extremely hard for me to take. We had gone to basic training together and had become close friends. Then after we graduated, we went to Fort Bliss together as our duty station. I couldn't get Spencer's image out of my head. I could still see him smiling the day I had come in first in our company in the two-mile run. "The reason *you* can run so fast," he said, "is because you are used to chasing gazelles and wild animals in *Africa!*"

"How do they hunt wild game in Africa?" he wanted to know. "Do they use spears or guns? Is it like deer hunting?" He was full of questions, and I tried to answer them for him. He wanted so much to visit Africa with me in the future and see all the wild animals for himself. But instead, he sacrificed his life for his country at the young age of twenty-three.

It seemed that progress was slow, but still we were gaining ground in making things safer, especially in the COP Thrasher area. From time to time we would find large caches of explosives that the enemy had stored. One such cache was deadly chlorine explosives—but then, *every* kind of explosive posed a serious threat. My constant prayer was that God would help us bring peace to that country so its people could enjoy their freedom. The children were always my first concern because they were innocent victims and didn't understand what the war was all about. Sometimes they would tell us that they would like to go to America someday and have a new life.

When August came, we had another thing to deal with—the intense summer *heat*. One day we were told the temperature had reached 118 degrees, and with our heavy gear, it felt like we were on fire! Of course, *without* protection, we would have been ready targets for the enemy. But by that time, we were beginning to count the weeks until our term of deployment would end.

August was also a month when we were visited by members of the top brass. Among the dignitaries were General Odierno and General Campbell, plus British and Iraqi generals. We were also visited that month by General Petraeus, who came along with several congressmen. When we took General Odierno with us, our Major Pirog told him our vehicle looked like the United Nations, because its passengers were so diverse.

Each time we took one of the generals on a tour of our sector, IEDs would go off. I could never figure out how the enemy always *knew* when we were carrying a VIP aboard—but fortunately, there were no bad incidents during those tours.

The visiting dignitaries complimented us on the fine job we were doing in our sector. And we too were pleased with the progress we had made in working with the Iraqi leaders. Our Lieutenant Commander Nickolas was especially good at dealing with the people in Ghazaliyah; he often bought cookies and treats from the local shopkeepers, and he developed good relationships with many of the other locals. With everyone working together, we were accomplishing what we had come there to do.

In September, tragedy struck my platoon again when Specialist Brandon Thorsen was accidentally killed by friendly fire. He was a great guy, always good-natured. He had been in my platoon in Fort Bliss and was looking forward to working with wildlife—maybe as a ranger after his contract ended. He was engaged to be married the following April, and I felt very sorry for his fiancé, whose dreams had been shattered.

Our deployment was soon coming to an end, and we were counting down the days. On Thanksgiving Day, we went on our regular mission outside the wire, and then we came back to our base for dinner. The chow hall was especially crowded that day, and the line was long, but they had prepared a fine meal for us. And a special guest—Senator Joe Lieberman—joined us for Thanksgiving dinner. That was our last holiday in Iraq.

December 3 was the final mission outside the wire for us as TAC team for 2-12 Cavalry. We completed our mission and returned safely to our base, with great joy and thanks to our Father in heaven for his mercy on us during our deployment. I had a US flag in my turret with me as a sign of victory for us after we'd spent so many months in the war zone.

The time had finally come for us to return to the United States, and it was an emotional moment for everyone. It was hard to keep our composure in the face of the many challenges we had faced together. After more than a year of fighting at least fifty times a week, by the end of our tour things had turned around to the point we were averaging only *one* attack a week. What we had accomplished was nothing short of *amazing!*

Our wedding Day, July 8, 2006.

(Left to right) Mayom Ngor Deng, Kiir Bol Giir, Dominic, Mahalet, Birukitawi, and Lual Joach Akec.

Dominic Malual, after a
firefight in the Gee Spot.

Dominic sharing water
with Iraqi children.

SPC Barker, Iraqi soldier, and
Dominic at the unfinished
Al-Rahman Mosque in
Baghdad, Iraq.

Dominic, right of flag, at
the Iraq Monument to the
Unknown Soldier in Baghdad.

CHAPTER 5

Transition

Like the proverbial bad penny, some problems always return! When I came back from Iraq, there was a bill for more than eight thousand dollars awaiting me. My car deal woes were not over after all. It turned out that the vehicle I had unknowingly cosigned for had been sold for much less than what was still owed on it. But the credit company offered me a deal. They said if I would give them three thousand dollars, the rest of the eight thousand would be forgiven. Americans have a saying that "you can't get blood out of a turnip," so I gave up on trying to locate the man who had cheated me, and to protect my *own* credit from going bad, I went ahead and paid the three thousand dollars. After the credit company received the money, they mailed me a "Paid in Full" receipt, which I still have.

I have learned that both failure and success are the results of one's own struggles. We are responsible or our *own* dreams; only *we* can fulfill them. And if we fail to fulfill them, we can only blame the guy we see in the mirror—not our family or anyone else. I have had to forgive the man, because what he did to me was wrong, but the ordeal with him and the car was a *learning* experience for me.

When I first came to the States, I was in debt for more than sixteen hundred dollars for travel documents for myself and my cousin Deng Makuac, who came with me. That was a small fortune for someone like me without a job.

Since then I have taken out loans for my education and have paid off all my debts in full. I struggle to be who I am today, because of what I went through during the war in Sudan. Although I lived with my parents for only seven years, during that time they instilled in me values that have stayed with me throughout my life. I was taught to be honest and to respect others and their belongings, and that includes being financially responsible.

After we returned to Fort Bliss, a stone monument was erected as a tribute to our unit's fallen comrades. The parents of Specialist Brandon Thorsen, who had died in August, were there for the ceremony. They came to pay tribute not only to *their* son, but to *all* the soldiers who had been killed in the Iraq war. Brandon's mother was in tears as she saw the stone with the list of names engraved on it. That, of course, affected all of us, and we couldn't help but weep again with her. These brave men had joined the army just as I had—but they had paid the ultimate price for freedom.

In February 2008, Mahalet went to the doctor for a checkup because she suspected she might be pregnant. When she came back home, I asked her what she found out.

"I'm not pregnant," she said. Her test was actually *positive*, but she wanted to tease me a little to see my reaction. Of course, I was very excited when I found out we were having another child.

Everything about the pregnancy was going well, and during Mahalet's fifth month we started walking exercises together and would go out every evening when I got off from work. I wanted her to have an easy delivery of the baby, and I knew walking would help keep her in shape. Except for dealing with my back injury, I was doing quite well myself. But after a few weeks I began having nightmares and confusion almost nightly. A few disturbing incidents occurred while we were still living in El Paso.

I got out of bed about two o'clock one morning. I washed up and shaved and then woke Mahalet. "Get up," I told her. "We need to go to Walmart and to the bank." She didn't think much about it. She just thought I wanted to go to Walmart for some things because the store was open all night. We got ready and went to the car, placed baby Achuei in her car seat, and then I got in and drove off toward Walmart. We had gone no more than three blocks when I woke up *completely*. I noticed the sky was still dark, and I looked at my wife. "What *time* is it?" I asked.

"Three o'clock in the *morning*," she said. "It's pretty *early* to go shopping, and the bank isn't open yet." I started laughing to myself, and I told her that something went wrong for me to get up at such a crazy hour. So I turned the car around, and we went back home.

I could see that the sleep disturbances and nightmares were becoming a serious problem, so I made an appointment to see a doctor about them. I told him everything that was going on with me at that time, and he said I was having flashbacks from the war. He told me that it was common for soldiers returning from the war zone to experience such flashbacks, and I was given a caseworker to monitor my situation. I saw the caseworker twice a month, and she kept updates on everything from my dreams to any other kind of problems I was having.

Then I had *another* incident. I woke Mahalet up at one o'clock in the morning and told her to call the hospital so that they could make an appointment for me. But this time she *knew* not to get up. She told me that one o'clock was the wrong time to call the hospital for an appointment. Then I realized that I was having another nightmare.

It was very confusing. Sometimes I felt as if I were on another *planet*! Every night I would dream that I was in Baghdad—or I would have a dream *within a dream*. Sometimes I would get up early in the morning after I'd had a dream, and I would think that I had been dreaming back in *Iraq* instead of being in Texas. I would dream of patrolling outside the wire. There would be roadside bombs, IEDs, small-arms fire, and ambushes going on. I was constantly *reliving* the war!

It was strange, because I never had these kinds of dreams about war when I was a boy in the South Sudan conflict, which took two and a half million lives. But my wife helped me to work through these nightmares. She would guide me and help me to get *completely* awake, and I would be okay. Even now, after all these years, I'm *still* having dreams of war—but at least I'm not sleepwalking like I was back then.

Mahalet's doctor had set her due date for September 28th, and everything was going well. Then her doctor told her to stop doing the walking exercises that I'd been having her do. "No," I told her, "your doctor is *wrong* about that. Walking is the *best* thing for you—and you aren't having any problems, so just keep it up and you'll have an easy delivery." We continued to walk together, despite her doctor's advice.

A short time later, the doctor told Mahalet that the baby was in the wrong position for birth, and he made an appointment for her to come in and have the baby turned so that its head was facing downward. "Then if there are any complications, we'll take the baby by cesarean right away to keep it from suffocating."

The appointment was made for the second week in September— two weeks before the baby's due date. But I began to have a bad feeling about it and had her cancel the appointment when the doctor's office called to remind her. This didn't set well with her doctor. "Okay," she said, "if you don't come in and let us turn the baby, I'll put a note for them to *automatically* take the baby by cesarean when you come in."

When Mahalet got off the phone with the doctor, she broke down and cried. I was displeased with the doctor for worrying my wife as she had. I took Mahalet in my arms and tried to console her. "The doctor is not *God*," I said. "Just be patient, and you will have this baby *naturally* just the way you had Achuei."

September 28th came on a Sunday, and my wife and I got up and went to church that morning. The priest said a special blessing for Mahalet and told her he thought the baby might come that day. He told her that *he* had been born on Sunday too. We came home from church and had our lunch as usual. Then at around five forty-five in the evening, Mahalet told me she was going into labor. I packed up the things she would need at the hospital and then got Achuei out of her crib and into her car seat, and we left quickly. We lived only five minutes from the hospital, but when we were halfway there, Mahalet's water broke.

At the hospital, they put Mahalet into a wheelchair and pushed her directly to the delivery room. I went into the room with her, carrying Achuei in my arms. The maternity nurse looked at me questioningly. "Would you step *outside* the room, please?"

"No!" Mahalet told her. "He's my *husband*, and I want him to *stay* with me."

The nurse was obviously unhappy with my being there, so I asked her, "Why should I go outside?" But she didn't answer me.

Mahalet's contractions were now very close together. Then while she was pushing the baby, one of the nurses opened up the computer, and my wife's information popped up on the screen. It said that she was scheduled to have a *cesarean*, but it gave no reason. Within a minute, at six thirty-five, my wife gave birth to the baby naturally. It took her only twenty minutes from the time we left home to have the baby!

After the baby had been cleaned up, we were alone in the room with the maternity nurse. Of course, she was aware of the drama with the computer message. "There was no *reason* for that baby to be taken by cesarean," she said. "Some doctors recommend cesareans because it cuts down on the length of time they have to stay with their patients." I was shocked when she told us that. There are unethical doctors, and there are good ones. It seems that some of them see money as more important than their patients. God only knows how many unnecessary cesareans that doctor performed on women.

It didn't make sense to me that someone would go to school for so many years to do something good for her patients and then take advantage of them. I don't want to go too far in blaming doctors, but they should remember the wise saying, "What *goes* around *comes* around."

I thanked Almighty God for showing me the right way each time my wife had a baby, and I thanked him for allowing my two daughters to be born on Sundays. I named my second daughter Hawathiya after my mother because of the way she encouraged me when I was in the war. I remembered what she had said when I called and talked to her before our first baby was born and had told her I was serving in the US Army. "You will be fine," she said. "God will *protect* you. Even if you sleep in the fire, you will come out of the problem like a fragile egg comes out of a bird unbroken." My mother was a very wise woman.

God is always there for my family and for me. I have a lot yet to learn, but God is already showing me ways to serve others. When my time comes, I will never use my power to do something that would hurt other people. I would be so grateful if Almighty God would give me the wisdom of King Solomon in the Bible, who settled the problem between two women who were fighting over a baby.

My contract with the army had come to an end, and there was nothing to keep me in El Paso. So my wife and I decided to move back to Michigan, where I had cousins and friends. It was December 2008 when we packed our basic needs into our cars, a Ford Explorer and a Pontiac Sunfire, for the journey to Michigan. I arranged for our household goods to be shipped to us once we had established a permanent address. We planned to stop in Fort Worth on the way and visit my cousins Arop and Ayiik.

I paid our apartment mechanic, whom we referred to as "amigo," to hook our small car up to the Ford Explorer so that we could tow it. That way, Mahalet and I could travel together in the truck and take turns driving, and she could nurse the baby whenever she needed to. But we had no sooner gotten onto the interstate than the tow chain broke, so I stopped the truck and unhooked the broken chain. I told Mahalet I would drive the truck with the two girls, and she could follow close behind me in the Sunfire.

She did a great job of following me, and I was careful to watch that cars didn't get between us and block her view of me. We stopped from time to time for her to nurse the baby, so it took us twelve hours to reach Dallas. Then we called my cousins in Fort Worth, and they directed us to their home. Our original plans were to spend the night and set out the next day for Louisville, Kentucky—but Achuei had gotten carsick, and we stayed a couple extra days until she was feeling better.

We started our journey again and drove to Louisville, where my two aunts, Nyanuer and Achol, live—but by the time we got there, we could see that driving two vehicles was not practical. It was nerve-racking trying to stay together on the highway, plus very *expensive* having to fuel two gas tanks.

I checked with a rental company to see about getting proper towing equipment to pull the car, but that didn't work out, so we gave up on the idea of taking both vehicles to Michigan. We decided to leave the Sunfire there in Kentucky. We hated leaving it after bringing it so far, but the rest of the trip was definitely more enjoyable without it. I drove the Explorer, and Mahalet could nurse the baby without our having to stop—so we had an easy time the rest of the way.

Finding affordable housing in Grand Rapids proved to be a challenge. When I had lived there before, it had been with three of my cousins—but *now* I had a wife and kids to think about. We rented a hotel room when we first arrived, but because of the expense, we sought help for housing through the local veterans' office. We explained our situation, and they referred us to the Department of Housing for Low Income People, and a man who was himself a veteran directed us to someone for assistance.

The process was frustrating to my wife because the agency had us returning every day and it was the dead of winter, plus we were running low on funds. After we were shown a house we felt was unfit and in a bad neighborhood, the lady in the office gave us thirty days to find our *own* apartment. I went right away to check out an apartment complex not far from where I had lived before. Our application was accepted, and we took care of the necessary paperwork and moved in on January 9, 2009.

We were relieved to have found a place and were just waiting for our furniture and household goods to arrive from El Paso. In the meantime, we slept on a large air bed I had purchased—and the very day our furniture arrived, the kids were playing on the air bed and it went flat. What good timing!

My *next* move was to find a job so that I could continue to support my family. Unfortunately, the Michigan economy was in hot water and few places were hiring. We were hanging in the sky, so to speak, but thanks to the government and taxpayers, we were getting food stamps until my veteran's disability payments kicked in. Fortunately, the lady in the veterans' office got me in touch with someone who could expedite my disability paperwork, and it went through very quickly.

It was time to file my taxes, and when I did, I saw that I would be getting a refund. I had not seen my mother since I was seven years old, and she was getting on in years, so I made plans to go home and reunite with my family. It was a trip I had long dreamed of taking, and I thought it would be best to go before I started a new job.

CHAPTER 6

Return from Exile

I t was a bad time to be going to Sudan. The International Court was going after Sudanese President Omar al-Bashir, for the brutal genocide that had been taking place in Darfur and other parts of the country under his watch. When I bought my ticket from Grand Rapids, Michigan, to Khartoum, Sudan, my family members were understandably uneasy. They were concerned about my landing in Khartoum, because I was both a Lost Boy *and* an American soldier—two things that would not sit well with the Sudanese government.

"Don't worry about me—I'm a *veteran*," I reminded them. "I'm not currently enlisted. And I'm not going there for *political* purposes or to be involved in the northern Sudan crisis—not without *backup* from the United States."

My flight left from the airport in Grand Rapids for Chicago, and then I flew to Khartoum, Sudan, via London and Lebanon. It was two o'clock in the morning when we landed in Khartoum. There in the airport, things turned ugly at first for me and for an Indian gentleman. *He* had made the mistake of going to Sudan with no knowledge of either Arabic or English. The airport officials were talking of deporting him back to his own country or to wherever he had come from. Then it was *my* turn. I was *born* in Sudan. The problem was, I was carrying a US passport and had not gotten a visa for Sudan. The officials started to give *me* a hard time too. But I gave them my full name and explained to them that Sudan was my birthplace and that two of my brothers, Garang Malual and Ajuong Malual, were living there in Khartoum at the time.

It was the middle of the night, and my brothers were at home waiting for me to land at the Khartoum airport. But they had been watching a soccer game on TV and had fallen asleep. They were just waking up when one of the agents at the airport called Garang on his cell phone and told him I was there.

I was at the window paying the airport customs for my visa when my brothers showed up. They checked in, and when the airport customs official looked at their identification cards, he saw that their names matched the name on my passport ... and my brothers also *look* like me. The customs agent then asked them what their mother's name was, and when he saw that it matched the name *I* had given them, we were all cleared.

When I had first gotten off the plane in Khartoum, I was confused. My initial thought was that I had landed at the *Baghdad* airport by mistake, because the people in northern Sudan are Arabs and look much like the Iraqi people. The *sight* of them woke up my war flashbacks. Also, when I was outside the terminal, I could hear the sounds of prayers coming from the nearby mosque, and they were the same sounds I had heard from people at prayer in Iraq.

I had never been to northern Sudan, and I knew nothing of what life there had been like for the black natives of the south. Whole families from South Sudan had been taken to the north by force during the struggles, and their lives had been most unpleasant. Those people were still living in mud houses, in extreme contrast to the homes of first-class Arab citizens. There was clearly no justice for the black natives of Sudan, so I had *reasons* to feel uneasy.

Thanks to my brothers, my patience, and my basic knowledge of English as well as a few words in Arabic, I was able to deal with the people at the Khartoum airport. Otherwise, they would have deported me back to America without my getting to see my family after so many years apart.

The next day in Khartoum, I went to the American embassy to register for my stay in the country. I met first with one of the northern officers, and then I asked to speak to the ambassador. The officer went inside and put my social security number in the system, and he came back to me with some questions. "Are you a *soldier*?" he wanted to know.

"Who told you that?" I asked. He told me that he was working in the embassy with the American ambassador, so I explained to him that I had been in the army, but I was now a *veteran* and a student. He then stepped back inside the office and sent the ambassador out to speak with me. The ambassador advised me to *leave* the country right away, for my own safety because of the current political situation in Sudan.

I then told the ambassador that I had been away for many years and had not seen my family since I was a child. My story *amazed* him. He then asked me to leave a telephone number where I could be reached, and so I could contact the necessary authorities in case something happened to me while on my way south. I gave him my brother's phone number, and he let me go.

Two days later people in Khartoum began to go crazy when they heard that the International Criminal Court wanted to arrest President Omar al-Bashir for the genocide of people in western Sudan. But Omar was out there boldly campaigning and giving the people all kinds of speeches saying he *had been* and *still was* the right president for Sudan. Meanwhile, people were running in the streets and chanting, "Death to Americans and their allies!" I was beginning to see why the ambassador had warned me to leave.

When I called my family back in Michigan, they were very concerned about my being in Khartoum, but I didn't let them know just how dangerous things actually were. "Don't worry," I told them. "I'm just a normal person—a *civilian*." But when my brothers took me to get my visitor's ID, I became concerned *myself*. The people in charge at that office said they needed to see my birth certificate. I thought to myself, *Boy, am I in the wrong place at the wrong time!* Then my brother spoke up and told them I had attended school in Uganda and was now studying in America—so they asked to see my ID. Then I showed them my Michigan driver's license and my student ID from Grand Rapids Community College, and they were satisfied.

My brother Ajuong had gone to Khartoum some months earlier in hopes of finding work. But he'd found it was nearly impossible for a native of southern Sudan to make a living there—*especially* without an education. But while Ajuong was still there, my brother Garang's daughter became very ill, and he had brought her to the hospital in Khartoum for treatment. He had been staying with Ajuong so he could be near her. Then before we left Khartoum, I went with my brothers to the hospital to see my niece. Fortunately, she did recover and was able to go home soon afterward.

After I'd been in Khartoum for eleven days, my brothers and I took a slow bus to South Sudan. We encountered some difficult times on the way. Our bus broke down *four* times because the roads between northern and southern Sudan were not maintained. In fact, there were stretches where there was no real road at all—just rough, rocky ground. We spent a night at a bus stop on the way without sleeping—it was not safe to sleep there unguarded. After that, my brothers and I took turns sleeping in two-hour shifts until we reached our town of Turalei.

When we arrived in Turalei, I stepped off the bus and retrieved the three small bags I had brought with me. Then my brothers and I set out on foot for the seven-mile trek to our family compound in our village of Wunriang. It was hard to believe that I was really coming *home*. I wondered about friends and families I had left years ago—would I recognize the people I had known, and would they know *me*? Many people had died during my absence, but many more had been born—brothers and sisters, nieces and nephews. But the one person I wanted to see most of all was my *mommy*. As we talked on our way, my brothers said they wondered if she would recognize me—after all, I was only *seven* when I left home, and I was now almost thirty.

As soon as we were close enough to be seen, a group of friends and relatives came to meet us. They all seemed happy—some were crying as we embraced. It was a very emotional time. My brothers then led the way to a large spreading tree, where a frail gray-haired woman who looked like my *grandmother* sat. I recognized my mother's features, but I was shocked at how much she had aged during my absence. One of my brothers asked her to look at the group and point me out from among them. Then she looked directly at me. "Is that *you*, my son?" she asked. "Is that *you*, my son?" Then again, a third time, "Is that *you*, my son?"

"Yes, Mommy," I answered. "It's *me*, Deng." At that, she slumped down in her chair and passed out. She was completely out for a few minutes. I was frightened—I thought the excitement had been too much for her and she was dead. But then she came to, and I reached down and held her as tears coursed down my cheeks. She was wet with perspiration, and I could feel her rapid heartbeat against my chest. She leaned back so she could search my face again.

"My *son*," she said, "I will not fail to recognize you even if you spend a *hundred years* away from me!"

The rest of the family moved on and let the two of us have privacy. I was weak with emotion too as I sat down to talk with my mother. She began telling me how she had continued to search for me for five years. At that point she had quit looking, but she had never given up hope that I was still alive. She thought perhaps I had been kidnapped and taken to northern Sudan—or that I had gone with the other missing villagers to wherever they had fled to. I was suddenly struck with the reality of the life my mother was living. She looked as if she'd barely eaten for weeks, and she clearly had no strength.

She told me about things that had happened in the years since I left and how my father's death had affected everyone. Life in our village had *always* been a struggle because of the constant raids by the government from the north. Yet despite that, my dad had worked very hard maintaining the cattle camps and had provided well for his wives and children. But it was after he was killed, my mother said, that things really fell apart. My dad had been considered a wealthy man by the standards of our community. He had owned hundreds of cattle plus large numbers of other livestock and poultry. But when his cattle camp was raided, his entire herd of cattle had been taken away and he was murdered in the process. I didn't press my mother for the details of his death at this time, because I could tell it was much too painful for her—but I *did* plan to talk to my brothers about it later.

With the source of family income vanishing overnight, it fell on my mother to care for my dad's other wives and their children. In Dinka culture, the first wife is the matriarch of the family and the role model for the other wives. If her husband dies, *she* is the one who must take his place and shoulder the responsibility for the extended family. She had to do the farming with her own hands, trying to provide food for everyone, and the hardships had taken a toll on her. When word of my father's death reached me in the refugee camp, I knew things were going to be hard for my mother, but I had no idea what a cruel lot she had been dealt until I saw her now, a shadow of her former self.

There was so much my mother wanted to tell me; her words poured out as I sat and listened. "Son," she said, "*look* at your brothers' and sisters' children—and the other children in our village. They are not going to school because of the tough times we are going through. What are you going to *do* to help them get an education? Are you going to take them all to America so they can learn like you, and like all the children in America? *Please* do something!"

Then she told me that from the time I came out of her womb she had known I would be the one to bring hope to our family. Then she thought of something amusing. "Do you remember when your sister Achuei was married and you stood up and asked her father-in-law for a pregnant cow and a calf?

"Yes" I answered, chuckling, "I still remember that." We laughed, and I wished the man had been there to make good on his promise.

I know he will someday—he's a man of his word—but I did not see him during my visit.

It had been evening when we sat down to talk, and now the sun was creeping above the horizon; we had talked *all* night long. As happy as I had been to see my mother, I was now burdened with all of the cares she had endured. I looked at her dusty calloused feet, and I wondered if she even *owned* a pair of sandals—or if she walked from place to place barefoot. And the dress she wore ... was it the only one she owned?

Her home was not a fit place for anyone to live; rats raced through the hut at night, making it dirty and unsafe—yet she had tried to stay *strong* for the rest of her family. I was shocked by her plight to the point I could not express myself. True, I am *rich* by my family's standards, but back home in America, I am *anything* but wealthy!

One thing I was glad to observe about my mother was that she didn't *drink*. She told me that she would die without drinking, and she begged me that if I did *not* drink, to never start. I told her I don't drink, and I made a promise to her that I never will. I intend to keep that promise for life. I don't even drink sodas, because I believe water is much healthier for me. I was saddened to see that many of our women had taken to drinking sorghum wine—something that was unheard of in the past. But I believe this has come about because of the hopelessness our people feel—it's their way of shutting out the sadness.

I was troubled to see my older sister, Achuei, behaving strangely. She is a good woman who has raised children, but something was not right with her. She sat on the ground all alone, singing throughout the night until daybreak. I watched but didn't interrupt her, because she seemed focused on what she was doing. I recognized some of the songs, *old* songs about life and about spirits ... anything from happiness to sorrow, and other songs that I had never even heard before. She did this all night long, oblivious to anyone or anything around her.

"What is wrong with Achuei?" I asked my mother.

"I don't know why she does that," Mother told me, "but she does this about twice a week. Some people believe she has a mental problem, and some think she has some kind of spirit taking over her body." Mother told me my sister also carried *spears*—and Dinka women don't carry spears. But I noticed as she sat singing, that she had placed spears in the ground in a circle, and she sat in the middle of the circle facing east as she sang.

My sister's behavior was a mystery to me, and I felt sad for her. I wondered if there was anything I could do for her. I thought if I could take her to church with me so she could learn about God and be baptized, she might be okay. Still, when I *spoke* with Achuei, we had a good conversation. She even *encouraged* me. "My brother," she said, "the God who took care of you for many years as a child will take care of you now and in the future." She asked me how many children I had, and I told her about my two little girls. She said God would take me safely back to my wife and that he would give me a *son*, and I would name him after my father and grandfather.

In Dinka culture, as in most cultures, naming a boy for his father or grandfather is a sign of great honor and pride. Both my father and my grandfather were highly respected leaders in our clan. They were very wise men who had much wealth—mainly in property and great herds of cattle, sheep, and goats. They also had many wives and children and were admired by other tribesmen for the way they cared for their families. It is because of this family pride that we name our children in each generation after the previous parent or grandparent.

My brother Garang was having problems too. His life had been fraught with tragedy. He was still trying to cope with the death of our father. And now his wife had just died after giving birth to a little girl, and his mother-in-law, who lived some distance away, was caring for the infant. He had two other daughters, ages three and six, who had both been very ill and were in the hospital. We visited one of his daughters at the hospital in Khartoum when I first arrived there. His other daughter had been treated in the small hospital in Turalei, and fortunately, both of the girls recovered and came home.

I saw that Garang had become very depressed—to the point where he was ready to give up on caring for his family. It was difficult for me to see my brother in so much pain, and I felt helpless. He no longer interacted with others. He would sit surrounded by people, but he wouldn't join in and speak—or if he *did* speak, it would be a single word.

Then one day I sat down with him—just the two of us—and we had a conversation about his life. He told me he would like to leave his family and look for work in the city because life in the village had nothing left to offer. But that would have been pointless, because few jobs were available to people with no education. I urged him not to give up, because his family *needed* him, and I promised to support him financially from home so he could keep the families together.

"Always remember the kind of man our *father* was," I told him. "Be strong and follow in his footsteps."

It was sad for me to hear Garang talk about the need for education. "You know, Deng," he said, "I may have been *born* before you, but *you* are the older brother. You have an education, and that makes you wiser. People who are educated grow up much faster than those who are not."

My brother is very intelligent, and I know he could have accomplished so much if he'd had the same opportunity to learn that I've been given.

When I left Sudan as a child, I was thinking only of survival, but like Joseph in the Bible, what the enemy meant for *evil*, God meant for *good*. I now look back upon those dark years, when death and starvation stalked us relentlessly, and I thank God. It was through those hardships I endured that I was given the opportunity to *learn*.

I am most thankful for the Bible classes I had the good fortune to attend. Without the word of God, I am not strong—but with his power and glory, I will *always* be strong. "I can do *all* things through Christ who strengthens me"(Philippians 4:13 NKJV).

I saw my younger half brothers and sisters for the first time—the ones who were born during my absence. Like myself, my brothers and sisters have children of their own, and I made a point to become acquainted with them. I visited with my uncles and my cousins, and *everyone* had endless questions for me. They were curious about my years in the jungle ... how I had survived. "How did you handle life with no *family*? What did you think when you got *sick*, or when you went for days without *food*?"

They also wondered about the cultural differences I had faced. "How did you manage being with people who spoke a different *language*—and how were you able to *learn* other languages, like Arabic and English?" They were especially interested in school and how I had obtained my education. This made me sad because they had such a *desire* to learn but had so little opportunity. My people have very sharp minds, but only a few have been taught to read and write.

I saw my cousin Achuei Bol, who is now married and the mother of several children. She still remembered the time she cooked the beans and sorghum and accidentally spilled it on me. "I learned my lesson from *that*!" she said. "I am very cautious now when I'm cooking because I don't want anything like that to happen to one of *my* children!" It was good to see Achuei again and to see that she is doing well.

I understand that I'm nobody special, but to my family, it was as though they were welcoming royalty when I arrived. In fact, they crowned me with the title of "king." They said, "Welcome home, King," and "Long live the king!" It was a very humbling experience to see and feel their outpouring of love. People cried and ladies danced—and they were singing their traditional songs of war and of praise to my *daddy*, who had been the leader of our clan. Some of the elders came and poured water on me, while the older women washed my feet—all as signs of welcome in our Dinka tradition.

My family celebrated my homecoming with a great feast, killing a goat, an ox, and several chickens. We got the ox from a neighbor, and I made arrangements to pay him back when I returned to the United States. And I gave my family money to buy the goat.

To the Dinkas, who delight in celebrations, *everything* is worthy of a ceremony. After the men killed the ox, they called to me as they stood around the dead animal's body. "Jump *over* it, Deng," someone yelled. After I jumped, I was handed an AK-47 rifle. "Now fire several bullets up into the air as a sign of happiness! We know about the sadness and the hardships you have been through—but you have jumped *over*, and you will now be *safer* than you were before." I went along with their celebration because of the joy it brought my family. But I knew it was Almighty God, not a dead ox, who would continue to be my protection.

After the men had completed their job of killing and dressing the animals, the women took over and prepared the meat. Some of it was made into a delicious stew, and the rest was roasted over the fire. There was a constant air of celebration as the women worked and sang and cooked all night long until after daybreak. Neighbors too came with traditional foods they had prepared—mostly foods made from milk and from sorghum meal, including sorghum wine. Everything they did was with hearts full of rejoicing over my return after so many years away.

The celebration went on for four days, with many kinds of activities. People were dancing and singing while carrying spears, sticks, and other items. Some of the women waved shakers made from gourds, keeping time as they sang. And the men had a competition to see who could dance the best. They were actually very good. Then my cousins Dut Ajuong and Dut Malual showed me how to fight in traditional war with spears. It was amazing to see how quick they were at dodging and missing their opponent's spear. They also taught me how to play a simple ground game with a row of shallow holes where stones were tossed. These were all things I would have grown up doing, had I never left the village. The activities were much like the ones at Dinka wedding celebrations, which also last for days.

Young people came forward with AK-47s and spears to protect me as they walked with me in the village, and they gave me my *own* AK-47 to carry during my stay. While I did carry it at times, I often chose a spear instead, as that had been the *traditional* Dinka weapon—the one I was more comfortable with.

The boys explained to me why I always needed to be armed. They told me that a traveler like me was considered an "odd," or a stranger, and that people could take advantage of me if they were to see me walking about unarmed.

I traveled from village to village with my "bodyguards," and I always carried my video camera with me. I recorded scenes of life in the villages … of children who walk to school a distance of more than eight miles, of children swimming in the dirty rivers where cattle are standing, and of my people drinking water from those same rivers, because the villages are without wells for fresh drinking water.

The people asked me to dig a well for them, because I came from America. They said that since people in America went to the moon, surely there were some good Americans who could help to improve their lives in the villages. I broke down and wept when they spoke to me like that, because I felt so helpless. "Yes," I told them, "there are Good Samaritans in America. But America is far away, and it is not easy to send help to Africa, because there are many complications and rules to follow when we help in other countries." They pleaded with me to do something to help their hopeless situation. The people in the villages have suffered for many years, and their suffering still continues. How different their lives would be if they could have clean drinking water, hospitals, and other essential things needed to support their lives.

Now that South Sudan has gained its independence, I hope it will become a good country with a real democracy where people are given equal opportunities. I'm able to sleep in a comfortable house, I have a good job, and my children eat healthy foods. My people back home don't have those luxuries. Everything in their lives is a constant struggle. My own family members told me they eat one meal a day—and that meal is small. Instead of books and tablets, many schoolchildren still use sticks to write on the ground; other children don't go to school at all. Some teachers in the schools have little education, but they are willing to share what knowledge they have with those children, who are so hungry to learn.

When my time came to return home to the United States, my brother Ajuong and I walked together to the bus station in Turalei, and I purchased two tickets to Khartoum at a cost 160 Sudanese pounds. We had gotten our tickets on time, but we spent about six hours at the bus station because the driver would not leave until all the seats had been filled. It was late afternoon when our two-day journey to Khartoum finally got under way.

Because of the militia, we had to be constantly on guard as we rode. I was told that people were being killed on that same route nearly every week. If the militia stopped a bus in order to loot passengers' belongings, there was no way to stop them. Two weeks earlier, when we left Khartoum to go to South Sudan, we were told that eleven people had been killed on buses by the militia the previous week. The government doesn't intervene in those situations, because the militia is funded by the government in order to continually terrorize southerners at the border.

As we continued on our way to Khartoum, we were searched at every checkpoint by northern Sudanese soldiers and police officers. They were bribed by the drivers at each checkpoint, and that is the way they do their jobs. Those drivers who are driving buses between the north and South Sudan are very brave. They are doing a good job, because they know the system. They understand that the militia will not hesitate to kill, so they try to protect the lives of their passengers during robberies by telling them not to resist when they are being robbed.

We saw gangs of militia at various points along the way. Some of them were taking care of their cows, and some were wandering at the borders with their AK-47s on their backs. Southern Sudanese living and traveling near the border are the militia's primary target. Those poor people are truly living in the second hell on this planet.

When we arrived in Khartoum, I called Mahalet to let her know where I was and to assure her that I was okay. Everyone back home was relieved to get my report, but they remained uneasy because I was still in Sudan. They told me later that they had prayed for me from the time my flight was scheduled to leave Khartoum until I called again from London's Heathrow Airport, because they couldn't be sure I was actually on the plane. From Heathrow, I also called my brothers to let them know that I was in England and was safe.

I made many observations during the twenty days I spent in northern Sudan. I saw cars being driven around the streets of Khartoum with pictures of Osama bin Laden on them. That wasn't strange to the people there, because they liked Osama bin Laden. He had lived in northern Sudan in 1996, and it was said that he had operated businesses there under the names of various other people. I was also told that he had helped supply the weapons that the militia used in the raids against my people.

I returned safely to Michigan at the end of March 2009. It was a relief to be back where I no longer had to think about my safety. But most of all, I was glad to be back home with my wife and my little girls and to sleep comfortably in my own bed again. I was eager for Mahalet to see the pictures and the video footage I had taken in Sudan. Viewing them with her in the safety of our apartment made me realize just how truly blessed I am.

With my brothers by the Anaam River in Turalei.

Friends and family rush to welcome me and carry my bags.

I finally reach my village of Wunriang.

So much had changed in the world since I last saw my mother more than twenty years ago: The United States had an African American president. I left as a child and returned as a man. And, I took a selfie with my mother!

So much was just as I remembered it: baby animals are born. And, Adior Giir, my father's third wife, was still cooking over an open fire.

My mother, sister, and I are together again
sharing stories in our family home.

CHAPTER 7

Reminiscing

How can one cram twenty years of memories into a two-week period? It is impossible. After returning from Sudan, I realized just how inadequate my time there had been, as far as catching up on the news and events of my family. There was still *one* question that continued to haunt me—but I had not wanted to spoil our good times together by talking about unpleasant things. As close as I had been to my daddy as a child, I needed to know just how this great man had died. I knew he had been killed by the northern militia during the last great cattle raid when our family lost everything. But I didn't know just *how* it had happened.

Now that I could reach Garang by phone, we could reflect and talk about our childhood memories. It was a great way to reconnect and become closer to my brother and get answers to many troubling questions. This was good for Garang too, because he was coming out of his shell of depression and was talking much more than he had been when I was visiting. He had not forgotten those things from our early years, and he seemed glad to revisit the past with me. And when the time was right, I would ask him what he knew about our daddy's death.

"Do you remember that night when Mother carried food to the men at the headquarters?" he asked. "We were so *scared* because we had been left alone." I remembered it well.

At night in the villages, the moon is the only source of light unless an outdoor fire has been built. But on nights when the moon doesn't shine to illuminate the sky, people are in *total* darkness. That was how it was one night in 1987, not long before I became a Lost Boy. Because of the frequent raids, the men of the families were sleeping at the outskirts of the village, where they could watch for the enemy and alert people of danger. Since safety was a priority, my father sent his men regularly to patrol the borders of the villages and camps.

The headquarters for the men was about two and a half miles from home, and the women in the village would gather with my mother in the afternoon to prepare food for the men. Since it was usually dark by the time the women had delivered the food, one of the men would walk them back home, because it was dangerous for the women to walk through the forest without protection—especially after dark.

On this particular day, there had been a heavy rain and the other women didn't venture out to come to our house and help with the cooking. That evening my mother prepared the food by herself and delivered it to the men. We worried about her taking the long walk alone, laden down with enough food for the whole crew of hungry men. My sister Achuei begged Mother to let her go with her—but Mother told her no because the rest of us were still too young to be left by ourselves.

After Mother left, Achuei secured the door from inside the hut. Then we children huddled together in the darkness to wait until Mother returned. It was the growing season for crops—the time of year when forest animals roamed back and forth through the fields looking for food. Mother had been gone for about thirty minutes when we heard a loud racket at the door. We recognized the sound as that of a wild animal—and judging from the noise it made, it was not small. Whatever it was, it was determined to come inside, and it began clawing and bouncing against the door until we thought it would rip it off. The animal was making weird noises, and we tried to make noises back, hoping to scare it away. But we were so frightened that we couldn't get the sounds to come out of our throats.

The animal noises grew louder, and Achuei grabbed a piece of wood and began banging on the inside of the door. Her idea worked. The banging frightened the animal away, and we could hear it running off through the field. But we were still afraid. What if it came back later and ripped the door off?

We were greatly relieved when we heard Mother come home about an hour later. One of our uncles had walked back through the dark with her. We were nervous and excited as we told what had happened while Mother had been gone, and how *terrified* we had all been.

"You are very lucky," my uncle said. "It could have been a hyena or a young lion at the door. And the way it was tearing at the door, it must have been very hungry." He spent the night with us, and in the morning when it was light, we went outside with him to investigate. On the ground by the door we saw footprints that appeared to be from either a leopard or a young lion. Because of our close call, one of our uncles came and stayed with us until my older brother, Mayom, could come home from the cattle camp and protect the family.

We always kept a few cows in the village to provide milk for our own use. It was the job of my brothers Ajuong and Garang to care for those cattle and take them to graze close to home. The grass there wasn't as good as it was where the herds fed, but my brothers were afraid to take the cows very far from home because of wild animals in the forest. So after Mayom returned from the cattle camp, he decided to take the family cattle away from the village for a day to where there was lush grass for grazing. It would be a special treat for them.

Later in the day as he was leading the cattle back home, he encountered a lion. The lion was hungry and made a great leap toward the back of one of the cows—but fortunately missed it. The frightened cows took off running toward the house, with the lion in hot pursuit. Mayom was chasing the lion, screaming at the top of his voice as he ran. "Don't touch my cows, or I'll spear you!" When the cows neared our compound, the lion stopped and the cows ran into the safety of the barn. We had heard Mayom screaming and had gone outside to see what all the commotion was about. But when we caught a glimpse of the lion, we dashed back inside our hut. Then Mayom came in, panting and out of breath, and told us what had happened.

We could hear the lion making strange noises in the distance as it walked away from the compound. Some of the villagers had heard the noises too, and they thought the lion had *attacked* us. Then once the lion was safely out of the way, my brother went out to the barn and checked on the cows to make sure none were missing—and that was the *last* time he ever took the cattle that far away from home to graze!

South Sudan, like any other nation, has its share of mental illness. Depression too is common, especially today, because our people have lost hope. Yet even as a child, I saw strange behavior among our people.

"Do you remember our crazy cousin Makueen—Aunt Agom's son?" Garang asked me. How could I *forget*? I've never known another person like Makueen. "Do you remember the time he tried to give his mother a *bath*?" he asked.

"Yes, I remember that," I told him, and the details began to unfold in my mind.

It was a pleasant midafternoon, and my friends and I were playing near my aunt Agom's house when Makueen came by singing one of the many crazy songs that he'd made up. His mother was sitting under a large tree in their compound making rope, and everything was fine. Then Makueen went into the house and got a large cooking pot—one that held about five gallons of water—and filled it and put it on to boil over the fire in the traditional kitchen.

Later on, Makueen came outside carrying some ropes and tied his mother's hands together, and then he tied her legs together. All the time she was trying to fight him off, but he overpowered her. Then he brought the pot of scalding water out and set it down beside my aunt Agom. "Mother," he said, "it's been a *long* time since you've taken a shower with hot water." He had a large ladle made from a gourd in his hand, and as he talked to his mother he began dipping the ladle into the water and pouring it on her as she cried out in pain. The water was burning Makueen's hands too, and he stopped just long enough to dip them in cool water. Then he continued to talk to his mother in a soothing voice. "Just be *calm*, Mother. I'm going to wash you like a baby because it's been a long time since you took a shower with boiling water. Do you remember how you used to wash *us* with hot water when we were kids? Now it's *my* turn to take care of *you* like a child—to pay you back for your good ways, Mom. I love you so much because you are a *special* mother." He continued babbling nonsense.

We had watched Makueen as we played, but it hadn't really registered with us what he was doing until we heard Aunt Agom frantically screaming for help. Then we rushed over to where the two were, and she begged us to get her away from her son. One of the boys ran to my house for help, while the rest of us ran back and forth carrying cold water to pour onto Aunt Agom's burns and to mix with the scalding water in the pot to cool it down. We were all jumping and running from Makueen because we were afraid of him—we didn't want him to beat us. Moments later, my daddy came running and rescued his sister from her crazy son.

The reason Makueen had used hot water to wash his mother was that Dinka mothers wash their kids with very warm water from the time they are born until they are two years of age to protect them from stomach pains. They also believe it helps kids to sleep better at night. Of course, they didn't use *boiling* water, but he didn't understand that, because he was mentally ill.

Just a few days after the "hot shower," Makueen decided he would do away with his older brother, Deng Agom, by burying him *alive*. He went out into the field and dug a deep grave and waited for his brother to come home. Makueen was very strong, and when Deng came home he grabbed him. "I believe our family will be better off without you," he told Deng. "But I'm not going to *kill* you—I'm going to bury you *alive*. No one needs to question me about this, because I have the right to do it. I can choose when and how I should bury you."

Then he wrestled Deng into the grave. Deng remained surprisingly calm. "This grave is *deep*," he said. "You're going to need help filling it in, so go and get some men to help you." Then Makueen turned away to grab a shovel, and Deng leaped from the grave and ran. Makueen, who was known for his swiftness, proved to be no match for Deng, who was running for his life.

Makueen didn't let the grave go to waste, however. He got busy and fashioned a man out of clay and let it dry the way they dry bricks. He then placed the clay figure in the grave and covered it with dirt, claiming it was his brother Deng. "There is no need to mention Deng's name anymore," he told his family. "I have buried him alive, and *I* am now the man of the house."

Nobody knew what to do with Makueen. He was clearly a danger at times, but there was no way to get help for him. People had even tried to *chain* him, but he always freed himself and went on about his craziness.

The villagers called Makueen a "ghost runner" because of the way he ran. Sometimes he would run eight to ten miles without stopping at all to rest. He would travel from place to place without eating food or drinking water, but at *other* times he would eat really *strange* things, such as raw goat meat.

One time after he was running, he jumped into a deep well, thinking he could easily get back out—but he found that he couldn't. He remained in the well overnight, and the next day some of the local men dropped ropes down for him to fasten himself to, and they pulled him out.

Makueen knew no fear. Once as he was walking between two villages, he saw a lioness about to give birth beneath a tree. He was excited and wanted to witness the birth up close, so he crept up behind the lioness and grabbed her firmly by the tail. A struggle ensued as the animal tried desperately to free herself, but Makueen was determined to watch the birth. About that time two men came walking by. All they could see was Makueen holding the tail, and they ran toward him thinking he might need help. As soon as the frightened lioness saw the men, she bolted free, nearly knocking my cousin over as she escaped.

The two men began to laugh when they realized Makueen had been holding onto the tail of a *lioness*. They had seen the back of a brown animal and thought he was assisting a cow that was in labor. The poor lioness had been in pain, but it had taken the arrival of the two men on the scene to cause her adrenalin to kick in and allow her to free herself from Makueen's grip.

The two men stopped by our house afterward and told us what they had just witnessed. Then we all went out to see the place where the incident had occurred. There were footprints everywhere, indicating a struggle, and a wet spot in the sand where the pregnant animal's water had broken during the encounter. The men were still laughing at the sight of Makueen trying to restrain a wild lioness by her tail!

Some people might have said Makueen was extremely hyperactive—but it went far beyond that. One day two of my brothers and I were playing under a tree when Makueen came strolling by. My mother had gone to fetch water from a stream, and we were alone at the time. Makueen glanced at the steep conical roof of our house and decided to climb to the top and roll back down. It was a climb of about twenty feet, and we laughed at his antics as he reached the top, curled himself into a ball, and rolled to the ground. He did this several times, and then he sat down under the tree for a moment until his craziness kicked in again. This time he climbed to the top and didn't roll, but *leaped* like a frog and landed on the ground.

He then left and went to our chicken house. It was now evening, and the chickens—about forty of them—were roosting. There were fresh eggs to be gathered, and brood hens were sitting on their nests. Makueen closed the door to the chicken house and set it on fire. The flames spread quickly, and the straw building, along with an attached grass silo, was quickly engulfed in flames. We could hear eggs popping in the heat, making sounds like gunshots as they burst. My brothers and I quickly got sand and threw it on the flaming building, but we were too little to understand much about firefighting. Our neighbors saw the smoke and flames and came running—but the fire was out of control, and the buildings burned quickly to the ground.

When Mother arrived home with the water, she almost went into shock. It was a tremendous loss to our family—the chicken house, the silo, and forty chickens, all *gone*. But she looked at the positive side; it was just *chickens*, not *children*, that had perished in the flames. Many of the chickens had burned to ashes, but some were just roasted through, so we salvaged what we could from the roasted fowl and shared it with our neighbors.

When I went home to visit the first time, I asked my mother about our cousin Makueen and was very surprised by what she told me. As Makueen got a little older, his mind became perfectly sound. He got married and had two fine sons. People were amazed when they saw him with his family—farming, fishing, and leading a productive life. It was hard for them to believe it was really Makueen.

No one knows *why* he had behaved as he did, but some people believed he was driven by evil spirits in his body. My mother told me that Makueen died of natural causes while his boys were still young—and long before his death he made peace with his older brother, Deng, whom he had once tried to bury alive.

I continued to call Garang, and each visit with him awakened old memories from my childhood. But the one question that continued to haunt me concerned my daddy. How did he *really* die? Was it a quick death, I wanted to know, or did he suffer? Were there any witnesses to the tragic event?

No one knows for certain if my dad had predicted his own death just four months before he died. But as he was a man of unusual insight, I'm inclined to believe that he did. He told my brother Garang to leave the cattle camp and go to another city that was far away from our town of Turalei. He said that the weather was not good at that time, and he should just go to the city and stay for at least six months. But he should come back when he got news from home—whether it was *good* or *bad*. Garang didn't like the idea of being sent away, and he argued with my dad. He felt Daddy was just using the weather as an excuse, and he wanted to know the *real* reason why Daddy wanted him to leave camp—but he never got a satisfactory answer.

My dad and my brother discussed the matter for two days, but Garang *still* resisted. Then my dad approached my brother-in-law Nyoul Matong and my uncle Mayombek Malual and asked them to talk to Garang. My brother-in-law didn't really *like* the idea of Garang leaving, but he respected my dad's authority as our leader and convinced my brother to go. So my father gave Garang enough money for his expenses, and he went to the city as he had been instructed to do.

My father had lost me years earlier, and saying good-bye to another son likely was more difficult than he outwardly let on. But after Garang had been gone for a while, my father told my uncle why he had made him leave. "Ever since his brother Deng disappeared, Garang has stayed by my side, and I know him very well. If something *bad* ever happened—if we were ever in real danger—Garang would *refuse* to leave me, and the enemies would kill us *both*. I don't want our families to be left in the darkness with no one to care for them."

What my father said was very true. Garang told me that through the years he was like my daddy's shadow, following him everywhere he went. Garang kept an eye on things in the camp and notified my dad when anything went wrong. I could understand my brother's loyalty. I would have been the same way. I would have *died* with my daddy, had I been faced with losing him.

My brother Mayom was still living in the family compound at the time. My father had paid eighty-five cows for a wife for Mayom, leaving the family with a herd of five hundred. Mayom's wife was now pregnant, and he needed to stay close to her—so there was no talk of *him* being the one to leave.

It was 1996 when the government militia from the north came again to Twic County and attacked and raided the cattle camps—and this time, they meant *business*! A dozen or more family members were living and working with Daddy in the camp, including my young cousin Ayoom Madul and his parents, but Ayoom had become the closest to him. He was perhaps thirteen, and he seemed more like a *son* as he followed my dad around the camp the way I had done as a child.

Each time the herds were moved and a new camp was set up, Ayoom would help the men prepare the camp by driving sturdy wooden stakes into the ground—one for each cow. Then in the midafternoon when the cattle were through grazing, they would come and stand, each in its own spot, and wait for workers to secure them to their stakes with heavy leather leashes until morning.

Once the cattle had been tethered to their stakes, the milk cows would be milked. Workers did this using containers made from large gourds that could hold several gallons. Milking was a lengthy task because the cows had to be milked one udder at a time, directly into the small neck of the jug. There was plenty fresh milk for drinking and cooking in the camp, and the rest was made into cheese and yogurt, which could be exchanged for sorghum, clothing, or even more cattle.

When the milking was finished, a large fire would be built and the evening meal would be prepared. Then when everyone had eaten, it was *family* time. It was a time to talk about the day's events and perhaps to dance and sing and tell stories. The fire, usually fueled by dried cow dung, kept mosquitoes and other insects away and provided the only light in the otherwise darkened camp. And that was how life in the cattle camp was for my cousin Ayoom.

On the night of the raid, Ayoom had helped the men with the evening chores and had joined the family around the fire before settling down to sleep. But he was awakened abruptly around three o'clock in the morning by a thunderous blast of gunfire. He jumped up quickly to see what was going on and soon realized that the enemy had crept in during the night and was completely surrounding the camps. After the first blast, shots continued from every direction as people fled—some trying desperately to rescue an animal or two, only to be gunned down by the enemy. Some of the brave men in the camp tried to fight back with spears, but they were no match for the enemy's vast and powerful army.

The attack had been strategically planned. Smoke from the fires in the various camps had led the enemy to their exact locations, and they knew what time the camp workers would be sleeping. While there is no way to know just how large the attacking army was, it has been estimated to have been around two thousand men, and possibly many more. The soldiers had entered from every side, surrounding the perimeter of the six cattle camps, an area covering roughly fifteen square miles.

The militia moved in quickly, brandishing machetes as they slashed the leather straps and loosened the cattle from their stakes. The sheep, goats, and donkeys were not tethered, but they were corralled, making it easy for the enemy to take them away.

A few people from the camps *did* escape, but others were taken captive as slaves—most of those being women and young girls. Some of them later managed to flee from their captors because the enemy was concentrating more on the cattle herds than on the people. One of the women who had been captured and later escaped was Ayoom's mother. Ayoom's daddy was shot in the arm and lost a lot of blood and barely escaped with his life.

The bloody raid continued for five hours as animals were gathered from the six camps my daddy oversaw. By eight o'clock in the morning, fifteen thousand head of cattle plus a few thousand goats, sheep, and donkeys had been swept away by the enemy, leaving our people with no means of livelihood. Then to make certain the job was finished, the enemy came back to the camp and set fire to the makeshift tents used for shelters, and to all the people's personal belongings.

All during the raid, Ayoom had stayed right by my daddy's side. The leader of a cattle camp is somewhat like the captain of a ship—he doesn't desert his people or his animals. Refusing to run away, Daddy followed the enemy with Ayoom trailing close behind him. After he had followed for a distance, he turned and shouted to Ayoom, "Leave *now!*" But Ayoom would not desert his uncle. Daddy then grabbed a stick and whipped the boy for disobeying, and Ayoom then turned and left.

Ayoom knew that his uncle had beaten him with the stick to save his life—yet he was reluctant to return to the burned-out camp alone. So he hid in the bush where he could follow my daddy unseen as he continued to run to catch up with the enemy and the vanishing herds. When Daddy finally reached the enemy, they stopped and ordered him to go back, but he refused and continued to follow them. When they saw that he was not going to give up, the men looked for a way to stop him and began to argue among themselves. Some wanted to take him with them as a prisoner, while others were in favor of tying him to a tree so he *couldn't* follow them. Still others didn't want to do *anything*.

As two of the men continued to squabble, another man jumped up and grabbed my daddy's spear. He then turned and thrust the spear through his belly, the spear entering his right side and exiting his left. With that, Daddy slumped to his knees and the two men began fighting and arguing again. One of the leaders stepped in and separated the two, angrily reminding them that they were still in enemy territory. Ayoom was in shock from what he had just witnessed, and he stood frozen, unable to move for about thirty minutes. By this time, it was midmorning and the enemy soldiers had left the dying man and continued on their way north with the herds.

Ayoom crept warily out into the open space where his uncle's now dead body knelt in a pool of blood. He moved slowly toward the body, scanning the area for any enemy that might be watching. Then he carefully laid my daddy down and closed his eyes before taking off, running the fifteen-mile trek to the family compound. Other family members and neighbors had returned earlier and were waiting anxiously for my daddy and Ayoom to arrive.

Ayoom ran for six hours. His legs ached and his sides hurt as he reached the compound. When he got there, he couldn't speak. Each time he opened his mouth to try to say something, the words failed to come. "The boy has been poisoned!" someone said. "The *enemy* did this to him, and he can no longer speak." Family members gave him water to drink and had him sit down and rest for a few minutes, and then he began to cry. When they saw him crying, they all began to weep because they *knew* something tragic had happened to my daddy.

Ayoom told the family everything he had seen and heard, and he told them where he had left his uncle's body. Upon hearing the terrible news, some of the men grabbed their spears and threatened suicide, but others were quick to grab the spears from them before they could harm themselves. Some were so determined to kill themselves that they had to be restrained with chains until they calmed down. Then a few men and some of the women ran to find my daddy's body, and they carried it back as far as the cattle camp. There at the camp, the men dug a grave for him and buried him before sundown.

News travels swiftly, even in places like Sudan. My brother Garang learned of his father's death and rushed home to be with my mother and family. Many people came to the funeral, which was held to honor my daddy as a great leader in the community and as their hero. In Dinka tradition, a couple cows from the compound were killed to feed the crowd that had gathered during the week of the funeral rites. Four months after the raid, my brother Mayom's wife gave birth to a son. They named the baby Lok, which in Dinka means "born after," because he was born after my daddy's death. After Lok, they had three more children.

Our village would never again be the same. The people had not only lost a great leader and counselor, but they had also lost their only means of livelihood and survival. It was hard to even *imagine* life without cattle camps, because that was the only life our people had known. It was the sale of livestock, milk, cheese, and butter that had provided them money for their daily necessities. In addition to what they had already lost, they lost *hope*.

Some of the cattlemen went back to the village and farmed,

keeping only two or three milk cows for their families. Some joined the rebel forces to protect what was left of the village. Still others began to arm themselves with AK-47s in order to protect their families. They were determined that no more lives would be lost without the enemy losing lives in return. When I spoke with some of the young men during my visit, they told me it would take some time for them to give up these weapons, even if the government of South Sudan becomes stable, because their nights are still haunted by visions of war.

One day during my visit, I saw a young man bolt up from where he was sitting when something reminded him of what he had witnessed in the camp during the raid. He was shaking at the memory of his ordeal. He told me how during the raid, he had taken shelter in a small grove and hid under a large tree. Powerful bullets ripped through overhead, causing the tree to split and fall on top of him. He was not injured, but he was pinned against the ground by the tree's massive size. Unable to free himself from the heavy weight, he had to dig the ground beneath him to make enough clearance for him to escape. "I had nothing to dig with but my bare hands," he said, "and the enemies were returning, searching for any survivors."

It had taken him two grueling hours to free himself from the trap. "The ground was so hard I didn't think I could make it. At the time, I was wishing that instead of hands, I'd had *paws* with sharp claws like an animal. When I finally pulled myself out, I looked at my hands. They were full of mud and were bleeding, but I was just glad to be *free*." He told me that after he had freed himself, he was *still* in fear for his life and ran, hiding between trees as shots continued to ring out from all directions.

"If I'd had a weapon back *then*," he told me, "the enemy would have paid the price for raiding our camp and taking away our cattle." Even now the man is looking to get an AK-47 ... *just in case*. And like most young men, he has dreams for the future. If South Sudan remains at peace, he would like to get an education and become a businessman. He would like to save money, marry, and have a family—but he is still haunted by the devastation of the war. The people were left without food and not enough milk for their children, and he watched as people around him starved to death. They were truly at a dead end with nowhere to turn.

I am one of the *lucky* ones. Countless people disappeared from South Sudan during the civil war raids and have never been heard from since. Many are believed to have died, but many others are being held as prisoners in the north, just because they are from southern Sudan. Still others were kidnapped and are serving as *slaves* in the homes of Arabs in northern Sudan. There is no closure for families of the missing. One of my cousins was captured by the militia from the north twenty years ago. His family still wonders if he was killed or if he was able to run and is still alive somewhere in the north.

The question now is what will be done to *locate* the missing people. Some entire families vanished, never to be heard from again. Will the United Nations step up and aid in the search? The missing people who are still alive certainly *know* who they are, as do their captors. And if the missing people were returned to the south, would they feel at home again, or would they have trouble adapting?

A few months after I returned home, I learned that Garang's infant daughter, who was being cared for by her grandmother, had died. Within a *two-year* period, he had lost his wife and baby girl and had seen one of his older daughters come very close to death. There is so much sickness and disease in my country, and much of it can be traced to contaminated drinking water.

Not *all* stories of the Sudan war are negative, however. Many miracles happened during the struggle as people became smarter and wiser than the militia. As the raids continued in Twic County, which is close to Abyei at the border where the worst of the conflict was centered, something *amazing* happened. The militia had been coming from the north through Abyei to Twic, wiping out everything in their path. They were taking cattle, personal belongings, and even people's crops, and they were terrorizing the villagers and leaving many people dead.

But there was a very brilliant man who had built a large hut in his village—large enough to house his extended family. From the *outside* the house looked like any other large hut, but inside something was completely *different*. The hut had a solid floor and a trapdoor that was not readily visible. From the trapdoor, there was a drop of perhaps twenty feet to a room below and a rope ladder that allowed safe entrance to the lower area. From the lower room, the man had dug a long tunnel that led to the middle of his farm, a good distance away.

The man called his family together and told them that the government militia had changed their tactics. Instead of coming to the villages, shooting people and burning their houses, they had a *new* approach. They would now come in the middle of the night and knock on the door to rouse a family member. They would then order that person to awaken everyone else in the house and bring them out. The soldiers would then kill family members, rape the women, and take others to be slaves in northern Sudan. With this being done in the night, neighbors would not be aware of what was happening until there was a knock at *their* door too.

The man told his family about his *thongpiny* plan. The word *thongpiny*, meaning "mouth down" in English, referred to the secret trapdoor, or mouth, in the floor of the house. The man explained in detail how they would use the thongpiny door to escape.

One night some men from the government militia knocked on this man's door. He got up slowly and told his family to be quiet, saying that he was going to the door to see for sure who it was. He then went to the door and greeted the officers, and they ordered him to awaken everyone in the house and bring them outside. He went back inside and quickly roused everyone, calling out, "*Thongpiny, thongpiny, thongpiny!* Get up!"

Everyone in the house got up quickly and quietly and headed to the thongpiny opening in the floor. One by one they climbed down the rope ladder and escaped through the long tunnel. As they emerged from the opening far away from his hut, they raced and alerted everyone in the village that the government militia was there. The man had given instructions that the *last* person to escape was to whistle four times from the distant tunnel exit so that he too could escape. He paused a few minutes with his ear alert to the sound of the whistle, and then he too climbed down through the hole. When his feet hit the ground below, he removed the ladder behind him and followed the escape route the others had taken.

About fifteen minutes had passed since the knock at the door. The government militia then realized there must be a problem with the people inside, so they sent a soldier in to check. The soldier had heard the man calling, "*Thongpiny,*" so he did the same. He walked through the house, groping for people in the pitch-darkness shouting, "*Thongpiny, thongpiny, thongpiny!* Get up!" Then he came to the open hole in the floor, but he couldn't see it in the dark and fell twenty feet, breaking his neck in the fall.

When the soldiers waiting outside heard no sound coming from the house, they thought the family had attacked and killed the soldier, and they sent two armed men in to investigate. The two soldiers walked through the house in the dark before stumbling into the same gaping hole and falling to their deaths as the first man had done.

The government militia was alarmed, not knowing what was happening to their men, so they entered the house very cautiously carrying flashlights. Then they discovered the downward door with the three dead soldiers on the floor below. "Oh, no!" they cried. "So *this* is the thongpiny the man was talking about!" The remaining soldiers tried to retaliate by shooting at the villager's houses and destroying their belongings and crops, but the people had all escaped to safety and all of their lives were spared.

This man quickly became a local hero. He had outsmarted the enemy, killing three of their men without the use of spears or any other weapons. After the raid, the people began seeking advice from him on various matters. They also showered him with gifts of cows and goats to express their gratitude. I hope someday to meet and speak with this man's relatives, because he is a true symbol of the struggles our people have endured.

Now that I was home, I began at once to apply for work. I went to two places where I had previously been employed in Grand Rapids, and both places gladly accepted my application. One of my former bosses interviewed me and promised me a part-time job. He praised me for coming back and for serving our country, and I was pleased by what he said. But he called me a week later and said he was unable to hire me because I had left for the army without telling him good-bye. This wasn't true, because I had given him a week's notice before leaving.

That upset me at first, but I let it go because of my belief that we should forgive one another. I know some people don't support the military—but they forget that it's the enlisted men and women who have sacrificed their lives for the nation during times of war. Every nation around the world depends on its military for protection.

Having been in the army, I thought it would be easy to find security work once I returned home, but I found that was not the case. I worked only four days that year, and that was with DK Security during a large outdoor concert in the small town of Rothbury, about seventy miles from Grand Rapids. It was July, and a lot of musicians had been booked for the event. People were camping out for the weekend while attending the concert. It was hard to imagine, after serving our country in the war zone, this was all the work I was able to find after returning home.

Fortunately, my wife was hired by a temp agency soon after I returned from my trip. It was a night shift job, and it was working out well for her. I studied and took care of the house and the babies during the day while she slept, and we survived that way until the end of 2009.

The following April I was fortunate to be offered a job as a security guard at the Gerald R. Ford International Airport. I accepted the offer and started working while continuing with my education at the University of Phoenix West Michigan Campus, where I was studying for a career in criminal justice. I want to state how truly grateful I am for those who proposed the GI bill so that those serving our country in the military can get help obtaining their education.

Dominic, security guard at Gerald R. Ford International Airport.

Dominic, left, in class with students at the University of Phoenix.

CHAPTER 8

Our Family Grows!

In November 2010, I had another one of my dreams. In the dream, I was sitting beside the swimming pool at our apartment complex when a man began speaking to me. All I could see was his face. He was African, and he told me that I was going to have a son. But, he went on to say, there was a *curse* that must be broken before a son could be born. In my dream, I felt puzzled over this, but then again, my people do believe in curses being mysteriously placed on individuals. The man then explained that in order to *break* the curse, I would need to take a clay pot—such as the ones the women of Sudan use for cooking—and *break* it. I woke up and remembered the crazy dream I'd just had, but I didn't really give it much thought, because it made no sense to me at all.

At two forty-five the next morning, I was on my way to my job at the airport when two deer ran across the road in front of my car, and I narrowly missed hitting them. It was a close call that left me quite shaken, and when I got to work, I called Mahalet to tell her about it. While I was on the phone, I also told her about the crazy dream I'd had about sitting by the pool. When I got home from work in the morning, I went to the kitchen and got a glass of water to drink—but the glass slipped from my hand, hit the floor, and shattered. Right away I thought of the dream. Of course, it was just a drinking glass, not a clay pot, that had broken. But I couldn't help but be reminded again of the crazy dream.

Mahalet was continuing her temp job doing assembly work for an auto parts company. Meanwhile, things were becoming increasingly stressful at home because of our tight schedules. I had my own job, plus I watched the kids while Mahalet worked, and I was also trying to study and keep up with my classes. All these responsibilities left me very little time to sleep. Mahalet was feeling the effects of things too. She looked pale and very stressed and tired. One day she came home from work and said, "The girls at work told me I looked *pregnant*. They even said I was going to have a baby boy."

"But you're *not* pregnant," I said. "So, what did you *tell* them?"

"I told them to just leave me alone—that they didn't know what they were talking about. I told them I'm *not* pregnant! But they kept on needling me—they told me my pregnancy was nothing to hide."

I could see that the job was putting too much pressure on my wife. The extra income had helped, but with two toddlers to care for, we decided it would be better for Mahalet to quit work and be a stay-at-home mom. That would take a big load off me, plus she was much happier when she wasn't working. We could now focus on our plans to go to Ethiopia and search for Mahalet's family. And while I had been fortunate to have seen my own family, I couldn't wait to return to Sudan again and let my mother meet my beautiful wife and hold my little girls.

Then one day Mahalet told me that she had reason to believe she might *be* pregnant. "What are you *talking* about, woman?" I said. Then I went straight to Walmart, got a pregnancy test kit, and told her to check and make sure. When the test showed *negative*, we were both relieved. Then we began to wonder if we should *trust* the test—or if she should test herself again. So Mahalet tested herself a couple more times and informed me that she tested *positive*. This was *not* good news for her. "My husband!" she cried. "What have you *done* to me? Look—now our plans for me to go home have been destroyed, and I will have to wait another year!"

I told her *I* was just as shocked as she was, because neither of us had planned on this pregnancy. But we soon accepted it as being God's plan for our family, and Mahalet told me she was positive the baby was a boy. Then things changed with her completely, and she began to distance herself from me. Her hormones had her so messed up that she hated me like an enemy. She told me that just the *sight* of me made her throw up and she wished I would pack up and leave.

This was a very difficult time for me, because I didn't know how to help her, and there was no one else to turn to. I would come home every morning, prepare food for the day, and clean the apartment. But Mahalet couldn't eat any food I fixed, because she couldn't stand my being in the house. Whenever she threw up, it frightened Achuei and Hawathiya. "Mommy, are you okay?" they would ask. "Do you want our daddy to take you to the *hospital*?"

I became very discouraged when she couldn't keep her food down, and I wondered *why* she had gotten pregnant. This pregnancy was so unlike the others. When she was pregnant with the girls, she was always her normal self and was *happy* to be with me. I could see that I was in for some tough times ahead.

It was January 9, 2011. It was the second anniversary of the day we had moved into our apartment, and it was a joyful day for me *and* for my wife. *I* was happy because the day had finally arrived for the Lost Boys to go to Chicago and cast their votes for the separation of South Sudan from the north. My *wife* was happy because I was *going*! She even said she wished I would not come back. It was hard leaving her in the state she was in, but on the other hand, she needed a break from me, even if for just *one day*.

Around 9:00 a.m. Mahalet dropped me off at the Episcopal church in Grand Rapids, where the Lost Boys were gathering to board buses to Chicago. She and the girls would have the day to themselves until that evening, when I would return.

When I returned home from Chicago early that evening, I was shocked to see the apartment spotless and food cooking on the stove. I wondered who had come by to help my family while I was gone. Then I realized that Mahalet had done it *herself.* Not only that, but she hadn't gotten sick at all during my absence.

The serenity did not last, however. Almost immediately she began throwing up like a crazy woman. Then she broke down and cried. "Why did you have to come back and ruin my day? I was just *fine* while you were gone! Please do me a favor and go and stay with your Lost Boys. Stay with them until I have the baby; then you can come back home. I *love* you," she said, "but you just don't understand this pregnancy. What kind of baby am I carrying anyway? A baby that doesn't like me looking at you or even smelling you is a *big* problem!"

But leaving my wife would have presented an even *bigger* problem. I told her it wasn't safe to leave her alone with the kids. She was weak and needed my help. If we had been living in Africa, my sisters and family would all have been there to help her, and I could have stayed away until the birth of the baby and not be worried about anything. But living here, I was all she had. Mahalet was right—I did *not* understand. When she had been pregnant with our girls, she never had been sick and out of control—so why was she now?

Then as she went into her fourth month, her moods quickly changed. There was no more sickness and no more throwing up. I had my wife back—and she *liked* me! I set up a schedule for the two of us to begin exercising together as we had done during her previous pregnancy. I would get home from work at ten thirty in the morning, and we would put the girls into their strollers and go to a field and exercise together until noon. Then we would come home, and I would go to bed for two hours; then I would get up and help clean the apartment before settling down to study for my five o'clock classes. I would get home from school by 10 p.m., go to bed for three hours, and then get up and go to work again.

In May, Mama Rita VanderVen invited our family for dinner one evening. Her aunt Dorothy was visiting from Charlotte, North Carolina, and Rita was eager for us to meet. I had kept a detailed journal all during my military training and deployment in Iraq, and I had added to it my recollections from childhood and of my years with the Lost Boys. I hoped to get the material edited so it could be submitted for publication. Aunt Dorothy was retired but had a background in editing and writing, so I looked forward to meeting her.

Over a huge spread of tacos with *everything,* we all discussed my book project. Mahalet told them her own story of fleeing Ethiopia and Somalia as a child, and everyone was in disbelief at what she had been through. Aunt Dorothy was interested in seeing what I had written, so we gave her a copy of the rough manuscript to take home with her and read.

Back in North Carolina, she began the lengthy process of putting the material in order, and she invited Mahalet and me to bring the girls and come for a visit whenever we could get away. That interested me because I had been in Charlotte a few years earlier. I had enjoyed the city and wanted my family to experience it too. I had some vacation days coming, and we made plans to fly down the following month. Mahalet was now feeling well and was actually looking forward to getting out of the apartment for a few days. She bought Achuei and Hawathiya some matching outfits and shoes for the trip, and we soon had everything packed and ready to go.

At the airport, we thought we were early for our flight, so Mahalet and I sat down with the girls in one of the airport restaurants and ordered breakfast. We were just relaxing after our morning rush when a lady came over and said, "Excuse me, but your plane is about ready to *leave.*" I grabbed one of the bags and picked up our younger daughter and rushed toward the gate, which was a fair distance away. Mahalet grabbed the other bag, and she and Achuei ran after me. People were staring, wondering why this very pregnant woman was running so fast. We were the last passengers to board the plane, and we were very relieved after we realized how close we had come to missing our flight!

We had met Aunt Dorothy only that night at dinner, so I hoped she and my family would recognize each other in the Charlotte airport's crowded baggage area. But there was no problem. She saw me looking for my bags on the baggage conveyor and walked right up to me, while Achuei and Hawathiya ran to her, grabbing her around the legs and calling, "Grandma! Grandma! We're here—are you going to take us *home* with you?" Within minutes we had retrieved our bags and were headed across the street to Aunt Dorothy's van in the parking deck.

As we traveled along the highway to her home near the South Carolina border, I was curious about the trees in certain areas. They were strangely, but beautifully, shrouded in bright green leaves so that their trunks were not visible. "Oh, those are kudzu vines," Aunt Dorothy explained. "The vines grow and attach themselves to trees, poles ... anything they can reach." It was a beautiful vine, but she said it grows about a foot a day during the summer months and is impossible to control.

When she first mentioned the kudzu, I thought she was saying "cat zoo," and I tried to imagine a zoo housing nothing but cats. Then I realized she was speaking of the vines—but I *still* thought it was called "cat zoo" for some reason, and I wondered why the vine had been given such a strange name. I finally got the name straightened out.

When we reached her house, Aunt Dorothy introduced us to her son Norman. He was helping care for his disabled father, who was also named Norman, but everyone called him "Grandpa." Grandpa was happy to meet us. He loved kids and had fun playing with Achuei and Hawathiya. The next day he saw me and said, "Come here, Norman," thinking I was his son.

"I'm not Norman," I told him. "I'm Dominic."

But he insisted I was Norman and said, "Why are you *lying* to me, Norman?" Then Norman came in, and Grandpa was quiet. I told Norman what Grandpa had said, and he laughed. It was funny because I'm tall and very dark, and Norman is much shorter and light-skinned and wears his hair long.

We got settled into our room and had lunch, and then the girls went outside to explore the backyard. With a privacy fence surrounding the yard, it was a fun and safe place for them to play. The girls were excitedly picking green tomatoes from large potted plants on the patio when Aunt Dorothy came out and explained that the tomatoes had to turn *red* before picking. She directed them instead to some flowers they could gather. Playing in the yard was a real treat for the girls because they had no yard at home, and it gave them a chance to run and be free.

The girls were curious when they saw an open stairway leading up from the dining room, and they decided to explore the upstairs. They didn't know that Aunt Dorothy's grandsons, Corey and Kasey, were living with her while they attended college. Kasey was in his room watching television. He is a tall blond-haired young man with blue eyes and a big smile, and his presence took the girls quite by surprise. They came running downstairs, and Achuei was wide-eyed as she shouted, "There's a *giant boy* upstairs!" After that, we kidded Kasey, calling him the "giant boy."

On Sunday morning, we attended the Methodist church with Aunt Dorothy. Although I attend the Catholic church when I'm home, I enjoyed the service very much, especially the singing. I was amazed when her pastor read a passage from the book of Haggai: "Suppose a person carries in the fold of his clothes, some *meat* made holy for the Lord ..." (Haggai 2:12 NCV). The pastor commented on the verse and said people today would think that was *strange*—after all, who would carry *meat* folded in his *clothing*? I thought of those years with the Lost Boys and how when we were fortunate enough to *have* meat, we would carry it folded it in our shirts as we continued to walk. I felt like calling out and saying, "That's exactly how *we* carried it!"

That evening we all gathered in the living room, and I showed videos I had taken on my visit to South Sudan in 2009. Everyone was in awe of what they saw. When we got to the part where cows were standing in a muddy river, they couldn't believe that the river was also the source of my family's drinking water!

When it came time to return home, I realized that I had mistakenly purchased *one-way* tickets rather than round-trip—a very costly mistake. We went online and got what we felt was a good deal, in light of its being arranged at the last minute. Our flight was delayed because of a severe thunderstorm over Lake Michigan, and our plane was rerouted from Chicago to Detroit. The airline apologized for the delay and gave us meal vouchers, and we bought pizza. After we ate, the girls had fun running around the airport with me chasing after them while Mahalet tried to rest.

It was midnight when we landed in Grand Rapids—sixteen hours after we departed from Charlotte. I had to be back at the airport for work at 3:30 a.m., so the only sleep I was able to get was a two-hour nap. It had been a long, tough day, but we had returned home *safely*, and that was all that really mattered.

On August 24—just two months after our trip to North Carolina—we welcomed our firstborn son, Malual Deng Malual, into our family. It was six thirty in the morning, and I was at work when I got the first call from my wife saying she was feeling contractions. She said the contractions were "different" from the ones she'd felt a little earlier. "I just wanted you to know," she said, "in case the pains continue and I need to get to the hospital." My shift would not end for another three hours, but I recalled how my second daughter had come very *quickly* after my wife's first labor pains, so I knew there was a good chance I'd have to leave work early. No more than ten minutes later, Mahalet phoned again to say her contractions were increasing, so I got on the radio and called my supervisor to come to Gate 4, where I was working security. When he came, I told him our baby was on the way, and he arranged with the manager to have my station covered.

I reached our apartment at seven o'clock and found Mahalet and the kids all ready to go. I quickly changed out of my uniform, got the girls secured in their seats in the car, and grabbed extra clothes for them to change into, and we were on our way. When we reached the hospital parking lot, we didn't go inside immediately. Mahalet felt safe knowing we were just steps away from the entrance—but she wanted to wait until the pains were no more than five minutes apart. Remembering how the doctor in El Paso had wanted to take Hawathiya by cesarean, she didn't want to check in until the last minute.

It was 8:05 when we finally went inside. Mahalet was checked in, and a few minutes later we were ushered into the delivery room. I was amazed at how well behaved my usually rambunctious girls were while we waited. They seemed to understand just what was going on and wanted to comfort their mother in her pain. Three-year-old Hawathiya kept saying, "You'll be *okay*, Mommy. You'll be okay."

Mahalet had asked for something for the pain, and a nurse was busy trying to insert an IV into her arm, but the pressure from her pushing kept forcing the IV out. But there wasn't time for it anyway, because the baby's head was already coming, forcing the nurses to forget about the pain medication. The doctor held the baby's head for support as he emerged just before nine o'clock. Then he handed me a pair of scissors so I could cut the umbilical cord—the final step in my son's birth. Mahalet looked up at me and said, "Let's have *another* boy right away." But I thought about the crazy effect the early months of the pregnancy had had on her, and I told her we needed to wait a little while.

Achuei and Hawathiya were ecstatic. They wanted to hold their baby brother the moment they saw him, but I told them to let the nurse clean him up first. After he had been washed up, the nurse brought him back, snuggled in a soft blanket, and handed him to his mother. I then held him for the girls to see. It had been quite an experience for them, seeing their little brother make his entrance into the world.

"You *did* it, Mom," five-year-old Achuei said. "How, did you *do* it? Did you just push the baby out by *force*?" She looked at her little brother again. "When are we going home?" she asked. "We want to take our brother home and *play* with him!"

She was full of questions. "Will baby brother's skin be *dark* like Daddy's skin, or will he be *light* like you? I hope his skin is dark, because Hawathiya and I look like you, and our brother should look like Daddy." The nurses were still in the room as she continued chattering. She told them she was so happy that she got to see her little brother come out of her mom's stomach. "I'm going to be here *all* the time when my mom is having more baby brothers," she announced. She even told the nurse that she would be helping her mom change her brother's stinky diapers after they got him home. I had never seen my little girls' faces look so happy!

The whole family slept there that night, crowded into the small hospital room. I shared Mahalet's bed, and the girls slept on a small sofa bed. Every three hours a nurse would come in to check on the baby, and she would carry him to the nursery to take his temperature and see how he was eating. I would follow the nurse each time so I could see what they were doing to my son.

I had done the same thing when my girls were born, because I have always wanted to be there for my children. Maybe it's a cultural thing; Sudanese boys are trained from their youth to be *protectors* of their families. I love my wife very much and have always gone with her for her doctor's appointments because I want to know what's going on.

Mahalet and baby Malual checked out of the hospital the next day after the doctor had circumcised him. They told us he was doing well but that he was a little jaundiced and needed special light treatments to correct the problem. So the hospital sent someone to our apartment to set up the needed equipment. After one week with the treatments, Malual was all clear.

My little son's birth had been predicted by my family members back home, and he was now such a blessing to us. I thought of the hard times my wife had had during her first three months of pregnancy—how sick and emotional she had been. I also remembered how we would put the two girls into a stroller and go to a field where Mahalet and I would walk for more than four laps every day so she could stay in shape and have an easy delivery. Now it had all paid off.

The following May of 2012, I graduated from the University of Phoenix in Grand Rapids with a bachelor's degree in criminal justice administration. It was a big event for me and my family, and many of my *extended* family members were there for the ceremony. The ceremony was held at the Sunshine Community Church in Grand Rapids.

Mahalet's foster mom, Ann Dennis, was there, along with her foster brother. Aunt Dorothy was visiting from North Carolina and came to the ceremony with Mama Rita and her husband, and they sat with Mahalet and our children. Aunt Dorothy had brought with her a large suitcase with close to fifty pounds of clothing and flashlights for me to take to my village in Sudan the following month. I knew those gifts would be a godsend for my family.

Achuei, Mahalet, and Hawathiya.

Dad giving son Malual a driving lesson.

Our little Lina. God has blessed us!

Dominic graduated with a Bachelor of Arts degree
from University of Phoenix in May 2012.
Shown with Ann Dennis and Mahalet.

(Left to right) Mahalet with the girls, Dominic, Dad Gary, Mama
Rita, Aunt Dorothy, and cousin Dominic, with our son, Malual.

CHAPTER 9

Mahalet's Search

That night long ago at my cousins' apartment, when Mahalet had first told me her story of escaping to Somalia and going to Djibouti, I was very sad for her. She was just a little girl at the time and had been left all alone. It was hard to comprehend how abandoned she must have felt. She cried when she talked about her mother, because they had been so close. Now she was convinced she would *never* see her parents again. "Don't give up," I told her. "I *promise,* I will take you to Ethiopia someday, and we will search for your family."

We had previously made plans to go in 2011, but she had gotten pregnant with our son and we had to delay the trip. But now the time had come, and she was full of anticipation.

Our plan was to go to Africa and stay for two months. We would spend the first month in Ethiopia searching for, and hopefully *locating,* Mahalet's family. Then we would fly to South Sudan so Mahalet could meet my mother and the rest of my family. I knew Mother would be disappointed that we were not bringing Achuei and Hawathiya with us, but the cost of travel had made it out of the question. We would look for someone to keep the girls, but we would take baby Malual with us; he was nine months old, and Mahalet was still nursing him.

When Ann Dennis heard that we were making the trip, she offered to keep the children, but she wanted us to leave *all three.* She didn't think we should be taking a young baby to Africa, considering the poor sanitation and other factors. We had already purchased a ticket for Malual, but after listening to Ann, we decided she was probably right and took her advice. We would leave Malual *and* the girls with her and go by ourselves. (We realized later that "Grandma Ann" really *had* known best!)

When it came time to leave, we packed the children's clothing and supplies and took them to Ann's home in Fowlerville. Then with the help of Ann's pastor, we drew up a document giving her temporary guardianship in case any emergency came up during our absence. Mahalet was so happy to see her dream of searching for her family become a reality, but she was crying as she said good-bye to the children. Two months was a long time to be away from them, but we knew we were leaving them in *excellent* hands.

On June 4, we flew to Chicago from the Grand Rapids airport. From there we went to Istanbul, Turkey, and finally on to Addis Ababa, Ethiopia. It was a sixteen-hour flight, and we were glad when we finally landed in Addis Ababa, on the same date we had left home. Beautiful weather and pleasant people greeted us as we arrived.

The first thing we did was get our Ethiopian visas; then we collected our luggage and met Mahalet's foster brother, Monde, as he waited for us outside the airport terminal. Mahalet introduced us, and we all hugged each other; then Monde loaded our luggage into his small car. It was a 1960s vintage Ford that looked every year of its age.

Monde drove us to his house and introduced us to his wife, Esegenett, who gave us a warm welcome. We sat and talked for a while, and Esegenette wanted to set out a lunch for us. But we told her we were not hungry—just *tired,* and we needed to sleep. Tired as we were, we stayed up and continued to talk until six o'clock in the morning. Then Monde and Esegenett showed us to their bedroom and gave us each a bottle of water. We slept a few hours and then got up and had breakfast. Esegenett had set out a spread of several kinds of African bread, including, of course, Ethiopian *injera.*

We spent the day resting and planning our itinerary; then in the evening we went to the Ethiopian Airlines office and purchased three tickets to my wife's hometown of Dire Dawa. Monde had agreed to go with us, and he would be a real asset because he knew the country, while it was foreign to us. The next day we flew from the Bole Airport in Addis Ababa to Dire Dawa, where we would search for Mahalet's family. Taking the bus would have been much cheaper, but it was a thirteen-hour ride and we were eager to get on with our search.

They served us sandwiches on the plane, which was somewhat of a surprise, since the flight took only forty-five minutes. I watched Mahalet's face as we flew and could tell she was deep in thought about her family. I prayed that she would not be disappointed.

As we prepared to land, I looked out the window and saw cows and goats grazing peacefully on the hillsides. The last time I had seen Ethiopia, it was through the eyes of a frightened nine-year-old boy dodging bombs. A blast of hot air hit us as we stepped off the plane, but we didn't care; we were on a mission. I was anxious to find my wife's parents and have her introduce me to them as her husband and their son-in-law.

There at the airport, we got into a small blue taxi, paid the driver one hundred Ethiopian Birr, and asked him to take us downtown. "Have you booked your hotel yet?" he asked. We told him no, so he offered to take us to a hotel that was not far from the town center. He dropped us off, and we went inside the hotel and booked our rooms for the night. Then we went downtown to begin looking for Mahalet's family.

Mahalet studied the buildings as we walked through town. She said that things looked somewhat familiar, but she wasn't sure if we were looking in the best place. "Let's ask someone where there's an open-air market," she said. "A lot of people would be there, and we'd stand a better chance of finding someone who knew my mother." Monde stopped someone on the street to ask about open-air markets, and he was told that there was a place called Kafira, but it was not walking distance.

The common mode of transportation seemed to be the Bajaj, a three-wheeled covered motorcycle with bench seats. We rode the Bajaj to the Kafira open-air market, where we began our quest. The market was large, perhaps a quarter of a mile square, and we walked through every section from one end to the other, stopping people to ask if they knew Juara, my wife's mother, but no one had heard of her. It was well into the day, and it had turned very hot; our search had been fruitless, and we were exhausted. "We're not having any luck here," Monde said. "Let's go back to the hotel and get some rest, and we can look someplace else tomorrow."

Mahalet turned and looked at him sternly. "No!" she said. "We have to search until the sun goes down." Then a lady named Sanite—I call her our Good Samaritan—showed up and offered to help. "We will look for your family today," she said, "and if we don't find them, we will look again *tomorrow*. We'll keep looking until we *do* find them." Sanite's attitude was very positive—yet our search that day turned up *nothing*, and we reluctantly headed back to the hotel. Mahalet was crying again, and it seemed as though a cloud of darkness and despair had settled over everything.

"Maybe my mother was killed in Djibouti," she said. "Or maybe the rain here in Dire Dawa swept my family away after they returned from Djibouti." The reason she kept talking about her mother being dead was because of a dream she'd had back in the United States shortly before we left for Ethiopia.

In her dream, she saw her mother lying in a hospital bed. Her mother was blind and for some reason couldn't speak to her. Mahalet was crying in her dream and was asking the doctor, "Why didn't you treat my mother's eyes so she didn't go blind?" The doctor said, "I *tried* to treat your mother, but she refused my help."

Because her mother was blind in the dream, my wife insisted that her mother would never see her again. "After all we went through with the war and separation, I come back after all these years to ask my mother what she and my sister did while I was gone, and *now* she's not *talking* to me." Mahalet continued to sob. "What am I supposed to do *now*?"

"My sweetheart," I said, "let's be *positive* about this. We won't know what happened until we find your family. Let's just keep praying that we will find at least *one* family member who can tell us what happened during all those years." I looked at the clock. "It's three o'clock in the morning," I said. "Go and wash your face, and let's get to bed and get some rest."

Four hours later we were up having breakfast. Mahalet was still feeling depressed because we hadn't found her family the day before. Just then our Good Samaritan, Sanite, showed up. It turned out that a friend of Monde's wife, Esegenett, *knew* Sanite and had asked her to come and help us.

Sanite was an attractive businesswoman who marketed soft drinks in Dire Dawa. She was a Christian and wore American-style clothing. Sanite went back to the open-air market with us to help us continue our search. She began asking people again if they knew Juara. Several people did know someone by that name, and we followed up on every lead they gave us—but we didn't find Mahalet's mother.

"Who was Juara's *father*?" someone asked.

"I don't know my grandfather's name," my wife told them. "I was just a little girl when I left." We continued to plod through the marketplace, crisscrossing past purveyors of spices, beans, clothing, and live chickens, still turning up *nothing*.

"You *see*, my husband?" Mahalet said, sobbing. "I *told* you that my mother and my family are not alive!" We had turned to leave the market when we met a man who called himself Baby. He had been aware of our search, and he told us to turn around and go back to the market *again*. Baby joined us as we turned around and went back for the *third* time ... and that's when God brought my mother-in-law's best friend to the market.

The woman stopped and looked at my wife in disbelief and burst out crying. "I *know* this little girl!' she said. "She is my best friend's daughter. This is her little girl, Felisan, who disappeared years ago when she was very young. Now she's come *back*, and her mother is *dead!*" The woman was speaking in Oromiya, Mahalet's native tongue, but Mahalet no longer remembered the language, so we didn't have a clue what the woman had been saying. Monde understood her, however, but didn't say anything.

People were gathering around us to see what was happening, and the woman shouted to them, "*Please*, people," she said, "don't tell her that her mother is *dead*. She's traveled a long way; she's tired and needs to rest." The lady seemed to be in anguish as she spoke, but we still didn't know what she was so upset about. Finally, people told her to be *quiet*, or my wife would figure out what she was saying about Juara. Then the woman wandered off, still wailing as she went.

The crowd was getting larger and larger, with curious onlookers eager to know what all the commotion was about. Just then a very old and very short woman pushed her way to the front of the crowd to talk to Mahalet. She spoke in Amharic, so my wife listened. "*Come*, my child," she said. "Come to my house—I *know* you. If you don't believe me, I will show you pictures of your sister and your brother and your father. You are *my* family member too. Please follow me to my house."

A crowd of at least forty people joined us as we followed the old lady home. The people were perfect strangers, but they were eager to get in on the excitement these visitors from America had caused. About ten minutes later we arrived at the old woman's humble dwelling. She opened the door for us to enter and invited us to sit down on the padded mat on the floor. The crowd of onlookers gathered close to the door outside, hoping to catch bits of our conversation.

The woman disappeared for a moment and then came back with pictures in her hands. She held the pictures in front of my wife. "Look," she said, "this is your *brother*, and here is your sister Malika and this is your father, Beduru." Mahalet's eyes brimmed with tears as she held the pictures of her long-lost family. Curiously missing from the photos was her mother, Juara.

I was taking videos and snapshots of my wife talking with the old lady. Meanwhile, Sanite and the other folks huddled close and continued to converse in Oromiya. After studying the pictures,

Mahalet set them aside. "Now I'd like to go to my *mother's* house," she announced. The room suddenly grew quiet. "No, no," someone said. "You need to rest first; you've been traveling, and you're very tired." The people stalled as they tried to think of the best way to tell my wife the truth about her mother. Finally, Monde stepped over to me and whispered in my ear, "Juara is *dead*."

I felt a huge lump form in my throat, and I almost broke down; it was *not* what I wanted to hear, but I had to remain strong for my wife. Then Mahalet begin to cry because people were not allowing her to go to her mother's house. Finally, they broke the news to her—that her mother had passed away several years ago. For all the negative comments my wife had previously made about her family being dead, she had begun to have *hope* again after seeing the pictures. Now her hopes were shattered—initially, at least. Then she decided she was being *lied* to.

Mahalet refused to believe what they had told her. She was shaking as she spoke. "I *know* my mother is not *dead*!" she said. "She is *hiding* somewhere else." Now I was crying with her, yet trying desperately to stay strong for her.

"Mother," she cried. "I'm *here* for you. Come back to me, please! You are not dead, Mother! I'm here for you. Is *this* the way you're going to *welcome* me? Why did you disappear, Mom? I'm your daughter—I want to see you *alive*!" At times, she was speaking as though her mother was alive; then again, she spoke to her as if she was dead.

"How did you *die*, Mother? Did you die in Djibouti or in Dire Dawa, where I was born?" The ladies in the room could see that she was very distraught, and they tried to calm her down, but it was difficult. "Mom," she pleaded, "*please* tell me what happened to you. I want to share your pain. Did the bad gangs in Djibouti kill you, or did you die in Dire Dawa?"

Mahalet finally sighed with resignation. "Mother," she said, speaking more quietly, "I know that even if you *are* dead, you are *in* me. I will be strong, and I will take care of my brothers and sisters the way you used to take care of us." I was glad to see her a little calmer. Then came *more* bad news. They told her that her little brother had also passed away a year ago in the countryside, where he was living with his stepmother.

It was too much for Mahalet to handle, and she began to weep again. "Why did all these bad things happen to me while I was gone? I've lost my mother *and* my brother. What am I supposed to do *now*?" Her eyes were very red, and she was emotionally drained. People were telling her to be *strong* for her children and for her family members who were still alive. Meanwhile, I did my best to console her. Then someone came up with a good idea. They suggested we go to see Mahalet's sister Malika.

Malika lived about twenty-five miles away in a little town called Eresa. Five of us—Monde, Baby, Mahalet, and myself, plus another lady—all piled into a minibus. I was thankful the ride was no longer than it was, because it was a little unsettling. We traveled on a very winding road that snaked through hills overlooking deep valleys. I looked out the window of the bus and couldn't help but wonder if someone were to go off the road and roll down into the valley if they would ever be found.

After about forty-five minutes, we arrived at my sister-in-law's home. As we walked from the bus down the walkway to the house, I could see that Mahalet was fighting back tears. She said she was thinking about her young sister, wondering what hardships she may have gone through during the past several years without her mother being there for her. I was apprehensive myself; this time I wanted to hear some *good* news.

A woman was standing outside the mud-brick house, and we nodded to her and knocked on the door. Someone opened the door from inside and invited us in. The small living room was furnished with a traditional padded mat running along the wall for seating. A woman who we learned was one of Mahalet's stepmothers was seated on the mat. Baby introduced us to her, and then Mahalet said, "I want to see my *sister*." Her stepmother pointed toward a closed door. Mahalet opened the door and looked in, and she saw her sister lying down cradling a young baby in her arms. The room was dark and muggy and extremely warm. Flies were buzzing around and alighting on everything. Mahalet thought, in contrast, of her own infant son, who slept in a clean, comfortable bed, entertained by his two adoring sisters.

We pushed the door open wider to allow enough light for me to take pictures. "Hello," Mahalet said gently. "I'm *Felisan*, your sister," she told her, speaking in Amharic. Then she sat down close to Malika so she could talk to her. Malika, like my wife, was a beautiful girl, but there was no spark in her eyes—only sadness. Mahalet asked her what was going on in her life. She wanted to ask about the deaths of their mother and brother, but she could tell that Malika was nervous and didn't want to say much; she was afraid to talk about family secrets with so many people in the next room.

I went back to the living room and joined the others while my wife tried, unsuccessfully, to get information from her sister. A few minutes later Malika's husband arrived at the house along with a few relatives. He spoke in Oromiya and introduced himself as Bedasu. Baby told him who we were and explained that we had brought with us Malika's sister Felisan who had been away for many years. About twenty minutes later, Mahalet's father, Beduru, came with her young brother, Abdulnasir. They each carried small bunches of green leafy stalks called *mirra*, known in the drug world as "khat." Everyone in the room stood up to welcome my father-in-law, and Mahalet stepped from the bedroom to meet him.

Beduru looked at Mahalet in utter disbelief. "Welcome home, my daughter, who was lost for many years! How are you *doing*?" He spoke in Oromiya, so Baby translated for him. By this time, I was *really* glad we had brought Baby with us.

Abdulnasir was a handsome young man of seventeen. He had been born to Juara while his sister was gone, so he was meeting Mahalet for the first time. He greeted her shyly and gave her a kiss on the cheek. Then he turned to me and greeted me in the same manner, and we all sat down on the long mat, Mahalet taking a seat next to her father.

Then Beduru looked at me and asked Monde who *I* was. I knew the language and spoke for myself. "I'm Dominic, sir," I told him. "I'm your son-in-law. I'm from South Sudan. I married your daughter six years ago, and we now have three children—two girls and a boy."

"Did you leave your children in South Sudan?" he asked.

"No," I told him, "we left them in America." On hearing that bit of news, Beduru impulsively grabbed my wife and hugged her. He appeared to be very happy, but I could see that he was eying his daughter very closely. She was dressed in American clothing and was not wearing a hijab, implying that she was Christian rather than Muslim—an obvious disappointment to him.

Beduru was a medium-sized man with a red beard that I took to be dyed, because there were no traces of gray. "How old are you?" I asked. "I'm seventy," he answered. I thought he looked very good for a man his age. Beduru urged us to spend the night there in Eresa, but we told him we already had a room in Dire Dawa. "Felisan has a half sister, Sophia, in Eresa," he said. "She and her husband operate a shop in town. I'm sure she would like to see you." Beduru said he would go with us to Sophia's shop. He sounded proud of his daughter and of her business success.

Sophia and her children greeted us when we arrived—and like the rest of the family, they were in near-shock when they saw Mahalet. They didn't speak Amharic, only Oromiya, so once again Baby translated for us. Their shop was well stocked with clothing, food supplies, and household items. It was evident that Sophia's family was much better off than Malika's. We visited briefly, and they gave each of us a bottle of water to take with us as we left. We then visited another stepmother of Mahalet's, a diminutive older woman. Mahalet was surprised to learn that Beduru had been married six times, but it was clear that some of the wives lacked proper support.

When we left, Beduru got in the minibus and rode back to Dire Dawa with us. He sat in the front seat with Mahalet and the driver, while the rest of piled into the back. Mahalet began asking him questions about the family, but it was difficult because Beduru spoke only Oromiya, which Mahalet had completely forgotten. So her brother-in-law, Bedasu, translated the conversation.

It was afternoon when we reached Dire Dawa, and we went back to the home of the little lady with the pictures, who turned out to be Beduru's sister-in-law, Mahalet's Aunt Nafisa. Mahalet's half sister Warda, the daughter of wife number four, was also at the house. Warda was single and lived with her aunt Nafisa. We were thankful for Warda because she spoke Amharic and could answer my wife's questions without the need for an interpreter.

There was an open porch looking out onto an unpaved lane where children played and goats and chickens roamed freely. We congregated there on the porch to talk with a gathering of family members. It was a busy place, with curious neighbors stopping by to meet Nafisa's family. The place was becoming noisy. People were speaking back and forth in Amharic and Oromiya, so I was able to pick up only parts of the conversations.

Then I heard my wife in what sounded like a very heated dialogue with her father, her stepmother, and Warda. I listened more closely and realized the three were indeed arguing. Beduru didn't know what the women were saying until Warda began asking him questions for Mahalet. "Why did you marry so many wives and not take better care of them?" Warda told Mahalet that her father had waited *two years* before coming to see Mahalet's brothers and sisters after their mother, Juara, had died. Mahalet was now *very* angry.

"Why did you *do* that to our family?" she demanded to know. "Don't you even *care* about your kids? Our mother was *dead*, and you were supposed to come and show them *love*! And why didn't my brothers and sisters go to *school*?" Then she asked him the question that was consuming her. "How did my brother *die*?"

"I don't know," Beduru muttered. "Allah took him."

"Of course! How *would* you know when you didn't even *visit* him for two years!"

Warda had been listening to Mahalet's tirade. "Why are you complaining, Mahalet?" she wanted to know.

"When I was little, our father only visited us once a year," Mahalet told her. "What kind of father *is* he? He treated us like we weren't even his children!" Suddenly Mahalet remembered something from her childhood. "Father," she said, "I remember when I was a little girl, how you used to make my mother suffer." Mahalet continued to chastise Beduru. "Father, I will not forget the things that you used to do to my mother—she *lived* with pain, and she *died* with pain. But thanks to you, she is now at peace and living in a better place. Oh, she's *much* better off than living the horrible life she had with *you*! Father, don't forget—my mother is living in us because we are her children, and I am going to take care of my remaining siblings."

My wife's emotional state had the other women in tears, and Warda tried to soothe her. "Please, my sister," she said kindly. "I *know* the pain you are going through. I know losing a mother is not easy. I can't imagine losing my *own* mother—I don't know *what* I would do. Just take care of your brother and sister." Then Warda told her, "Just let it go. Forget the bad things of the past, and move on with your life. There's nothing you can do about our father; you can't change him. I know it's painful what he did to us—especially to *you*. Just forgive him because he is our father. He is the one who brought us into the world."

Warda was trying to be a peacemaker, but Mahalet didn't see it that way. What her father had done was not fair. It wasn't right for him to have married so many wives and not taken better care of them and his children. They continued to argue while everyone watched and listened. Then Mahalet asked, "Where is my *older* sister, Ahmetulah?"

"Your sister is in Djibouti, as far as I know," Beduru told her. "I don't have any connection with her, so don't ask me about her, because I don't know where she is right now. Maybe she has six children—or maybe more. I don't know."

Mahalet was more incensed than ever. "You know *what*, Father?" she said. "There is a reason why my Father in heaven took me away from you guys! Now I'm here for my siblings, and I will do something for *them* whether you like it or not."

Things were spinning out of control. "*Please* let it go," one of the ladies urged. "We know that is not easy to do, but just make peace so that you can go back peacefully to your children."

Beduru looked at Mahalet. "My daughter," he said, "*forgive* me, and let's make peace."

Everyone was happy and clapped their hands. Everyone, that is, except Mahalet. She was not ready to let go so easily. Warda gave her a hug, and the subject was changed as they talked about the long separation and how my wife had eventually ended up in America.

Things settled a bit, and some of the people sat and visited with Mahalet, asking her all kinds of questions. They were amazed when they heard how she had suffered as a little child without her parents, making her way alone from Djibouti back to Ethiopia and then to Addis Ababa. Then the visit ended.

It had been an exhausting day—especially for my wife. The timing of our trip had been of great significance to her family; just days before our arrival, they had declared Mahalet *dead*.

Mahalet and Malika had been looking for a chance to talk privately—but there seemed to be eyes and ears everywhere, making such a conversation impossible. Then Malika said, "Come with me, my sister. Let's go to the marketplace, because I need to buy diapers for the baby." Off the two walked, and Malika began to share her most unbelievable story with her big sister:

> After our mother died, our stepmother, Warda's mother, moved into the house our mother had built from her own earnings. Things had been hard for my brothers and me, because our father almost never came to see us and we were very young and

struggling. I had, however, been able to remain in school—until one day, not long before I turned fourteen.

I came home from school that day and found that our father had sent a couple women to take me shopping; they wanted to buy me a new dress. After we bought the dress, they took me to a house far from our home and told me that was where I would now be living. A strange man was there, and they told me his name was Bedasu and that I would now be his wife. I had been kidnapped—and my own father had arranged it!

I was terrified—I wasn't even fourteen yet. But the women left, and I was all alone with Bedasu. Within a few days, I had become the wife of a man whom I didn't like or even know. Then I got pregnant and was told to stay in the house where I was—that it now belonged to my new husband and me. But once again, I had been deceived. My half-sister Sophia and her family also lived in the house, and I was nothing more than a slave to them. I was treated very badly. I remember being beaten and told that I was just a useless woman. Sophia was my own half sister, my father's daughter, but she could be very cruel. She despised me because I was pregnant, and she told me she wished the baby I was carrying would die in my belly.

When it came time for my baby to be born, I was not allowed to go to the hospital as Sophia had for her babies. Instead, I was locked alone in the house for three days. Sophia and her children would come home at night, but they never checked to see how I was doing. I was now fourteen, and I was terrified because I was having a very difficult labor. I screamed out in pain, but no one was there to hear me.

Then Warda's mother, Zarah Abibi, came to my rescue. She stayed with me as I was pushing the baby and helped with the delivery. The birth was very difficult, and I lost so much blood that I was afraid I might die—but God helped me through it. I was grateful for Zarah's help; she had been a mother to me after our own mother died, and she was there for me when there was no one else to turn to. I knew very little about mothering, so Zarah stayed with me for a few days and showed me how to care for my infant son.

But as soon as Zarah left, I had to return to my job of waiting on Sophia's family. When I asked my sister why I had to do so much work alone for the whole family, she was not sympathetic. "You're a young woman," she told me. "You can do the work by yourself. You don't need help from anyone."

My worries were not about myself alone; I was concerned about my little brother, Abdulnasir. Sophia's children all attended school. They had all gotten a good education, and they now help run their family's business. But my little brother was not allowed to go to school, because my father needed him to work on the farm.

Malika told how their father made his living growing mirra, or khat (pronounced cot), a shrub with green leaves that are chewed as a drug and is sold at roadside stands because its use is unrestricted there. The branches are cut and tied into large bundles to be marketed, and her brother worked in the fields cutting and hauling the heavy bundles on his back. He was young—in his early teens—and the work was much too heavy for him. He now suffers from painful back problems. Malika continued with her story:

> My other brother, Abdulahi, had been born two years before me and had been sent to live with my stepmother, Haisha Hajih, in the countryside. He used to come to visit me and our little brother, Abdulnasir, and he saw what a miserable existence we had. "Don't worry, my sister," he told me. "I will take you out of this kind of life."
>
> He was the only one I had who would try to protect me. When I was kidnapped, he had fought with my husband and his family. "You will not stay with my sister for life," he told Bedasu, "not while I'm around!" He tried to defend me by throwing rocks at the family, but he was young and they overcame him. But he would still sneak and try to help me from time to time.
>
> Abdulahi knew that I was not being given enough to eat, so he would secretly bring food to me. This also gave him a chance to see what was going on in my life and to ask me questions. But when my husband and his family found out about my brother's visits, they were very angry and said disgusting things about him. "So, is your brother your husband now, or what?" Bedasu asked. "If your brother keeps coming to see you, then you are no longer my wife, but your brother's!"
>
> Bedasu's family threatened my brother to where he was afraid to come into my house anymore. I would see him standing outside and would ask him, "Why do you stand outside? Why don't you come in?"
>
> All he would say was, "Don't worry, my sister—I just wanted to see you."

My stepmother had no children, so my father had sent my brother Abdulahi to stay with her to do the farming for her. It was difficult work for my brother to handle by himself, but that didn't seem to concern Beduru. "You are a young man," he told him, "and if you don't do farming, you are useless." But my stepmother didn't appreciate my brother's help and didn't treat him like a family member, but more like a slave.

When Abdulahi could take it no longer, he went back to my father hoping he would help him. But Beduru didn't seem to care. "What kind of a father are you?" my brother asked. "My mother died, and my little sister got married at too young an age because of you. A real man takes care of his wives and children all the time."

"Please, give me money so I can live my own life," he begged. "Your wife is treating me so badly. I want to help my younger brother and sister so they don't have to live in this miserable existence anymore! And if you can't do that, Father, then just kill me so I can be in a better place like our mother is. She's in a much better place right now, in heaven."

With no help or understanding from my father, my brother returned to our stepmom's place in the countryside. A week later, my husband, Bedasu, came home with some of his family members. "Come on," he said. "We're going somewhere." He sounded very serious.

"Where?" I asked. But I couldn't imagine anything being any worse than my present environment.

"Don't worry," he told me. "But you are going to see something you don't want to know about now."

Then they took me by bus to the town near my stepmother Haisha Hajih's place in the countryside, where my brother was staying. From the bus, we walked for more than half an hour, finally reaching her house. No one had spoken on the way about the reason for our visit, but I had a very uneasy feeling about it. They opened the door and told me to go on inside. Then they showed me a coffin and said, "Here is your brother."

It was more than I could take, and I cried uncontrollably. "I lost my mother," I said. "And my two older sisters are not here, and I don't know where they are. Maybe they're not even alive—I don't know. And now I've lost my brother—the only one who ever fought for me." I was heartbroken, and no one was there to comfort me.

My father came for the burial, but not my little brother. He was most likely working in the mirra fields. I watched as they placed Abdulahi's casket in the ground; I was the only one crying. All they said as they covered the grave was, "He's gone. Allah took him, and there's nothing you can do about it." Then they said a prayer, and it was all over.

A week later I began to hear disturbing stories from people who had known my brother. They claimed my stepmother had poisoned him. Neighbors had heard him crying in pain, begging for help. He said, "Please, my stepmother—I know you don't like me, but just kill a goat for me. I don't know what happened to me right now, but I have a terrible pain in my stomach. Please! My stomach!" The reason he had asked for the goat was because that's what people fed to someone who is very sick and in pain. He felt that eating the goat meat would ease his pain and give him strength.

But my stepmother ignored my brother's cries and took her small herd of goats and left him to suffer alone. A neighbor lady heard my brother crying again, "Somebody come and help me, please! I'm going to die—my stomach is hurting so bad!" The neighbor hurried over and gave Abdulahi some traditional pain medicine, but it was too late. She saw foam coming from his mouth, and then moments later he was dead.

Shortly afterward, I was at Nafisa's house, and Warda's mother, Zarah, was there. She was the one who had moved into our mother's home and raised us. Our father was there too. Zarah was very angry and was arguing with him. "You see?" she scolded. "Now the boy is dead! Your wife poisoned him, and you are in on it too. The last time he fought with you, he begged you to give him money so he could manage his own business, and you refused! You knew how hard he was working doing farming for you and your wife, and you knew that she didn't feed him. He told you he hated that house and pleaded with you not to send him back. Now are you happy that he is dead?"

Beduru's anger had been building as he listened to his wife's rant, and when she had finished speaking, he grabbed her and beat her mercilessly. "Shut your big mouth, woman!" he shouted. "Or I will kill you too! Allah took him, and I have nothing to do with his death!" People who were in the room during the argument and fight had to step in and separate the two.

I burst into tears again after hearing everything. My sister, I know somebody killed our brother. He was very kind, but he was a fighter. I have lived with pain ever since I was forced into my marriage.

I am grateful to Warda's mother for moving into our mother's house and raising us after she died. So, my sister, Warda's mother is now our mother—but how painful it is to grow up without the love of our own mother.

They say our mother, Juara, was a very hardworking person. I heard stories about her working hard in the homes of people in Djibouti and getting beat up by the ones she worked for. But she stayed and worked until she earned enough money to return to Dire Dawa and start her own business selling fruits, vegetables, and breads. She then used the money she earned to build this small three-bedroom house for us. It was built by her money alone with nothing from our father.

What a strong mother we had! How I wish she were still alive. If she had lived, these people would not have taken advantage of me the way they did—and our brother would not have been killed.

Our mother said something strange before she died. She warned one of our cousins not to get too close to her and not to touch her body after she was dead, and not to come to her funeral. I don't know how long she was ill before she died, but they say she had been lying dead in her house for three days before anyone found her. And my brothers and I were there in the house with her all that time! I learned later that the cousin our mother warned not to touch her went in and took valuable jewelry that belonged to our mother. Apparently, Mother knew he was not to be trusted, and that's why she didn't want him around.

Some years later, our older sister, Ahmetulah, who had moved to Djibouti, returned to see the family. When she found that our mother was dead, she became hysterical with grief and cried until we thought she might die too. With her mother gone, she said there was no reason to stay around, so she went back to Djibouti. She came again two years later along with her infant daughter—a beautiful child about five months old.

While she was here, she confronted my cousin about our mother's jewelry. "I know you took Mother's jewelry," she said. "You always made trouble for us—I remember how you used to beat us up and curse at us. You're the reason I moved away from here. I'm 100 percent sure you did something to our mother. Our mother used to fight with you because of us. Now she's dead, and I believe your hands are guilty of her death. Now tell me where my mother's gold is. I want you to bring it back now!"

Our cousin was very angry, and he grabbed Ahmetulah and commenced to beat her and threw a heavy set of keys at her. They struck her in her head, leaving a deep gash that spurted blood. She grabbed her baby girl and ran bleeding to the house of our mother's brother. She stayed there with my uncle for a month, and then she went back to Djibouti. She left the infant with him. Unfortunately, the baby died shortly after she left, and that is the last the family has seen of our sister.

I don't know if our sister is dead or alive; maybe she will come back one day and surprise us the way you did. We all thought you were dead too—but now you are here. Thank God you are alive! Now my brother and I have a big sister again. We will look forward to talking to you in America by telephone. Please be strong, my sister. I know the things that have happened to us have been painful.

When you first came to the house to see me, I wanted to cry—but I didn't, because I was in shock. I was also afraid to attract attention from people in the house by telling family secrets, but now that I have seen you again, I will be telling you more and more, my sister.

Malika had talked for a very long time and had stayed strong; but as she finished her story, she broke down and wept, and Mahalet wept with her. I thought the crying would never stop, and I tried to console them.

"I lost my father too," I told them, "and I fled from home when I was young. My father was killed in a *horrible* way—they ran a spear through his stomach, in one side and out the other, as if he was not a human being. But do you know what? If I had not stayed *strong*, I would not be here talking to the two of you today. Each one of us has a day to die. It's okay to cry—but then move on with new life. You both need to carry on your mother's legacy, because you are both mothers now yourselves."

Then Abdulnasir spoke up. He had been listening to his sister's sad story, which he had overheard, and he began singing a song: "Let the dead sleep. Move on forward with new life, my sisters." Then he looked at Mahalet. "Your husband is *talking* to you, my sister, and you have children back home waiting for you to raise them. Just be strong, and pray to God that you and your husband can go back home safely."

It had been a tough day for Mahalet and her sister, and it had also been a very tiring day for Abdulnasir and me, listening to the talk of all the family problems. Our time with Mahalet's family came to a close, and we said good-bye to her brother and sister. They had wanted to walk to the bus station to see us off, but it was already almost 4:00 a.m., and we would be returning to see them again after we spent time with my family in South Sudan. Then we would leave for the United States.

It was a thirteen-hour bus ride to the airport in Addis Ababa, where we got our flight to Juba in South Sudan. We were weary from the bus ride, yet I was excited as we took off for Juba, because at last my wife would get to meet my family. The trip went smoothly because I was becoming more competent at traveling, and *this* time we had gotten our South Sudan visas at the South Sudan embassy before leaving.

At Kafira market, God sends Good Samaritan Sanite to help us.

(Left to right) Mahalet's foster brother, Monde, Mahalet, and Sanite search Dire Dawa for clues to finding Mahalet's family.

Mahalet finds her father, Beduru.

(Left to right) Mahalet is saddened by her sister Malika's story.

(Left to right) Mahalet and Malika speak with their father, Beduru.

(Seated left to right) Malika and Mahalet visit their
childhood home with half brother Abdulnasir

CHAPTER 10

Welcome to South Sudan

When we got off the plane in Juba, the agent checked our luggage and told my wife, "Welcome to South Sudan!" When the airport workers saw that she was from Ethiopia, they went out of their way to make her feel welcome and told her to make herself at home.

My cousin Ajuong Malual was at the airport to meet us, and he took us in his car to the Ethiopian Hotel, where we got a room for two nights. We had intended to spend just *one* night in Juba before taking the bus to Turalei, but Ajuong told us my family was still preparing a room for us, so we booked the room for an extra night. We thanked Ajuong and told him good-night, and he said he would meet us at our hotel the next day.

After we had gotten settled in our room, we went to the cafeteria and ordered some Ethiopian food, which was delicious. Mahalet especially enjoyed it because it was served with the traditional bread called *injera,* and it made her feel at home. After eating, we were ready to get some *sleep.* We had not been in bed long when it began to rain. The sounds of the raindrops were like music to our ears and helped us have a restful night, which we badly needed. In the morning, we went back to the cafeteria for breakfast and relaxed until my cousin came to pick us up.

It was afternoon when Ajuong returned, and he had brought with him my cousin Bol Mayom Malual. It was so good to see Bol again—he too was a Lost Boy. We had been together in the Kakuma camp in Kenya, but when we were being processed to come to America, he was one who didn't make it. Then after the peace agreement was signed in 2005, Bol decided to *leave* the camp and go to Juba and try to make a new life for himself.

That was a bold step for my cousin. It was touch-and-go for him during the first few years, but he was able to get training as a traffic policeman and then a job directing traffic for the police department in Juba. My cousin Ajuong is also in law enforcement as a lieutenant colonel with the Juba Police Department. It is extremely difficult to break away from life in the villages or the refugee camps and make a living in the cities, so I am extremely proud of my cousins for their hard work and persistence.

When evening came, Ajuong took us to his home, where he introduced us to his wife, Jacqueline, and his daughter, Nyiriou. Ajuong's niece and several cousins were also at the house waiting to see me and meet my wife. We had a great evening together sharing experiences from our days with the Lost Boys. I must say that *reminiscing* on those dark days was much more enjoyable than it had been *living* them!

It was raining hard the next morning, and the roads soon turned to mud. After the rain subsided, my cousin Majok Deng Malual picked us up at the hotel and took us to the bus station, where a car that served as a bus was waiting for us. We had purchased our tickets the day before, so we didn't have to wait at the bus station but could board right away. Mahalet and I got in the front seat next to the driver, and we began the long journey to Wau.

The ride was a rough one because, as *always*, the roads of South Sudan are not maintained, making nighttime travel especially unsafe. So rather than try to drive on through, we stopped and spent the night in a place they call Tony City. This was not far from Cueibet County, where Deng Nihal was killed. He was the man who was supposed to be the leader of South Sudan during the Anyanya One guerilla warfare.

Early in the morning we resumed our journey to Wau, and at every checkpoint officials asked to see Mahalet's passport. Her light skin was their reason for singling her out, because she was obviously not Sudanese. But when they noticed that we had the same middle and last names, I told them she was my wife, and they seemed pleased. "Welcome *home*, madam," they told her.

At one point, the vehicle we were traveling in broke down because the exhaust pipe had pulled apart. I got out and helped the driver tie the pipe back in place so we could be on our way again. In spite of any delays, we still reached Wau by 11 a.m.

I had heard that my sister Agom's son Feeth was in Wau to enroll in college—so I tried calling his number but didn't get an answer. Then just as I was wondering what to do next, I spotted Feeth's sister Aker charging her cell phone next to the bus station. I recognized her because we had met during my visit to Sudan in 2009. I don't know which of us was the more surprised at the meeting!

Aker was successful in reaching Feeth, and she told him we were at the bus station. He came and picked us up and took us to visit my mother's cousin who lived there in Wau. The cousin and his wife were out grocery shopping when we arrived, so we visited with their children until they got back. Then we stayed on for a couple of hours before having Feeth take us back to the bus station to get tickets to Kuajok, the capital of Warrap County.

After another rough ride of about two hours, we arrived in Kuajok, where we spent the night with my dad's brother Deng Malual Mayom. I was proud to introduce Mahalet to my uncle Deng. *Everyone* we had met liked her right away, and my uncle was no exception. He and I had so much to talk about, and I was especially interested in hearing stories from him about my father. We talked about our families in the village and about how much life in the villages had changed for them after the raids. Without the cattle camps to hold families together, change was inevitable.

My uncle and I had a special connection. It had been his son Madit who had walked with me as a Lost Boy. He was my "big brother"—my mentor. He had taught me to write my name in the sand when we were in Yoril. But Madit died on the way, possibly from heat stroke—but no one knows for sure.

I had gotten to see Madit's mother when I went home in 2009, because she lives in the Wunriang village near the rest of my family. She wept when she saw me. "Welcome back, my son!" she said. "We are relieved now that we have *seen* you, because we thought we had lost *all* of you." She had gone on to talk about her son Madit—about what a sweet and bright boy he had been. She said reports had come back to the village that we had all been killed by the northern militia. Other people claimed we had met our deaths at the jaws of hungry lions in the forest. That, unfortunately, *was* true of many of the boys.

My uncle Deng was fortunate to have gotten an education, and he was working in Kwajok in the financial department of the local government. He had a nice little two-bedroom home and seemed to be doing well, and he traveled to see his family in Wunriang from time to time.

In the morning, my uncle took us to Turalei, which was a couple hours' drive. It was early afternoon when we arrived. My family had been expecting us, and several relatives were at the bus station to welcome us, including my brother Ajuong. There was a hotel close to the bus station with benches out front where people could sit and visit. We congregated there with family and chatted, relieved to be on the last leg of our journey.

As we sat talking, a young man walked over to us. "*Deng!*" he said. "Is that *you?*" I recognized him at once as my friend Agel Adhardit, one of the Lost Boys.

"Agel," I answered. "I *wondered* what had happened to you after you left the camp in Kenya. It's good to *see* you!"

Agel told me that while I was being processed to come to the United States, he was processed to go with another group of boys to *Australia*. He had completed his education there and had since returned to Turalei to help improve things in his community. He was currently working with the local health department educating families and schoolchildren in preventing the spread of disease. I had not seen Agel since the year 2000, and so much had happened in both of our lives since then. He was in disbelief when I told him I had joined the US Army and had served in Iraq for more than a year.

The family members urged us not to go on to Wunriang, but to stay and spend the night at the hotel in Turalei—but we had already made up our minds to go. My uncle Garang was especially concerned about my taking Mahalet there at night. "*Please* don't take your wife to Wunriang," he begged. "The mosquitoes are very bad right now. Your wife is not from here, and she needs to be protected from things that can make her sick."

I was definitely anxious to see my mother, but it was Mahalet who would not be deterred. "I don't *care* if it's night or if it's dark," she said. "We *have* to go to where my mother-in-law is! We have to see her *tonight!*"

It was only a half hour's drive from Turalei to Wunriang, and we had been talking about hiring a car to take us. Mahalet was determined not to let anything stand in our way. "I don't care if we have to pay for a *donkey* to get there—and if there is no donkey, then we will *walk!*" Then Agel spoke up and offered us the use of his car for the trip, and one of my cousins, Mayom Ajuong, said he would drive.

It was after seven o'clock when we left with Mayom, but we stopped first at a market in Turalei to buy bread and to get some sugar for tea for the family. A half hour later we reached Wunriang. There are no roads leading up to the houses in the village, so we had to drive through fields to get to my stepmother's place, where my mother was staying.

The sight of headlights is unusual enough in the village, but my mother was especially surprised because she had assumed we would spend the night in Turalei rather than come after dark. When we told her we had *refused* to stay in town when she lived only two hours away by foot, she was very happy—especially because we would be spending the night there where she was staying.

Mother was overjoyed at meeting Mahalet, and I had to translate their greetings to each other as they talked excitedly. Then family members came and poured water on our feet to welcome us. That is a Dinka tradition, a type of blessing when one returns home.

My stepmom, Atak, showed us to the guest hut they had prepared for us. It was pleasant and represented much care and preparation on the part of my family. The hut was furnished with the traditional bed used in the villages, one made of thin leather straps crisscrossed and secured to a sturdy pole frame, and topped with a thin mattress, making a comfortable place to sleep.

After placing our bags inside the hut, we joined the family around the fire outside to catch up on what was happening. "What's been going *on* around here lately?" I asked, trying to start a conversation.

"We're *hungry*, and we have no *food*," someone said, and I was glad we had stopped for bread. I gave them the bread and the sugar, and they made tea for everyone. We enjoyed the hot drink and bread together and then retired for the night.

In the morning, I sent my stepsister Adhar Malual, and my brother Garang to Turalei to buy a supply of bread. I also had them buy corn flour so that they could bake extra bread at home, because family members would be coming to see us.

It broke my heart to see my family without food. Everyone was asking for money, but we simply didn't *have* it. They were not greedy—just *hungry*. They assume that everyone who comes from America is wealthy and comes with a good supply of money. They had worked hard planting crops last season so there would be enough food for the families—but heavy rains had come and *destroyed* their gardens, washing their food supply away.

It began to rain the day after we arrived—but this time they were *happy* to see the rain because it was planting season and my family was eager to put in new crops, hoping for a better outcome this time. Mahalet and I were up at five o'clock in the morning and out in the fields working the soil and planting with my family. Besides the regular crops they usually planted, we planted some seed corn I had brought with me from the United States. They don't have good tools to work with, so they do a lot of digging with their *bare hands*. We worked hard until eleven o'clock. By then it had become very hot, and our hands were sore with blisters.

Mahalet showed me her hands—they were bleeding. She felt sorry for my family and what they were going through to survive. "It's so *easy* to eat," she said, "but so *difficult* to do farming."

We had worked on the farm for three days when the family members came together and told me it was time to have a party to welcome my wife. They got a black-and-white ox from a neighbor, Chol Kuol, and I made arrangements to pay him for it.

Mahalet was excited; it was a great honor to see an ox being killed for her. I was happy too because I knew my family would have food to eat during the celebration, and I was pleased to see how much they loved and accepted my wife. The meat was prepared in various ways as they cooked it on fires beneath the trees at my stepmother's place. My half sister Adhar who was seventeen, and other young girls helped with the cooking and served food and water to the elders.

I bought traditional whiskey for the party too because there were those who wanted it for the celebration. There were people of all ages—young folks, small children, and elderly men and women—all joining in to welcome Mahalet into the family! It was good to see everyone so happy; they were dancing and singing songs for my wife, and she loved the attention. I was glad to see her smiling and cheerful after the sad and difficult experience she'd had in Ethiopia.

The young girls were fascinated with meeting someone who was not Sudanese. They wanted to know what her name was in the Dinka language. We told them that her name was Ayan Deng Malual, because that is the Dinka name I had given her, but the name she officially uses is still Mahalet Deng Malual. They were all talking to her excitedly, telling her all about Dinka customs and traditions, and I was busy trying to keep up with translating their conversations.

The girls reminded me of a bunch of young schoolgirls. They were begging for Mahalet to stay with them at my stepmother's place, but I told Adhar that she was not spending the night with *any* of them, but was staying with *me*. "Please leave Mahalet here when you leave, so we can teach her to speak Dinka," they begged. Of course, they were joking, because they knew that was not possible. But she told them if our *children* were with us, she would love to stay and help with the farming.

When the party was over, we gathered outside around the fireplace with my brothers Ajuong and Garang, and my mom and stepmother. My stepbrothers and sisters were there too, and we had a good family talk. The party had been a time of fun and celebration—but now we had to talk about *serious* matters.

They were all looking to me for a solution to their hunger problem, as well as the education of their children. They didn't realize that their expectations were not realistic. I gave them what money I could spare and kept only what we would need for our trip back home—but I knew money alone was *not* the solution.

"Stay *strong*," I told them, "and keep farming, like you've been doing. But you need to consider your *family size* too. Things are no longer the way they were in the days of the large cattle camps. Back then, there were resources to *support* large families—and it took the work of many hands to care for the large herds of cattle. But today the children are not in school; they are just playing at home and going hungry because there is no food. You need to have *family planning*."

We had a good family discussion, and everyone shared their thoughts—but in the end, we still had no good solution to the immediate problems they faced each day. They need to be strong and stand up for themselves, but I will continue to do my part to help them develop a stable community.

It had been a big day, and we were exhausted and ready to go to bed. It was completely dark away from the fire, so my wife armed herself with a small squeeze flashlight and went to our hut ahead of me. A moment later, she ran back out screaming hysterically, "*Snake inside the hut!*"

I grabbed a piece of burning wood from the fire and raced to the hut. Mahalet followed me with the flashlight and shined it inside. There I saw a large black snake moving slowly around the base of our bed. I crept close to it and attacked it with the burning piece of firewood and killed it. It was a venomous snake—a species responsible for the deaths of many villagers throughout the years.

Mahalet was visibly shaken and was afraid to go back into the hut to sleep. "The snake might climb the bed and come where we are *sleeping*," she said.

"No, sweetheart," I assured her. "The snake is *dead*. There are no more snakes." She reluctantly followed me back to the hut and went to bed. She pulled the covers up snugly about her for protection— *just in case*! Fortunately, there were no more snakes, but that was an experience my wife will remember for the rest of her life.

After hearing how my people have no sources of light except the fires, Aunt Dorothy had sent me a box of flashlights to take to my family. I purchased *more* of the lights and tried to give one to the head of each household—but they were still not enough. Family members and neighbors were begging me for more lights. "It's the *rainy* season," they said, "and snakes are *everywhere*. If your wife had not had a flashlight when she went into the hut, she would have been *bitten* by the snake." There are two kinds of venomous snakes coming into the huts in the villages, and only God is protecting the people from them.

Perhaps the most pressing need in the villages is *clean water*. A few weeks before my wife and I left for Africa, Aunt Dorothy called the Seychelle water filtration company to order water bottles for us to take to Sudan, and the owner of the company offered to send me several bottles for my family. My people were extremely grateful to Carl Palmer for his generosity, and it made me happy to see my mother drinking *pure* water for once, instead of the dirty water from the river where cattle were standing. Mahalet and I also used the water bottles while we were in the village, because we are not used to drinking contaminated water and I didn't want her to risk getting sick. The bottles were a *lifesaver* for us—we had no sickness at all during our trip.

My people don't understand about living in America. It's true, in comparison to them, I am rich, but by American standards I am far from wealthy. They are looking to me to solve their problems, and they gave me their "wish list" for when I return. They want more flashlights, a well for fresh water, a school for the children, and a tractor so they can farm enough crops to feed everyone. I wish it were that simple.

On our fifth day in Wunriang, we told my family that we would be leaving. This trip had mainly been Mahalet's trip, and we were returning to Dire Dawa to tell her family good-bye before we flew back to the United States. My mother was having problems with her eyes and needed to see a doctor, so we were going to take her to Wau on our way to Juba. My brother Ajuong would be coming along to see that she got to the hospital for treatment.

In all of my early childhood memories of Mother, she was *working*. With seven children, she was *always* working. And now her eyesight was failing, and the years of hard work had taken their toll on her. Mother approached me as we were preparing to go. "Son," she said, "let me tell you something before you leave with your wife." Mahalet was with me, and we stopped and listened to all that my mother had to say.

"Now I am old, and I don't have the energy I used to have. My hands are weak and can no longer do the farming. The day that I die, no bird will pass in my compound."

I thought that was a strange thing to say, so I asked Mother what she meant by those words.

"My son, I am the one who has been holding the family together. No one will take care of the family the way I have, unless you and your wife come here and take over the responsibility of raising the family the way I have done. For years now—ever since the death of your father—I have never rested.

"I did the farming and supported your father's wives and their children along with other family members here.

"The torch is in your hand, my son. I have seen your wife, and she is a beautiful woman with a very kind heart. She will be strong for you and your family. This is the kind of woman a man needs to raise his family.

"Now my eyes are having problems. Just take me with you and treat my eyes on the way before you go back to your children, my son. You can see how my hands are very weak. I am not strong enough anymore to do the farming. You and your wife are the only ones who can take care of the family, so just come back with her and grow the crops so there will be food.

"I know the American people will give you a tractor. Look! They gave you water bottles with filters and gave you flashlights. If Americans were bad, they would not do that. This is just the beginning of help to come. You brought these water bottles, which will help reduce sickness and death from drinking dirty water."

My wife was crying as my mother talked. She felt the pain that my mother went through for many years without a husband to support her—doing the farming all alone. She had suffered as Mahalet's mother, Juara, had, except Beduru was still alive while Juara had suffered.

"Mother," I said, "you know where I have come from. Things are not easy, but there are Good Samaritans in America. We suffered terribly in the camp—but afterward, people in America welcomed us into their homes. They shared their belongings with us and even provided cars for some of us to get to work and to school.

"The time will come, Mother, when people will help us get tractors, dig borehole wells, and build schools. Patience pays off, and one day things will change and no one will have to suffer in this area again. Take my word, Mother, and you will see the difference before you die."

She listened to all that I had to say. "Son, I've known your heart from the moment I gave birth to you, and I have no reason to doubt you—but your brothers and the families need your help. Just try in every direction by whatever means you can to find help for us here in this place."

We left for Turalei with Mother and my two brothers. A group of family members and neighbors walked with us to see us off. When we reached Turalei, we stopped at a market so I could buy sorghum meal for the families. Sorghum is one of the main food staples in South Sudan, and I bought four large bags—one each for my three brothers' wives and one for my stepmother Atak, who had been caring for my mother. It was too sad for me to see my own family going hungry every day. The bags weighed about a hundred pounds each—much too heavy to carry back to the village on foot. But the merchant agreed to keep the bags in his shop and let my brothers take small quantities of the meal each time they came into town.

We said good-bye to Garang at the bus station, and then we were on our way to Wau with Ajuong and my mother. We were not far from the town of Wunrok when the timing belt on our vehicle broke. Fortunately, our driver was a mechanic, but it was a half hour's walk to and from Wunrok for him to get a replacement part.

The breakdown caused us a two-hour delay, so it was getting dark by the time we reached Kwajok, and we decided to spend the night. We got our hotel rooms but had to go to bed without eating because Kwajok doesn't have twenty-four-hour food service. We were extremely hungry and couldn't wait for breakfast.

When we got up in the morning, our car was already waiting for us, so we had to leave without eating. We were very happy when, after an hour's ride, our driver stopped at a small café. We all went in, and I treated the driver and all the other passengers to tea and donuts. It is strange how uncomfortable I had been because I had gone to bed hungry. As a Lost Boy, I had accepted hunger as a fact of life, but now I had trouble when I missed a single meal.

The journey to Wau evoked memories for my mother. It was her first trip there since her pregnancy with my sister Abuk twenty-five years earlier. She said things looked somewhat familiar, but the roads had changed the most. They still needed improvement, but they were not as treacherous as they had been on that deadly trip. She will never forget the truck going off the road and so many passengers being injured or killed.

Believe it or not, our vehicle stalled again! This time we had run out of gas, and it was still a thirty-minute drive to Wau. We waited by the roadside begging for gas—but no one was able to help us, because we didn't have a siphon hose to get gas from one tank to the other. We had been waiting for two hours when we finally got help from a man who was headed to the city.

One of our passengers volunteered to ride into town with the man and bring back a can of gas. It was another hour's wait before the man returned with the fuel. He put it in the tank, and we were finally on our way. My mother had been praying, "Please, God, don't let the thing that happened twenty-five years ago happen again while my son and his wife are here. Please take them back safely to their children." A half hour later, we arrived at our destination in Wau, at the home of my mother's cousins.

After we had rested from the tiring trip, I asked Ajuong to go with me to the bus station to get our tickets to go to Juba the next day. We caught a ride in a Racha, one of the three-wheeled covered motorcycles used for transport in the city. It was the same as the Bajaj vehicles we had ridden in while in Ethiopia, but in Juba they called it a Racha. Three of us were riding—Ajuong, the driver, and I. Our vehicle was traveling straight down the highway when we saw a large truck speeding toward us before crossing the centerline into our lane. Our driver swerved to the left to avoid being hit head-on, and the truck barely missed us before plunging into the ditch upside down. If the truck had struck the little Racha, we would have stood no chance at survival.

Our driver pulled the Racha off the road and stopped to compose himself. He was visibly shaken as he took a deep breath. Then he looked at my brother and me and asked, "Who are you?"

"We're brothers," I told him. "Dominic and Ajuong." He just shook his head, still reeling from the near tragedy, and said, "Your God is very powerful!"

We did see our survival as a miracle, because the moment I saw the truck barreling toward us, I had said to myself, *We're dead men.* We saw the overturned vehicle again as we headed back from the bus station. Police were there checking out the scene, and we were told that the truck driver had been drunk and that he was in critical condition in the Wau hospital. We never knew whether or not he survived.

I was thankful my wife had not gone with us, because it would have made her fearful for the rest of our trip. Mother, who was always quick to see God's hand in situations, prayed. "Thank you, God, for protecting my children! May you continue to protect my children on their way home."

It had been an eventful day. That evening we cleared up any necessary details, and I gave Ajuong money so he could take Mother to the hospital after we were gone. In the morning we told Mother good-bye, and then Ajuong went with us to the bus station to see us off. Before we boarded the waiting Land Cruiser, I had my final talk with my brother.

"Ajuong," I said, "Mother needs you right now—so be strong for her and take care of her until I'm able to return and take over the family responsibilities." Even though I'm now living in America, I still want to follow the Dinka tradition of the youngest son taking responsibility for his aging parents. I might not return there to stay—but I will always be available to lead them in improving their living conditions and educating their children.

Ajuong thanked me again for my help and for the sorghum meal for the families. "Good-bye, brother," he said. "You and your wife take care and be safe on your way home to your children."

After fourteen hours in the Land Cruiser, it was good to arrive back in Juba. We had made plans to stay at the home of my cousin

Ajuong for a few days and were waiting to get our plane tickets to Addis Ababa when we realized that the city of Juba was preparing for South Sudan's first Independence Day celebration.

It had been one year since South Sudan became an independent nation after seceding from the Republic of Sudan, and I was thrilled to be in Juba, the nation's capital, for the very first anniversary of that momentous event. I hadn't planned our trip around the celebration—it just happened by chance. But now that we were in Juba, nothing could keep me away. The moment the clock struck midnight on the eve of the anniversary, revelers began driving cars up and down the streets, honking their horns and cheering; however, the actual festivities were still hours away.

As a Lost Boy from Sudan who had witnessed firsthand the brutality of a civil war that had claimed untold thousands of lives, I couldn't help but cry when the day came.

I still found it hard to believe that we were no longer under the oppressive rule of the Republic of Sudan. Mahalet was crying too—but for a different reason. She wept at the sight of the many disabled veterans who marched in front of the crowds. They had won their independence, but they would suffer the wounds of war for the rest of their lives.

The day was made even more meaningful to me as I paused to think about the two trips I had taken to Chicago just a year and a half earlier. The first trip had been to register to vote for the separation of South Sudan from the north, and the second trip had been to cast my vote for the separation. As Lost Boys, none of us thought we would ever get to vote for separation, but thank God it did happen, and it was cause for great excitement.

Thanks to the generosity of our fellow Dinka tribesman Luol Deng, who played for the Chicago Bulls at that time, a sizable group of us had been able to vote that day. Luol chartered two buses to take Lost Boys from Grand Rapids to the polling station in Chicago. Our bus driver was very kind, and we asked him if it was okay for us to sing as we rode, and he said it was. And sing we did! It was such a joyous occasion that we sang during the entire trip. We sang songs of sorrow and songs of happiness—whatever we felt like singing.

A lot of our friends were already at the polling station when we arrived, and it was wonderful to be together for that historic event. Our gentleman Luol Deng arrived and cast his vote for separation too, and we sang for him and presented him with an official red, green, and black South Sudan flag. He thanked us and wrapped the flag around his shoulders. We were touched by his showing up for us and voting with us on the same day—and especially for his generosity in providing the buses. It was because of him that we were all able to make the trip.

It had been a good day—one the Lost Boys of southern Sudan would not forget. January 9, 2010, will always be remembered in our history and the history of South Sudan. I saw the light and happiness in everyone's faces during the vote in Chicago. For the first time in decades our people had hope, and words could not describe what that meant.

The Independence Day celebration was indeed a time of triumph. Tanks rolled through the street, and soldiers marched, proud of the freedom they had fought for and won. People sang songs of war and of thanks to God, and tribal members performed traditional dances. A marching band wearing red uniforms took their place in the parade, undeterred by the sweltering heat, and helicopters flew overhead carrying the red, black, and green flag of the new nation of South Sudan.

When we first approached the John Garang Mausoleum, where the festivities were being held, I had my camera out and was taking videos, but an official at the gate stopped me and told me cameras were not allowed. Then Mahalet and I pulled out our American identification documents and showed them to the officer, and we became instant VIPs. We were then directed to sit in a private area along with the press, and I was allowed to record the celebration unrestricted.

There were speakers from various African nations; they all encouraged the Sudanese people to stand up and be strong for their country. One of the key speakers was Uganda's president, Yoweri Museveni. He said the problems of South Sudan should not have taken even two days to resolve, but for twenty years the world had refused to listen to the suffering of South Sudan's people. Those had been my own thoughts when I was running here and there with the Lost Boys. Then our own president, Salva Kiir, spoke of Museveni's commitment to the nation's economic growth and peaceful relations with Sudan.

A journalist we had met the night before, Christine Esipisu from Kenya, spotted us where we sat. "Wow!" she said. "How did they let you in?" She was not being rude—it was just that she had not expected to see us in the restricted area, seated along with the press. She and Mahalet had met the evening prior at a salon where they were both getting their hair braided, and they had struck up a conversation. After Mahalet had given Christine a little of my background, she wanted to interview me, so we met with her later at a restaurant next to the hotel where she was staying.

"What does this day mean to you?" Christine asked.

"It's a new day in South Sudan's history," I told her. Words failed me as I tried to describe the depth of my feelings. She became very interested after learning that I had spent time in a refugee camp in Kenya before coming to the United States as a Lost Boy. She then asked Mahalet about her life history, and she wanted to know how we two had met in America and become husband and wife.

Christine begged us to stay another day in Juba so that she could hear more of our stories, but we told her we had to leave the next day. She did, however, interview my cousin Ajuong Manyiel Malual while she was in Juba. We told her good-bye, and the next day we caught our flight back to Ethiopia.

As we flew from Juba, I still couldn't believe our good fortune in being there for such a momentous occasion. I began to reflect on the painful years of Sudan's civil war. As Lost Boys, we were wandering for many years and nobody heard our voices and our cries. We were like dogs without owners. Justice had no place in Sudan's conflicts. People of South Sudan had been buried in deep wells by the devil's government in northern Sudan. We were second-class citizens who had no voice. Now we are the first-class citizens of a new nation. The world will see the truth of South Sudan, but it's the world leaders who will have to provide a solution for Abyei and the other critical places at the nation's northern border.

Abyei was taken to southern Kordufon in the north by the agreement of Deng Mijok, the former leader of the Dinka Abyei people. But not everyone in Kordufon has the right to vote for separation— only the people who were taken there. Clearly, Abyei belongs to South Sudan, because all Sudan rightly belongs to the black natives of Sudan. The Arabic meaning of the name Sudan is the land of black, not brown. So the name itself confirms that Sudan is a land of black people.

Abyei County will not be fooled again the way the government of northern Sudan fooled our people for so many years. We will come out of this darkness, and the world is watching. My mother is from Abyei, and the Dinka Abyei people did not migrate from the Middle East a long time ago. We know who came from the Middle East and who didn't come from the Middle East in Sudan's history. We have legal rights—and the truth of the matter is that the time is coming for the thieves, and they will be caught in the Abyei solutions.

Monde met us at the airport again when we arrived back in Addis Ababa. On the way home, he stopped at the market where livestock are sold for the butcheries. He selected a nice lamb and brought it home to serve to us as his honored guests. He killed the lamb and prepared the meat in various ways throughout the week. Each preparation was delicious and was accompanied with injera, soup, and traditional Ethiopian breads—a real treat for us!

I was missing my kids and wondered how they were handling being away from us for so long, so I called Ann Dennis so I could speak with them. I told the girls that we were visiting Monde and Esegenette and that they had children too. Then I let the couple's son, Henok, and his sister, Salaam, talk on the phone with my girls. It was a new experience for all of them to talk to someone who lived so far away. Then it came time to tell Monde's family good-bye, and we caught a bus to Dire Dawa to see Malika and Bedasu before we flew back to the United States.

When we arrived at Dire Dawa, we went again to the home of Sophia, Mahalet's older half sister—the one who owned the shop. Mahalet also wanted to get her citizenship papers while we were in the country, but it became complicated because her name did not appear in any of the birth records. The man in the office where birth certificates were issued refused to give her one when his search failed to pull up her name. The problem was that when her family had come back from Djibouti during the war, she was no longer with them and her parents assumed she was dead. They didn't put her name on the census list—and now the official was refusing to accept her story without documented proof.

"What do you want from me?" Mahalet asked, brushing tears from her eyes. "I brought family members with me as witnesses," she said, referring to Malika's husband, Bedasu, who had accompanied us. "When I was a little girl, I got separated from my family before they came back from Djibouti. Now I'm happy to see the rest of my family again, and I'm proud to have been born in Ethiopia."

The man could see how distressed Mahalet had become. "I believe you are Ethiopian," he finally told her. "And I know your family. Just go to the boss in the office, and ask him to give you a letter requesting the document." Then when we looked at the time, we realized the "boss's" office was now closed for lunch.

"Your half sister's husband wants to see you back at the house," Bedasu told Mahalet.

"Why do we need to go back there?" she asked. "We just came from Sophia's place. Just let me get my paperwork and get my business here taken care of. Tell them we'll be there tomorrow. Also, I need to get an appointment with my half sister Warda."

"Don't worry about Warda," Bedasu said. "I'll talk to her—you can meet with her tomorrow. Right now, I want you to go to Sophia's home.

You haven't met her husband, Yassin, yet." Bedasu was so insistent in the matter that we didn't feel we had any choice but to go with him.

Things were quiet in the house when we arrived. Then someone said we should have *Duwa*, meaning prayer—which they did while chewing green mirra leaves. Then they asked us to sit down and hear what they had to say to my wife.

"You wonder why Malika was given in marriage at such a young age," Yassin said. "When she got married, it was because we didn't want her to end up married to some other man—someone who might hurt her. We did this so that she could be close to us and be taken care of." He gestured toward the adjoining room. "Look at these two rooms," he said. "Your sister used to live here, but she moved out because little kids were fighting here and hurting each other. But we are family."

"And your brother … we put Abdulahi in school, but he refused to go. Then we gave him a job, and he refused to work. There was nothing more we could do with him. Then he went to the countryside and got sick and died there." He looked at Mahalet. "What we want to know now is, what are you going to do about your sister and little brother? Are you planning to take them to America?"

"I don't have any plans now," she told him," but I will do my best to support them here so that the children can go to school."

My wife had listened to the simple explanation she'd just been given concerning her sister and brother—but she kept quiet. It was a far different story from the one Malika had told her.

Yassin spoke up again. "I want you to not separate your sister and her husband. If you want to take Malika and Bedasu with you, then take them. But you must leave their children here with me so I can put them in school … I have money." He then talked about the success of his own family.

"My oldest son is attending school in Sweden now and is doing very well. My children living here are also doing well in school—and their GPAs are amazing. Your sister's children will receive the same education as mine have when they enter school."

"I have no intention of separating my sister from her husband," Mahalet assured him. With that being said, the meeting ended, and we were told we should spend the night in Yassin's house.

"Thank you," I said, "but we want to go to our hotel. We have a room already paid for." We wished them good-night and told them we would be back in the morning.

The next morning, we went to Yassin's shop, and food had been brought in for everyone to eat. All the while people chattered away in both Oromiya and Amharic. Yassin is a well-known businessman in the area, and he had arranged for the "boss" to come to the shop and meet Mahalet. He told her to give him her passport picture and said he would handle the paperwork right away for her to get a birth certificate. We stayed around for the next couple hours or so, and the man returned with her citizenship papers and birth certificate showing that she was born in Ethiopia—not Somalia.

We took the papers back to our hotel and rested for a bit. We had promised to go back to Yassin's place, but someone called and told us not to come, because there had been a death in the family and they were going to the funeral. Instead, we went to the bus station and bought our tickets to Addis Ababa. Then we took Malika shopping and bought clothes for her baby. Our time in Dire Dawa had come to an end, and we told Malika good-bye and went on to Addis Ababa to catch our flight back to the United States.

After we landed in Grand Rapids, we were exhausted and went directly to our apartment and spent the night. In the morning, we drove to Ann Dennis's to pick up the children. Our girls were so happy to see us; they had so much to talk about. And little Malual was standing up and trying to walk. He didn't actually take his first steps until sometime later, and I was glad for that because that was something I wanted to be there to see.

We were so thankful to Ann for keeping the children for us— she has been a blessing to our family and a wonderful grandmother to our kids. We took the girls back to our apartment in Grand Rapids, and they were happy to be home and to see their own room again. We didn't have a lot of unpacking to do, because we had traveled very light so that we could take things to our families. Once we had gone out and shopped for groceries, our household was back to normal again.

Achuei and Hawathiya were full of questions about our trip, so I played the videos for them that I had taken of both of our families. It was important for the girls to see their two living grandparents and to learn a little about life in Africa. We hope to make the trip again someday and take all three children with us. I pray that my mother's health allows her to live to experience this family reunion.

I received some disturbing news from my brother Ajuong not long after we returned home. Ajuong had been staying with relatives in Wau close to where we had taken Mother. He went over to see her one morning and was surprised to find her gone. Her cousin hadn't seen her leave and assumed she was just sleeping late. Ajuong was greatly concerned because of her eyes—it wasn't safe for her to venture away from the house alone.

Then his gut instinct told him to check the open well in the yard. It was a very deep uncovered well from which they were getting their water. He peered down the well shaft but couldn't see anything … but when he called Mother's name, she answered. Apparently, she had been sleepwalking when she slipped into the well. It had been completely dark at the time, so they guessed it had happened about five o'clock that morning. Although the well was deep, the water came only to her waist, but it was uncomfortably cold. Ajuong got some men to help him pass a long rope down the shaft to rescue Mother from the chilling water, which she had been standing in for at least four hours. She told us she had tried to call for help, but due to the depth of the well, she couldn't be heard from any distance.

A few months later, Mother became ill and was diagnosed with both typhoid fever and malaria. Mosquitoes are bad in the area and often result in cases of malaria, while contaminated food and drinking water are usually responsible for typhoid. I sent money to Ajuong to pay for her treatment, and she made a good recovery. Medical science has come a long way in treating those diseases, which were often fatal in times past.

I continued to stay in close touch with my family and was pleased with some of the news I was getting. Garang said they appreciated the bags of sorghum I had purchased for the families before returning home—it had provided them bread when they had had none. But he told me the crop of sorghum my wife and I had helped them plant while we were there had done very well, and I would not need to buy any more for them at this time. I had also bought a female goat for them to keep for milk, and she had recently given birth to a kid. And because the chickens feed on sorghum, the crop they had harvested would provide feed for them as well, and hopefully they could increase their little flock.

They were by no means out of the woods, so to speak, but it was a start. They were fortunate with the year's crops—but in another year there could be flooding, which always brings destruction. The important thing is that for the first time since my father's death and since the birth of South Sudan as a new nation, my family was beginning to have hope.

Friends and family dancing to celebrate our visit.

Mahalet (left) meets my mother (right) for the first time.

Sitting with my grandmother, Achol Akec.

Mahalet visits with my mother and grandmother.

Dominic (left) helps plant seeds while his half sister Adhar Malual goes to the river to fetch water.

My stepmother, Atak Lual, cooks food for us.

Lual Deng and Dominic in Chicago to vote (2011).

What an honor for Mahalet and me to sit in the press area for the celebration.

I never dreamed that eighteen months after South Sudan's independence, I would be in Juba for the first anniversary celebration!

CHAPTER 11

"Come Back, Deng"

For Mahalet and me, the missing pieces of our lives were finally coming together. I had at last learned the details of my daddy's tragic death, and Mahalet had found her father and two of her siblings. I had yet to hear my family's account of the raid the evening I went missing. As a Lost Boy, I had searched diligently for them for years wondering if they were still alive and if I would ever see them again. I recalled how emotional the first meeting with my mother had been, and I did not want to put her through the ordeal of returning to the painful past. She told me that she had looked for me for five years, but she didn't give me much detail, so I needed to ask another family member.

My brother Garang had been in his early teens at the time of the raid, and I wanted to know what *he* remembered. I was keeping in close touch with him by phone and helping his family as I had promised to do. I called to ask him what happened to my family that night.

"Where were *you*," I asked, "when the enemy attacked our village? I don't remember seeing you."

"Deng, you forgot—I was taking care of the family's cows. I had taken them out to graze, and our father came to help bring them back for the evening. He was home from the cattle camp at the time."

The herd we had kept in the village was small—maybe ten or twelve cows. After my brother Mayom's close encounter with a lion while taking the cows away to graze, my daddy was cautious about my brothers bringing them home alone, so he had gone with Garang that evening. But Garang told me that as the two of them headed back to the village with the cows, they were suddenly under attack. They saw people running and screaming and heard shots being fired all around them, and their small herd was quickly seized by armed militia.

"Daddy took off running and told me to follow him," Garang said. "He was heading for the cattle camp, hoping to get there ahead of the militia and rescue the valuable herds. It was a good thing, too, because when we got there, soldiers were already driving the cattle away. But we did manage to run away with 150 cows."

"Where did you *take* them?" I asked.

"Well, the camp wasn't that far from the Lol River. We knew if we could get the cows to the other side of the Lol, they would be safe. When we reached the river, we got a lead cow to swim across, and the rest of the herd followed."

Garang told me that the militia had already taken a hundred cows, but he and my daddy had been able to return for the rest of the herd and take them across the Lol River too. The two stayed there with the cattle for two weeks.

"And what about Mother?" I asked. "How did you reunite with her?"

"Oh, our daddy was so *worried* about her! He didn't know what had happened to her and to our brother Ajuong. He didn't know if they were safe or if the enemy had taken them away—but all the time Mother had been searching for *us* and found us camped by the Lol River two weeks after the raid."

I remembered that Mother had been preparing the evening meal when the raid took place. She had ground flour for bread and had put two-year-old Abuk on her back to go to the river to fetch water for us. She was near the river when the attacks began. She later told Garang and my father what had happened. She too had heard gunfire, and she set her water pot down and ran, but in a *different* direction from where Garang and my daddy had gone.

"You and Ajuong were the ones we still worried about," Garang told me. "So we kept searching. Finally, after a *month* we found Ajuong in a nearby village with one of our uncles in what we called the "hideout" place, and we all returned home. But we couldn't rest until we had found *you*, because our family was not complete.

"We searched *so* hard for you. The whole family searched and searched, going from cattle camp to cattle camp, because that's where we figured you might be—but there was no trace of you. And people told us *conflicting* stories. Some people said they saw you running *west* toward the sunset—remember, it was in the evening. Then some people told us you were heading *east* when they saw you. Someone else said, 'We saw Deng going south.' And other people said they saw you heading north with the militia. Since we didn't know *where* to look, we looked *every* direction. Mother went west to search for you, and Daddy went east. Ajuong went north, and that's how he ended up *living* in the north. They had me continue going from cattle camp to cattle camp. We were not going to give up on finding you, because we all loved you so much. We were finally convinced you had been captured by the militia and taken to the north. Mother cried and cried for you and was nearly out of her mind with grief."

Then Garang remembered the nickname my mother had given me as a baby—Deng Achol Angom. "She called you by *all* the nicknames you had been known by. She would stand outside and call loudly, 'Deng Achel Angom! Deng Monychinweng! Deng Aleu! Come back, Deng, Come back, my son! You are a *fighter* and a leader of your own life. Take care of yourself, and come back to me! You are a wise boy with the brain of a *man* living in the jungle.' And there were times when she would sing songs while gazing up into the sky, with the hope that you would fly home like a bird. The name Monychinweng means 'a boy without cows who left us here.' She kept saying, 'My son is *somewhere*—and I can feel that he is *alive*. One day my son will come back, and I will see him.' Our father had his own nickname for you. When you were with him in the cattle camp, he called you Deng Mithawech, and pretty soon everyone in the camp called you that. Mithawech means 'a wild bird that knows how to hide.'

"Those names had real meaning," Garang said. "They defined who you were: a boy without cows—that is, without *milk*—living in the jungle. They defined you well as a jungle boy."

I don't know why people liked to give me all of those nicknames—but I guess they did have meaning at the time. I remember my father calling me Malual Pouchlei Junior because *he* had been called Malual Pouchlei, meaning "the lion that wakes up the other animals" (to warn them of impending danger).

I told Garang how I had cried as I looked for him and for the rest of my family, but I didn't realize at the time just how much pain my leaving had caused *them*. Oh, I knew they would *look* for me if they had also survived—but as time went on, I had doubts that they were even *alive*.

"As I went to the different cattle camps searching for you," Garang said, "I had to beg for food because I was walking for many miles. Strangers were very kind and helpful. They gave me food and a place to sleep as if I were a member of their own family. People were astonished when I told them that I was looking for my little brother who was lost."

"But just what was going through *your* mind during all of this?" I asked.

"I was thinking, *This is my brother I'm looking for!* Somehow, I believed you were alive. I believed the people who said you were taken to north Sudan. One reason I believed you were alive is because we had been to the places where the dead were taken after the raid, and we didn't find you. It was a very difficult thing, searching for you among all the bodies—but we *had* to know. Since we didn't find you there, I had hopes that you were alive and would come back someday. And as I continued searching, I realized many *other* children were still missing. A lot of them were found in nearby cattle camps where they had sought shelter. But some of the families were not so lucky—some of them found their missing children among the dead."

I wondered about the cattle that Garang and my daddy had rescued and had eventually taken back to the camp. "Who was minding the cattle camp while you and the family were searching for me?" I asked. "And how long did our father stay away from the camp to search?"

"Our uncles and others from the village helped out with the cattle," he said. "But our father's search continued off and on, my brother. You *know* our father—he always liked to have matters settled promptly. It was difficult for him, because he still had the cattle and the rest of the family to think about. He had taught you to hide in the jungle when there was trouble, so he looked in the places where people used to hide. He never gave up, but he finally said we should just be patient because everything has its own results. But Mother's search continued for several years. She searched the whole western part of the country, inquiring with people as she walked mile after mile."

"Some of our relatives were going north to look for their children who had been kidnapped by the northern soldiers, and Ajuong joined them so he could continue to look for you. They walked from Twic County to Abyei County and got transportation from there, stopping in various towns on the way before going deep into Khartoum. Ajuong knew a little bit of Arabic, so our dad told the relatives to take care of Ajuong and he in turn would help them by serving as their interpreter."

Garang told me how painful Ajuong's search for me had been. After looking everywhere, he finally had to stop and try to find a job to support himself. I remembered Khartoum from my visit in 2009. Black Sudanese people were living in deplorable conditions and being treated as second-class citizens by the local Arabs. Some of those people had been kidnapped and taken there by force, while others had gone there to avoid being kidnapped or killed by the Sudanese government. I knew my brother's stay there had not been pleasant, but he was there on a mission. He was determined to learn of my whereabouts.

I was happy to be having the conversation with my brother Garang, because I'd had so many unanswered questions. Back in the village our family was very close; but hearing Garang tell of the anguish that my disappearance had caused our family was extremely humbling.

"Garang, I remember when our cousin Dut left to return to the village. He had been walking with our group when he got terribly sick and said he couldn't go on. It was probably a good thing, because not long after he left, our cousins Madit and Ajuong Arop both died very suddenly. Dut *knew* where we were heading … did he tell you he had been with me?"

"We didn't know what to think about Dut," Garang said. "He returned to the village some weeks after the raid looking so thin, like he hadn't been eating. He told us how he had walked with the group for some time but had gotten sick and couldn't walk any farther. You know, he was only about seven at the time, like you. He said he found a family to stay with until he was well enough to walk again, and he told us that you had gone with your group to the camp in Ethiopia. But we didn't know whether or not to *believe* Dut, because other people had told us something different. He was surprised when he returned to the village and learned that his brother James Mum Ajuong was *also* missing.

"Dut was right," I said. "We walked south at first to Yoril, and then we went east to Ethiopia. I had wondered about him after he left us. I was afraid he wouldn't make it back to the village alive."

"He did look pretty bad," Garang said. "He had lost so much weight, and we assumed that you had gotten thin like that too and that you might not survive. But we kept our fingers crossed and hoped that someday you would return."

"Here *I* was crying because I thought all of you had been *killed*," I said. "I thought I was the only one from our family who had survived. And all the while *you* were searching for *me*! Each time we went to a different camp, I would ask people if they had seen any of my family members. And people would tell me that you might be in one of the *other* camps, because there were three camps in Ethiopia. But I was too young to leave my group and go looking for you alone. I just stayed in my camp until we went back to southern Sudan, and the three camps became one as we settled in Pakok, Kapoeta, Nairus, Lokichogio, and then Kakuma in 1992. That's where I met up with James Mum Ajuong."

"During all those years when you were in the camp, you were thinking we were all *killed*?" Garang asked.

"Yes," I told him. "When you are young and you don't see family members around, it's easy to believe they are dead. The enemy had us *separated* from each other in the villages and cattle camps. This is the kind of damage the government was causing families in South Sudan. A lot of families still have members missing. And many of them will never be found, because they are already dead."

"You are right, my brother. Look, our father kept looking for *you* hoping to find you alive. And now you have come back—and our father is *dead*. It is all very painful, and we are going to have to live with that pain for the rest of our lives. You returned here as a man, but you were just a child when you left. Twenty years is a long time. Even though Dut Ajuong came back and told us you had gone to the camp, we didn't fully believe him—but we held onto our hope that you were alive. It was hard to believe that you could survive in the jungle for so many years. Now we are happy—but it's not *complete* happiness, because our father has not been here to witness your comeback from nowhere."

When my brother spoke of pain, I knew *he* had endured more pain than most. After all, he had been very reluctant to leave when my father ordered him to go far away from our village. But he finally gave in out of respect for our father, and that was the last they ever saw of each other. He must have wondered if things might have turned out differently if he had stayed home. He would have been at Daddy's side during the raid and would have died for him. But he had followed Daddy's orders, and it was now in the past. Just before my first visit to Sudan, Garang had lost his wife. And soon after I left, his infant daughter had died. I was glad that my return had brought him some measure of happiness.

"But our *father* ..." I said. "Did he believe I was alive, or dead?"

"Our father was a wise man. His thoughts were somewhere in the middle. He told us, 'If Deng is alive, he will come back. And if he is dead, someone will let us know *how* he died. I taught him how to hide from danger, and I know my son very well.' When you talked to us the very first time, it was unbelievable to hear your voice, my brother. You have a special place in our lives. You are 'running the show' now in our family because of your education and all the experiences you have had. You are like an *older* brother to us now." I understood what Garang meant. I *was* the older brother now, because I had crammed decades of experience into my thirty years of life.

"Ajuong missed you so much," he continued. "You two were like twin brothers—always together, playing hide-and-seek in the garden. After you left, no one was here to play with Ajuong the way you did."

Garang chuckled as an old memory surfaced. "Do you remember the time when you hid from Ajuong in the garden and found wildcats eating our chicken? You came running back to the house with your eyes almost out of their sockets—and you were too frightened to even speak at first. You said, 'A *hyena* was eating our *chicken*, and the hyena's brothers were about to eat me alive like they did the chicken!' From then on you refused to play inside the garden because of the wildcats. Ajuong was amused by your fear and was always scaring you whenever the wildcats wandered into our compound in the evening."

"Ha! Ha!" I laughed. "I *do* remember that! I thought the wildcats were hyenas because I didn't know the difference between cats and hyenas at the time. But during our struggles I saw *all kinds* of animals. I saw hyenas, lions, wolves, leopards, and everything else that lives in the wild. And some of those animals really did eat some of our people on our way to Ethiopia and back to South Sudan. My journey to the camp was not a simple walk. I will remember those days for the rest of my life."

"And were you thinking about *us* all that time during your journey?" Garang asked.

"Yes," I said. "I was thinking about my family all the time—but I had no choice but to stay where I was. There was no place to turn to." Then I told him how I had come close to being adopted by the old lady in Yoril, but had changed my mind when we broke up camp and moved. I told him her story about the Malual Agueng Ber, the human lions, and how my cousins and I had secretly escaped to keep from being eaten by the old lady.

"I've heard folks tell those stories too," he said. "And some people really *believe* them. You know, my brother, the world is *big*, and you have seen many things and many different people. Aside from our own people, *I* had only seen the *Arab* people, and that was when they attacked us. And I saw *white* people for the first time when they brought food to our country a few years after you disappeared. I was amazed at their colors and the way they talked. I didn't know before that there even *were* such people in the world. I thought there were only the black people of our own country."

My brother was right about all the people and places I had seen. Even though the circumstances were most tragic, it had all become a part of my education. How *could* he have known about other people and other cultures without someone to teach him? I thought about the white judges who questioned us before we left Kenya. Seeing *them* had been somewhat of a shock to me.

Garang told me about the first white people who arrived years ago in Africa. "People saw them and thought they were ghosts," he said. "Then they thought maybe there were still *other* colors besides the Arabs, the whites, and the black people."

I told Garang about an incident that happened when I first arrived in America and had gotten a job as host at a restaurant. A woman and her little girl came in and asked to be seated. While I was speaking with the woman, the little girl reached up and felt my hand. I think she was curious what black skin felt like. "Why is your skin a different color from mine?" she asked.

"Have you ever seen dogs and cats with different colors?" I asked.

"Yes," she said, "because God *created* them with different colors."

"That's right," I told her. "And just like the animals, God created *us* with different colors because it's beautiful to have different colors instead of everyone being the same."

"I wish my daddy had black skin like yours," she said, "so I could play with his skin when he comes home from work."

The woman was very embarrassed and apologized to me. "Don't be sorry," I told her. "It's natural for kids to be curious when they see something that looks different. That's how they learn."

Yes, I thought, *children are curious, and their minds are full of questions.* I remembered that early on my journey—after I left the old woman in Yoril—I was frightened every time I heard someone speak with a different dialect. I would keep my distance from them because of the woman's frightening tale of the Malual Aguen Ber. Just in case they had infiltrated our camp, I wasn't going to take any chances! It was easy to have that fear at the time, because the intense hunger we endured as we walked through the jungle to Ethiopia was almost *unbearable*—but I never once heard of our people practicing cannibalism.

My conversation with Garang had been a lengthy one, but it was good to finally have another chapter of my life come to a close. I am so thankful to all my family for the months and years they spent searching for me—and especially my mother, who refused to give up. After hearing Garang tell of her unrelenting search, I could close my eyes and see her standing, gazing up into the African sky, and I could hear her familiar voice calling, "Come back! Come back, my son. Come back, Deng."

CHAPTER 12

The Lost Boys

The name "Lost Boys" was the label given to more than twenty thousand children from the Dinka and Nuer tribes who fled southern Sudan during the second civil war in that country. During the years that followed, their parents searched for them in anguish, not knowing whether they were dead or alive—they were simply *lost*.

The Sudan government was doing the same thing to us that the Egyptians had done to the Israelite children. It's hard to believe, but that was the true picture of the government of the Republic of Sudan. Remember, the Lost Boys' journey from Sudan to Ethiopia took place from 1986 to 1990. They were running for their lives, trying to survive, never dreaming that the end of the road for many of them would be in America.

We have lost land, properties, brothers, sisters, mothers, fathers, and other relatives—you can name them—because of the civil war in Sudan. Our own government's soldiers did *unspeakable* things to their own people. Young females were raped and made wives of the northern Sudanese soldiers. And when those soldiers raided homes and found families together, they forced the young males in the families to rape their mothers or sisters. If they *refused*, they were immediately beheaded. These are the reasons why the Lost Boys of Sudan ran away from their families and country to look for new lives.

Another reason for running was the enslavement of the people in southern Sudan by the government in the north. The northern soldiers would kidnap people from the south, take them back north as slaves, and then get *money* from the UN for taking care of "refugees." Yet the government of Sudan never admitted to violating the human rights of our people by killing them or forcing them into slavery.

Greed was behind the genocide in our country. Southern Sudan is like a beautiful woman—a virgin girl compared to other nations on the globe. God gave her much wealth from the creation of the world: oil, gold, fertile land, large rivers, many wild animals, the beauty of the country, and everything else that Sudan has. The enemy wanted to strip this all away.

My journey from Sudan to Ethiopia was like the Israelites' journey from Egypt to the promised land of Canaan. Along the way, we saw devils' eyes—thirst, diseases, and wild animals. But most frightening of all was the ever-present northern militia, constantly raiding us in the air and on the ground like eagles and hawks tirelessly hunting for food.

I have memories—horrible nightmares—in the back of my head. My childhood friends and many young kids who were related to me set out on foot with the same hopes I held of reaching freedom. But they never made it to Ethiopia or any other destination in their lifetime. Their bones can be traced back to the stomachs of lions and crocodiles, or to the great anthills of the African deserts. I watched in terror as lions, crocodiles, and wild birds snatched and killed people on the way and then ate them.

We had no hope, and we never even dreamed that one day some of us would see the home of the brave, the United States of America. Whenever someone close to us died, the next thought that came to our minds was, *Will I be next in line to die on the way?* Mentally, I compared us to goats on a farm. When a farmer wants to kill or sell one goat, he will choose a good-looking one to bring money to him or good meat to his family.

We were subjected to everything that is dangerous to human beings on our journey to the Ethiopian highlands. Even the insects actually killed many Sudanese children and adults during our struggle between Sudan and Ethiopia. It took many, many months, and by the time we finally reached Ethiopia in the eighties and nineties, only *half* of our original number remained alive.

CHAPTER 13

My Statement of Faith

I was born into a family in which some of the members are Christian, but some believe in traditional gods. My daddy and mother believed in traditional gods. My daddy was actually a spiritual leader in the community. He often would predict what would happen in the future around the community.

For example, he would dream that some thieves were coming to take away someone's belongings. If he alerted the people, they would move to a new area the next morning. Then the following day, the thieves would come and find nobody there. Some people in the community say that he predicted his own death when he told people in the cattle camp to move their cattle from where they were camping in the area with a lot of grass close to the river.

The years I spent running with the Lost Boys were unbelievably difficult. But there is also a bright side to the picture, because it was in the refugee camps that I was introduced to the God of the Bible. Once we settled in Kenya, food was scarce, but we learned to rely on our Christian faith. I thank God for the Catholic Church, for the way it reached out to help us. The afternoon Bible classes became the bright spot of my day—I couldn't get enough of it! It was there in the Kenyan camp that I was confirmed and baptized.

When I came to America with a large group of Lost Boys, it was the local churches that reached out to us. I will never forget the kindness of Christian friends who made us feel welcome in our new homeland.

Then when I joined the army and was deployed to Iraq, my Christian faith grew much stronger. I had my Bible with me and read Psalm 91 every day before leaving my barracks. I saw many people die in the war zone, but I was never afraid. I prayed for God's protection, yet I was ready to die if it was my time.

I finally returned home to Sudan to see my family after twenty years away, and I was happy to learn that a number of my family members are now Christians. I would like to see a church and school built near my village so the children can have the opportunity not only for an education, but also to learn about God.

I received my master's degree in 2017.
I thank God for my education.

CHAPTER 14

My Assessment of the War

Why did we *go* there? Did we go so we could do something to be remembered? You can ask politicians for the right answers. We were *soldiers*—the protectors of the nation—and we did our part when we were called. We will be remembered by the Iraqi people who got their freedom, and by American people for fighting for them. The Iraqi children will remember us for giving them sweets, clothing, and soccer balls—and for being there to protect them.

The children often thought of American soldiers as the Army Santa Claus. The soldiers often used their own money to buy gifts for the children, hoping to build a positive relationship with the families of Iraq.

Dominic greeting Iraqi children in Bagdad (2007).

The Iraqi children often rushed to see what the American soldiers brought for them.

Businesses came back to life, and schools were reopened in the "ghost city" that had been abandoned by the citizens of Ghazaliyah because of war. Roads were fixed, and fear was not in the cup anymore. All the neighbors were in good shape after a year of violence in the area. They thanked us and praised God for our hard work in their city.

Thirty minutes of intense fighting was like a whole day. That's how it was one day in the infamous "Gee Spot," or JSS Thrasher. I was on the gun when we saw the enemy shoot at us. They killed our second vehicle, and the firefight continued for thirty minutes. I had never come so close to being killed before, and I thank God that we didn't lose a single soldier in that fight. I joked about it later and said that what saved me was my very dark skin. My vehicle was the first of several vehicles to get hit by sniper fire. The bad guys were aiming at the drivers' *faces,* and when they aimed at *me,* the reflection of the sun's rays back to the enemy helped the round to land in the engine rather than on my face!

The ghosts of the war are never far from us. They are always living with us—the rich and the poor alike. And I'm not alone in my feelings—I speak also for my brothers and sisters in arms. Who has the power to heal the wounded soldiers both physically and mentally? I carry wounds in my body, my mind, my heart, and my dreams. I'm not the same guy I used to be. Suicide is common among veterans who are unable to deal with the pains of war. I have been asked by my friends and my doctors, "Do you ever want to *kill* yourself because of the war?"

My answer to that question is, "Those who *did* kill themselves didn't *tell* anyone they were going to do it." And while the feelings and the flashbacks were too painful to those who took their own lives, I'm not going to let those things destroy me.

Serving in the military can be disillusioning. Newly enlisted soldiers are looked upon with pride and respect, but *after* the war they are often seen as having little value. Many veterans end up homeless and living on the streets. According to statistics reported by the Center for American Progress, on any given night in January 2010, there were sixty-seven thousand homeless veterans on the streets. The same organization has reported that in 2010, nearly a million veterans were living in poverty and one and a half million veterans were at risk of becoming homeless. As a nation, we have got to do better at caring for these men and women who have risked their very lives protecting us.

THE AUTHORS

A Lost Boy from Sudan and a US Army veteran, Dominic Malual lives in Grand Rapids, Michigan, with his wife and four children. He is involved in the political and social affairs of the local South Sudanese community. Dominic has earned a BS degree in criminal justice and recently completed a masters degree of science in management.

Dominic Malual

Dorothy Fanberg Bakker

Dorothy Fanberg Bakker is a freelance writer who makes her home in Charlotte, North Carolina. She previously coauthored *The Agony of Deception* with Ron Rigsbee and *The Miracle of Touching* with Dr. John Hornbrook. She has also written numerous children's stories. Dorothy has shared a true interest in the people of South Sudan since she met and began working with Dominic.

Printed in the United States
By Bookmasters